TIMOTHY

Series Editor

COMMON CORE Mathematics in a PLC at Work™

GRADES 3–5

Matthew R. Larson
Francis (Skip) Fennell
Thomasenia Lott Adams
Juli K. Dixon
Beth McCord Kobett
Jonathan A. Wray

FOREWORD BY Rebecca DuFour

A Joint Publication With

NCTM
NATIONAL COUNCIL OF TEACHERS OF MATHEMATICS

555 North Morton Street
Bloomington, IN 47404

800.733.6786 (toll free) / 812.336.7700
FAX: 812.336.7790

email: info@solution-tree.com
solution-tree.com

Visit **go.solution-tree.com/commoncore** to download the reproducibles in this book.

Printed in the United States of America

16 15 14   6 7 8 9 10

FSC
www.fsc.org
MIX
Paper from responsible sources
FSC® C011935

Library of Congress Cataloging-in-Publication Data
Common core mathematics in a PLC at work. Grades 3-5 / Matthew R. Larson ... [et al.] ; Timothy D. Kanold, series editor ; foreword by Rebecca DuFour.
p. cm.
Includes bibliographical references and index.
ISBN 978-1-936764-00-6 (perfect bound : alk. paper) -- ISBN 978-1-936764-01-3 (library ed. : alk. paper)
1. Mathematics--Study and teaching (Elementary)--Standards--United States. 2. Professional learning communities. I. Larson, Matthew R. II. Kanold, Timothy D.
QA13.C5655 2012
372.702'1873--dc23

2012004128

Solution Tree
Jeffrey C. Jones, CEO
Edmund M. Ackerman, President

Solution Tree Press
President: Douglas M. Rife
Publisher: Robert D. Clouse
Vice President of Production: Gretchen Knapp
Managing Production Editor: Caroline Wise
Senior Production Editor: Joan Irwin
Copy Editor: Sarah Payne-Mills
Text Designer: Amy Shock
Cover Designer: Jenn Taylor

Acknowledgments

To Tammy, who supports my being gone from home way more than I have a right to expect.

—Matthew R. Larson

To Nita, Brett, Heather, and Stacey for their love, support, encouragement, and patience.

—Francis (Skip) Fennell

Any testament of my success would be incomplete without a statement of thanks to Larry, Blake, Phillip, and Kurt. They help me believe that the impossible is possible.

—Thomasenia Lott Adams

To my children, Alex and Jessica, who have helped me to see mathematics through their eyes, and to my husband, Marc, who supports my efforts to do so.

—Juli K. Dixon

To Tim, Hannah, and Jenna—thank you for all of your love and support.

—Beth McCord Kobett

To Alanna, Jordan, and Annika, who are among America's first elementary school–aged Common Core pioneers.

—Jonathan A. Wray

My heartfelt thanks to Thomasenia, Juli, Skip, Matt, Beth, and Jon for their dedicated, creative, and tireless effort to turn the idea of this book into a collaborative reality.

Special thanks to Solution Tree—Jeff, Douglas, Gretchen, Joan, and Sarah—for believing in the importance of this work for the mathematics community.

Sincere thanks to the National Council of Teachers of Mathematics and the Educational Materials Committee for their support of this series and their leadership in the mathematics education of teachers and students.

Finally, thanks to all of the authors and reviewers for this series. Many of their great ideas surface across the books and serve to bring coherence to the Common Core mathematics message.

—Timothy D. Kanold

Solution Tree Press would like to thank the following reviewers:

Honi J. Bamberger
Professor, Department of Mathematics
Towson University
Towson, Maryland

Rebecca DuFour
Author and Consultant
Moneta, Virginia

Laura Hunovice
Mathematics Resource Teacher
Hampstead Elementary School and Linton Springs Elementary School
Carroll County, Maryland

Karen Karp
Distinguished Teaching Professor, Department of Teaching and Learning
University of Louisville
Louisville, Kentucky

Mari Muri
Mathematics Consultant
Project to Increase Mastery of Mathematics and Science (PIMMS)
Wesleyan University
Cromwell, Connecticut

John SanGiovanni
Instructional Facilitator, Elementary Mathematics
Howard County School System
Ellicott City, Maryland

Visit **go.solution-tree.com/commoncore** to download the reproducibles in this book.

Table of Contents

About the Series Editor

Timothy D. Kanold, PhD, is a mathematics educator, author, and consultant. He is former director of mathematics and science and superintendent of Adlai E. Stevenson High School District 125, a model professional learning community district in Lincolnshire, Illinois.

Dr. Kanold is committed to equity and excellence for students, faculty, and school administrators. He conducts highly motivational professional development leadership seminars worldwide with a focus on turning school vision into realized action that creates greater equity for students through the effective delivery of professional learning communities for faculty and administrators.

He is a past president of the National Council of Supervisors of Mathematics and coauthor of several best-selling mathematics textbooks over several decades. He has served on writing commissions for the National Council of Teachers of Mathematics. He has authored numerous articles and chapters on school mathematics, leadership, and development for education publications.

In 2010, Dr. Kanold received the prestigious international Damen Award for outstanding contributions to the leadership field of education from Loyola University Chicago. He also received the Outstanding Administrator Award from the Illinois State Board of Education in 1994 and the Presidential Award for Excellence in Mathematics and Science Teaching in 1986. He now serves as an adjunct faculty member for the graduate school at Loyola University Chicago.

Dr. Kanold earned a bachelor's degree in education and a master's degree in mathematics from Illinois State University. He completed a master's in educational administration at the University of Illinois and received a doctorate in educational leadership and counseling psychology from Loyola University Chicago.

To learn more about Dr. Kanold's work, visit his blog Turning Vision Into Action at http://tkanold.blogspot.com, or follow @tkanold on Twitter.

To book Dr. Kanold for professional development, contact pd@solution-tree.com.

About the Authors

Matthew R. Larson, PhD, is a school district administrator, author, and nationally known speaker. He is the K–12 curriculum specialist for mathematics for Lincoln Public Schools, in Lincoln, Nebraska, where part of his work focuses on implementing effective professional learning communities to improve mathematics instruction and student achievement.

Dr. Larson has taught mathematics at elementary through college levels and has held an honorary appointment as a visiting associate professor of mathematics education at Teachers College, Columbia University. He is the coauthor of several elementary mathematics textbooks, professional books, and articles in mathematics education publications.

He is a member of the Board of Directors for the National Council of Teachers of Mathematics and has served on a variety of NCTM committees and task forces. Dr. Larson is a frequent and popular presenter at national and regional mathematics conferences, and his presentations are well known for their application of research findings to practice.

He earned his bachelor's degree and doctorate from the University of Nebraska–Lincoln.

Francis (Skip) Fennell, PhD, is the L. Stanley Bowlsbey professor of education and graduate and professional studies at McDaniel College in Westminster, Maryland, where he directs the Elementary Mathematics Specialists and Teacher Leaders Project (ems&tl). A mathematics educator who has experience as a classroom teacher, principal, and supervisor of instruction, he is a past president of the Association of Mathematics Teacher Educators and the National Council of Teachers of Mathematics.

Widely published in professional journals and textbooks related to elementary and middle-grade mathematics education, Dr. Fennell has also authored chapters in yearbooks and resource books. In addition, he has played key leadership roles for the Research Council on Mathematics Learning, Mathematical Sciences Education Board, National Science Foundation, Maryland Mathematics Commission, and U.S. National Commission on Mathematics Instruction. Dr. Fennell served as a writer for the *Principles and Standards for School Mathematics*, the *Curriculum Focal Points*, and the Common Core State Standards. He also served on the National Mathematics Advisory Panel, chairing the Conceptual Knowledge and Skills Task Group.

He has received numerous honors and awards, including Maryland's Outstanding Mathematics Educator, McDaniel College's Professor of the Year, the Glenn Gilbert National Leadership Award from the National Council of Supervisors of Mathematics, the Council for Advancement and Support of Education's Carnegie Foundation Professor of the Year, and the Association of Mathematics Teacher Educators' Distinguished Outstanding Teacher Educator.

He earned a bachelor's degree from Lock Haven University of Pennsylvania, a master's degree from Bloomsburg University of Pennsylvania, and a doctorate from Pennsylvania State University.

Thomasenia Lott Adams, PhD, is a professor of mathematics education and the interim associate dean of research in the College of Education at the University of Florida–Gainesville. Dr. Adams's research focuses on mathematics professional development and multicultural issues regarding teaching and learning mathematics.

Dr. Adams's scholarship includes funded grants; a commendable list of publications; and a vast array of international, national, regional, and state conference presentations. She has authored three publications with the National Council of Teachers of Mathematics and contributed to many other mathematics publications.

Her service to the discipline of mathematics education includes editorial and leadership roles in several NCTM journals. She has served as a board member of the Association of Mathematics Teacher Educators and the School Science and Mathematics Association and as president of the Florida Association of Mathematics Teacher Educators. Dr. Adams has reviewed proposals from the National Science Foundation and is a standing reviewer for the Fulbright Specialist Program. She is a recipient of the Mary L. Collins Teacher Educator of the Year Award for the Florida Association of Teacher Educators.

She received a bachelor of science in mathematics from South Carolina State College and a master of education and doctorate of philosophy in instruction and curriculum (with a focus in mathematics education) from the University of Florida.

Juli K. Dixon, PhD, is a professor of mathematics education at the University of Central Florida (UCF) in Orlando. She coordinates the award-winning Lockheed Martin/UCF Academy for Mathematics and Science. Dr. Dixon has also taught secondary mathematics at the University of Nevada–Las Vegas and mathematics in urban school settings at the elementary, middle, secondary, and postsecondary levels.

Dr. Dixon is an active researcher focused on professional development in mathematics and science. She has contributed to a multitude of publications, including books, textbooks, book chapters, articles, and international-, national-, and state-invited presentations. She has served as the chair of the National Council of Teachers of Mathematics Student Explorations in Mathematics Editorial Panel and as a member of the Board of Directors for the Association of Mathematics Teacher Educators. At the state level, she has served on the boards of directors for the Nevada Mathematics Council and the Florida Association of Mathematics Teacher Educators.

She received bachelor's degrees in mathematics and education from SUNY–Potsdam, a master's degree in mathematics education from Syracuse University, and a doctorate in curriculum and instruction with an emphasis in mathematics education from the University of Florida.

Beth McCord Kobett is a mathematics educator and consultant. She is a former classroom teacher and mathematics specialist for Howard County, Maryland, public schools. Kobett is an assistant professor of education at Stevenson University, where she teaches courses in mathematics education for preservice teachers. She is also serving as the lead consultant for the Elementary Mathematics Specialists and Teacher Leaders Project. She serves as an adjunct faculty member at McDaniel College, where she teaches graduate-level courses in mathematics education.

Kobett conducts extensive professional development with elementary and middle school teachers focusing on diagnosing student needs and developing conceptual understanding through problem-based teaching. She also serves on the board of the Maryland Council of Teachers of Mathematics. Kobett has received the Maryland Council of Teachers of Mathematics' Outstanding Educator Award, the Johns Hopkins University Excellence in Teaching Award, and the Stevenson University Rose Dawson Excellence in Teaching Award.

She earned her bachelor's degree from the University of Missouri-Columbia and her master's degree from the Johns Hopkins University.

Jonathan A. Wray is a mathematics instructional facilitator in the Howard County, Maryland, public school system. He is president-elect of the Association of Maryland Mathematics Teacher Educators and past president of the Maryland Council of Teachers of Mathematics. Wray also serves as the manager of the Elementary Mathematics Specialists and Teacher Leaders Project and chair of the Core Learning Community's Core Challenge. He has experience as a primary and intermediate elementary classroom teacher, gifted/talented resource teacher, mathematics supervisor, grant project manager, and educational consultant.

Wray is professionally engaged in NCTM, serving on the board of directors. He also served on the editorial panels of *Teaching Children Mathematics* and *ON-Math* for NCTM. Named NCTM's Outstanding Teacher Mentor, he has also been recognized for his expertise in infusing technology in mathematics teaching, receiving the Outstanding Technology Leader in Education award for his school district from the Maryland Society for Education Technology (MSET).

He earned his bachelor's degree at Towson University and holds a master's degree from the Johns Hopkins University.

To book Matthew R. Larson, Francis (Skip) Fennell, Thomasenia Lott Adams, Juli K. Dixon, Beth McCord Kobett, or Jonathan A. Wray for professional development, contact pd@solution-tree.com.

Foreword

The publication of *Common Core Mathematics in a PLC at Work*™ could not be more timely as educators across the United States are gearing up to make the new standards the foundation of their mathematics curriculum, instruction, assessment, intervention, and professional development processes. The series editor and his team of authors are not only some of the United States' most highly regarded experts in the field of mathematics, but they also have a deep understanding of the steps educators must take to bring these standards to life in our classrooms. They recognize that if students are going to learn these rigorous skills, concepts, and ways of thinking that are essential to their success, then the educators serving those students must no longer work in traditional isolated classrooms but rather work as members of collaborative teams in schools and districts that function as professional learning communities (PLCs). As the authors state on page 12:

> It is one thing to be handed a set of written standards—even if the standards are clear, concise, coherent, focused, and individually understood. It is quite another to ensure that everyone on your team has a shared understanding of what those standards mean and what student demonstrations of that understanding, fluency, or proficiency look like.

Picture an elementary teacher working in a traditional school. He or she will likely be provided a copy of the Common Core document, may receive a few hours of training from someone in the district, and then essentially will be left to work in isolation for the rest of the year to interpret, teach, and assess each standard to the best of his or her ability. The degree to which the students assigned to that traditional classroom learn each standard will almost exclusively depend on that teacher's understanding of each standard and how much time and energy he or she is able and willing to devote to teaching the new standards.

Now imagine a team of teachers working in a school that embraces the PLC process. Each teacher will be provided a copy of the Common Core document and will become a student of the standards with his or her collaborative teammates. Teams will be provided time and support to study and discuss each standard in order to clarify, sequence, pace, and assess the standards in a common way across each grade level. Each team will be provided time to collaborate vertically with teams in the grade levels above and below its own to build a strong scope and sequence and a common language for mathematics as students progress from one grade to the next. Leadership at the school and district levels will not only provide each team with the necessary time, support, and ongoing training to engage in this critical collaborative work, but it will also put structures in place and empower staffs to build schoolwide systems of intervention, extension, and enrichment for students—providing time and support for each student to take his or her own learning to the next level.

I am honored to write the foreword for this book, written and edited by dear friends and respected colleagues. I am confident it will provide you, my heroes working in schools and districts each day, with information, strategies, tools, and resources to help you bring the Common Core for mathematics to life for the students entrusted to you each day.

—Rebecca DuFour

Introduction

These Standards are not intended to be new names for old ways of doing business. They are a call to take the next step. It is time for states to work together to build on lessons learned from two decades of standards based reforms. It is time to recognize that standards are not just promises to our children, but promises we intend to keep.

—National Governors Association Center for Best Practices & Council of Chief State School Officers

One of the greatest concerns for mathematics instruction, and instruction in general in most school districts, is that it is too inconsistent from elementary classroom to elementary classroom, school to school, and district to district (Morris & Hiebert, 2011). How much mathematics a third-, fourth-, or fifth-grade student in the United States learns, and how deeply he or she learns it, is largely determined by the school the student attends and, even more significantly, the teacher to whom the student is randomly (usually) assigned within that school. The inconsistencies teachers develop in their professional development practice—often random and in isolation from other teachers—create great inequities in students' mathematics instructional and assessment learning experiences that ultimately and significantly contribute to the year-by-year achievement gap (Ferrini-Mundy, Graham, Johnson, & Mills, 1998). This issue is especially true in a vertically connected curriculum like mathematics.

The hope and the promise of *Common Core Mathematics in a PLC at Work, Grades 3–5* is to provide the guidance and teacher focus needed to work outside of existing paradigms regarding mathematics teaching and learning. The resources in this book will enable you to focus your time and energy on issues and actions that will lead to addressing the Common Core State Standards (CCSS) for mathematics challenge: *All students successfully learning rigorous standards for college or career-preparatory mathematics.*

Most of what you will read and use in this book, as well as this series, has been part of the national discussion on mathematics reform and improvement since the National Council of Teachers of Mathematics' (NCTM) release of the *Curriculum and Evaluation Standards* in 1989. In 2000, NCTM refocused the nation's vision for K–12 mathematics teaching, learning, and assessing in *Principles and Standards for School Mathematics* (PSSM), and the National Research Council (NRC) followed by providing supportive research in the groundbreaking book *Adding It Up* (NRC, 2001). The significance of these developments for your professional development is discussed in chapters 2 and 3.

So, what would cause you, as a classroom teacher, to believe the national, state, and local responses to the CCSS for mathematics will be any different this time than previous reform efforts and recommendations? What would cause you to think that your professional learning opportunities and activities will be any different this time than those that accompanied previous changes in standards and curriculum programs?

The full implementation of the previous mathematics teaching and learning frameworks and standards was limited by the lack of a coherent vision *implementation* process at the local level. School districts and school leaders were *invited* to implement research-affirmed changes in mathematics grade-level content, instruction, and assessment, but the changes were not mandated, nor were they reflected in the widely variant state assessments in mathematics. In many cases, the very system of the previous states' standards mathematics *assessments* caused local district resistance to teaching the deeper, richer mathematics curriculum described in the CCSS. This resistance was primarily due to state testing that reflected only the lower cognitive, procedural knowledge aspects of the states' standards. In many school districts, it often felt like a race to get through the grade-level or course curriculum before April of each school year as the *wytiwyg* phenomenon—what you test is what you get—kicked in.

Since 1989, mathematics teaching and learning in the United States has been mostly characterized by *pockets of excellence* that reflect the national recommendations of improved student learning, disposition, and confidence for doing mathematics well. The lack of coherent and sustained change toward effective practice has been partially caused by a general attempt to make only modest changes to existing practices. In this context, professional learning opportunities in mathematics were often limited or, in some cases, nonexistent. This situation is defined as *first-order change*—change that produces marginal disturbance to existing knowledge, skills, and practices favored by faculty and school leaders who are closest to the action.

The CCSS expectations for teaching and learning and the new state assessments of that learning usher in an opportunity for unprecedented *second-order change*. In contrast to first-order change, second-order change requires working outside the existing system by embracing new paradigms for how you think and practice (Waters, Marzano, & McNulty, 2003). The CCSS will be your catalyst for providing the support you need as elementary school teachers and leaders to effect real change.

In this book for grades 3–5 teachers and teacher leaders, the five chapters focus on five fundamental areas required to prepare every teacher for successful implementation of CCSS for mathematics leading to the general improvement of teaching and learning for all students. These areas provide the framework within which second-order change can be successfully achieved. The five critical areas are the following.

1. **Collaboration:** The CCSS require a shift in the *grain size of change* beyond the individual isolated teacher or leader. It is the grade-level or course-based collaborative learning team (collaborative team) within a Professional Learning Community (PLC) at Work culture that will develop the expanded teacher

knowledge capacity necessary to bring coherence to the implementation of the CCSS for mathematics. The grain size of change now lies within the power and voice of your collaborative team in a PLC.

2. **Instruction:** The CCSS require a shift to daily lesson designs that include plans for student Mathematical Practices that focus on the process of learning and developing deep student understanding of the standards. This change requires teaching for procedural fluency *and* student understanding of the grade-level CCSS content. One should not exist at the expense of the other. This will require your collaborative team's commitment to the use of student-engaged learning around common high-cognitive-demand mathematical tasks used in every classroom.
3. **Content:** The CCSS require a shift to *less* (fewer standards) is *more* (deeper rigor with understanding) at each grade level. This will require new levels of knowledge and skill development for every teacher of mathematics to understand *what* the CCSS expect students to learn at each grade level blended with *how* they expect students to learn it. What are the mathematical knowledge, skills, understandings, and dispositions that should be the result of each unit of mathematics instruction? A school and mathematics program committed to helping all students learn ensures great clarity and low teacher-to-teacher variance on the questions, What should students learn? How should they learn it?
4. **Assessment:** The CCSS require a shift to assessments that are a *means* within the teaching-assessing-learning cycle and not used as an *end* to the cycle. These assessments must reflect the rigor of the standards and model the expectations for and benefits of formative assessment practices around all forms of assessment, including traditional instruments such as tests and quizzes. *How will you know* if each student is learning the essential mathematics skills, concepts, understandings, and dispositions the CCSS deem most essential? *How will you know* if your students are prepared for the more rigorous state assessment consortia expectations from the Partnership for Assessment of Readiness for College and Careers (PARCC) and the SMARTER Balanced Assessment Consortium (SBAC)?
5. **Intervention:** The CCSS require a shift in your team and school response to intervention (RTI). Much like the CCSS vision for teaching and learning, RTI can no longer be invitational. That is, the response to intervention becomes R^2TI—a required response to intervention. Stakeholder implementation of RTI programs includes a process that *requires* students to participate and attend. How will you *respond* and act on evidence (or lack of evidence) of student learning?

Second-order change is never easy. It will require your willingness to break away (or to help a fellow teacher break away) from the past practice of teaching one-standard-a-day mathematics lessons with low cognitive demand. This change will require teachers to break away from a past practice that provided few student opportunities for exploring, understanding, and actively engaging, and one that used assessment instruments that may or may not have honored a fidelity to accurate and timely formative feedback. Now every teacher will be required to embrace these new paradigms to meet the expectations of the CCSS in grades 3–5.

Based on a solid foundation in mathematics education research, *Common Core Mathematics in a PLC at Work, Grades 3–5* is designed to support teachers and all those involved in delivering meaningful mathematics instruction and assessment within these five second-order change areas. It is our hope that the suggestions in these chapters will focus your work on actions that really matter for you and for your students.

Above all, as you do your work *together* and strive to achieve the PLC at Work school culture through your well-designed grade-level or vertical collaborative learning teams, your collective teacher knowledge capacity will grow and flourish. Each chapter's Extending My Understanding section has resources and tools you can use in collaborative teams to make sense of and reflect on the chapter recommendations. Then, as a collaborative learning team, you can make *great decisions* about teaching, learning, assessing, and how your response to learning will impact student mathematics achievement. We hope this book will help you make those great decisions—every day.

CHAPTER 1

Using High-Performing Collaborative Teams for Mathematics

Far too frequently, your mathematics professional development experience as a grades 3–5 elementary school teacher likely feels inadequate. Why? It could be because you receive little or no professional development time dedicated to teaching, learning, and assessing mathematics. Unless you are in the process of implementing a new mathematics curriculum, which may happen every six to eight years, the focus of most professional development time is in another major area of need—literacy.

To be certain, professional development in literacy for grades 3–5 is essential. After all, the evidence is clear that students who struggle to read in your class often struggle in mathematics as well. Skill in reading is necessary for success in mathematics (Gersten, Jordan, & Flojo, 2005; Jordan & Hanich, 2003). However, in order for you to transition to the Common Core State Standards for mathematics, you will need to shift the same amount of priority time to your professional development in mathematics (National Governors Association [NGA] Center for Best Practices & Council of Chief State School Officers [CCSSO], 2010).

Think about your most recent professional development experience in mathematics. What was it like? Was it a collection of short and disjointed *make- and take-it* workshops or *try-this* games? Or was it a robust and collaborative professional development experience that focused on tasks designed to improve the quality of instruction, connect to important mathematics, and advance student learning?

The expectations of the CCSS content standards and the CCSS Mathematical Practices (NGA & CCSSO, 2010), as well as the research on highly effective mathematics instruction, will require a new professional development learning emphasis on mathematics instruction for you and your colleagues who teach in grades 3–5. This will require using professional development resources—and, most significantly your, *time*—to learn the content and pedagogical shifts needed to teach for the depth and conceptual understanding expectations outlined in the CCSS for mathematics. You should not do so alone. This opening chapter examines the first of the second-order paradigm shifts necessary for successfully implementing the CCSS mathematics standards—the need for you to work within grade-level collaborative learning teams to expand your knowledge capacity and bring coherence to your interpretation and implementation of the CCSS. This opening chapter examines the role and activities of collaborative teams in making the necessary accommodations in professional development to ensure successful implementation of these new mathematics content standards and practices. Working together with your colleagues, you will be able to expand your knowledge and bring mutual understanding to CCSS implementation. Together, you will develop a common vocabulary that helps you to communicate more effectively about changes in your instructional practices. (See the introduction, pages 2–3, for descriptions of the five paradigm shifts.)

Effective Mathematics Professional Development

There is new clarity as to what constitutes effective professional development. Linda Darling-Hammond (2010) provides one of the best summaries of the research on effective professional development for teachers:

> Effective professional development is sustained, ongoing, content-focused, and embedded in professional learning communities where teachers work over time on problems of practice with other teachers in their subject area or school. Furthermore, it focuses on concrete tasks of teaching, assessment, observation, and reflection, looking at how students learn specific content in particular contexts. . . . It is often useful for teachers to be put in the position of studying the very material that they intend to teach to their own students. (pp. 226–227)

In other words, effective mathematics professional development is sustained and embedded within professional learning communities and focused on the actual tasks of teaching using the same materials you use with students. What is meant by *sustained?* It means *effective professional development*—programs that have demonstrated positive and significant effects on student achievement (gains of more than 20 percentile points) and somewhere between thirty and one hundred hours of contact time with teachers over the course of six to twelve months (Darling-Hammond, Wei, Andree, Richardson, & Orphanos, 2009; Garet et al., 2010).

We know with certainty that the most effective professional development immerses you in collaboratively studying the curriculum you will teach in a structured way with other teachers, as well as in assessing how your students will acquire that curriculum. This kind of professional learning is embedded in your instructional practice. At the lesson level, this approach ultimately leads to your deeper understanding and thus wider adoption of the curricular and instructional innovations sought (Penuel, Fishman, Yamaguchi, & Gallagher, 2007; Wayne, Kwang, Zhu, Cronen, & Garet, 2008). The capacity to provide this type of sustained and focused collaborative professional development for you as an elementary school teacher must be the vision for future professional development if mathematics instruction is to significantly improve and the vision of the CCSS for mathematics is to become a reality.

Professional learning communities have become ubiquitous in education, and you may equate PLCs with teacher collaboration. At the same time, various definitions and understandings regarding a PLC *culture* abound. In this book, we use the work of DuFour, DuFour, and Eaker's (2008) *Revisiting Professional Learning Communities at Work* and DuFour, DuFour, Eaker, and Many's (2010) *Learning by Doing* to define the conditions for collaborative mathematics learning teams in an authentic PLC school culture. For the purposes of this book, we will refer to grade-level groups of teachers working together in a PLC as *collaborative teams.*

Professional Development Paradigm Shift

An often-troubling problem with mathematics instruction and assessment is that they are too inconsistent from classroom to classroom, school to school, and district to district (Morris & Hiebert, 2011). Is this the case at your school? Would you be comfortable if your own child were assigned any fourth-grade teacher in your building?

How much mathematics a fourth grader in the United States learns, and how deeply he or she learns it, in many schools is largely determined by the student's school and, even more directly, the teacher the student is assigned to. Sometimes, the inconsistencies teachers develop in their isolated practice can create gaps in curriculum content with consequent inequities in students' instructional experiences and learning (Kanold, 2006). Noting that isolation is the enemy of improvement, Eaker (2002) observes, "The traditional school often functions as a collection of independent contractors united by a common parking lot" (as cited in Schmoker, 2006, p. 23).

Your students come to school with many challenges, and you are expected to ensure each student receives, understands, and masters the more rigorous content standards outlined in the CCSS. One of the characteristics of high-performing elementary schools successfully closing the achievement gap is their focus on teacher collaboration as a key to improving instruction and reaching all students (Education Trust, 2005; Kersaint, 2007). Only through a collaborative culture are you provided both the instructional knowledge and skills required to meet this challenge, as well as the energy and *support* necessary to reach all students (Leithwood & Seashore Louis, 1998). Seeley (2009) characterizes this challenge by noting that "alone we can accomplish great things . . . but together, with creativity, wisdom, energy, and, most of all commitment, there is no end to what we might do" (pp. 225–226).

Collaborative learning teams provide you the supportive environment necessary to share your creativity and wisdom and to harness the energy and persistence necessary to meet the demands of students' needs and the challenges of the CCSS.

Adequate Time for Collaborative Teams

Thus, mathematics professional development at the elementary school level must help you to work in a grade-level collaborative team within a PLC school culture. The best hope for you and your students to be successful in mathematics in the era of the Common Core State Standards for mathematics *requires* this shift. The effectiveness of your collaborative teams will depend on how well the standards are implemented. Effective implementation begins with the provision of adequate time for you to collaborate. The research indicates that significant achievement gains are only achieved when teacher teams are provided with sufficient and consistent time to collaborate (Saunders, Goldenberg, & Gallimore, 2009).

The world's highest-performing countries in mathematics or sustained educational improvers—Singapore, Hong Kong SAR, South Korea, Chinese Taipei, and Japan—allow significant time for elementary school mathematics teachers to collaborate and learn from one another (Barber & Mourshed, 2007; Stigler & Hiebert, 1999). This requires that school districts shift their priorities to support weekly collaborative professional development opportunities in the form of grade-level teacher collaboration time (Hiebert & Stigler, 2004). Teaching the grades 3–5 Common Core State Standards for mathematics is a much more complex endeavor than generally perceived if done with fidelity, and collaborative teams with regular time to meet will be necessary for successful implementation of the CCSS.

How much time? You should have a dedicated block of grade-level collaborative team time once a week, and each session should be at least sixty minutes long. This time needs to be embedded within your professional workday; that is, ideally, it should not be scheduled in the stereotypical arrangement of *every Tuesday after school, once a week* (Buffum, Mattos, & Weber, 2009). When such "professional development" is scheduled beyond the normal workday, after you have spent the entire day working with students, there are two problems. First, it sends the message to you and parents that your professional learning is not that important; if it were, it wouldn't be an add-on to a full day. Second, as you know, teaching is hard work, and teachers are tired at the end of the day. The type of collaborative work that needs to take place in grade-level collaborative teams requires you to be fresh and focused on the task at hand. Collaborative professional development work simply cannot be done as effectively in an after-school session at the end of a long day of hard work.

Some school systems that are implementing the PLC process have early-release or late-start days. There are objections to late-start or early-release schedules, particularly at the elementary level, when students cannot provide their own transportation, and there are concerns about the loss of instructional time. In addition, financial constraints may make it difficult for schools to implement late-start or early-release schedules. However, schools committed to teachers working collaboratively in learning teams have found a number of ways to find collaboration time that do not require money or result in a loss of instructional time (DuFour et al., 2010). Consider the following. (See www.allthingsplc.info for additional collaborative time scheduling ideas.)

- **Parallel scheduling:** Grade-level teachers in grades 3–5 can have a common preparation time by assigning specialists (music, art, physical education, and so on) to work with students across the entire grade at the same time. The grade-level team then can designate one day each week for collaborative planning rather than individual planning.
- **Shared classes:** Students across two different grade levels can be combined into one class while the other team engages in collaborative work once a week.

- **Extended faculty meeting time:** Time can be scheduled for teams to work together during faculty meeting time, changing the focus of faculty meetings from administrative communication to professional learning for teachers.

As an elementary teacher, you face another unique time challenge: how should you split collaborative team time equitably between literacy and mathematics? Note that the assumption is that you will work within your collaborative team to address both mathematics and literacy instruction for student learning. This is not an either/or choice but rather a matter of how you can most effectively do both. Literacy and mathematics both have new Common Core State Standards, both face new consortia assessments, both remain factors in a school's accountability calculation, and therefore both subjects must be addressed within collaborative teams.

Lezotte (1991) argues that one of the characteristics of the most effective schools is their willingness to declare that some subjects are more important than others and to assign more instructional time to those that are considered most important. It is time that administrators and faculty in elementary schools finally heed this advice and prioritize student instructional time, intervention time, and your professional learning time accordingly in favor of literacy *and* mathematics. In many school systems, because literacy typically dominates professional development time, this will require an increase in both the instructional focus and professional development work devoted to mathematics instruction.

There are three possible models we suggest you follow when allocating your collaborative team time to literacy and mathematics. These include:

1. Implementing an alternating schedule, designating every other week for mathematics or literacy
2. Spending two consecutive weeks a month on mathematics and two consecutive weeks on literacy
3. Spending half the time during each collaborative team session on literacy and half on mathematics

Regardless of the model you select, note that the third model—splitting each session between literacy and mathematics—is not recommended in the first year of implementation, unless you have a significant amount of collaboration time each week. The type of work outlined here requires significant and focused work, which cannot be effectively done in a once-weekly thirty-minute session. In the first year of implementation, you may consider devoting one semester of collaborative team time to mathematics and the other to language arts to allow sufficient time to focus on and experience the benefits of all the steps in the collaborative team process in one content area before tackling another.

The challenge of developing the content knowledge and content-specific pedagogical knowledge necessary to become a highly effective teacher of reading, language arts, and mathematics, particularly in the upper intermediate grades, is daunting. This has led some school districts to adopt a model in which individual teachers in the upper intermediate grades specialize in either literacy or mathematics instruction. Compelling arguments have been made in support of this organizational approach for mathematics instruction (Reys & Fennell, 2003). Although some research indicates that this model can have a positive effect on student achievement and that these achievement gains are cumulative across two to three years (Campbell, 2011), the research on the overall effectiveness of this approach is not substantial (National Mathematics Advisory Panel [NMAP], 2008). It may be that the most critical factor is your selection and implementation of effective instructional strategies, not the nature of your assignment. It is also worth noting that content specialization can isolate teachers and does not promote a collaborative school culture.

Therefore, particularly after year one of implementation, the most effective model to consider is the first—alternating weekly focus between literacy and mathematics instruction. As described later in this chapter and more fully in chapters 4 and 5, much of your work in collaborative teams is focused on responding to your students' performance on collaboratively developed assessments. Waiting two weeks to discuss students' performance on assessments and planning appropriate instructional responses in mathematics lets too much time pass between collaborative sessions and defeats the timely intervention response of collaborative teams.

Grade-Level Collaborative Mathematics Teams

Your collaborative work focuses on reaching agreement on the answers to the four critical PLC questions for student learning (DuFour et al., 2008):

1. What mathematics (content and practices) should students learn? (See chapters 2 and 3.)
2. How should we develop and use the common and coherent assessments to determine if students have learned the agreed-on curriculum? (See chapter 4.)
3. How should we respond when students don't learn the agreed-on curriculum? (See chapter 5.)
4. How should we respond when students do learn the agreed-on curriculum? (See chapter 5.)

It might seem that the CCSS have answered once and for all what students should learn and how they should engage in mathematics as they develop competence within the content domains and through the Mathematical Practices. To some degree, this is true, but there are still significant issues that you need to discuss in your grade-level collaborative team and reach agreement with respect to what students should learn and when they should learn it. While the CCSS at the elementary level (K–5) outline a clearly defined and coherent set of grade-level standards within the mathematics domains, all teachers at each grade level in your school should have a deep across-grades understanding, a deep grade-level understanding, and a deep understanding of the shifts in emphasis recommended in the CCSS. Knowing how to read the CCSS grade-level standards is an important first step in developing a common vocabulary within the collaborative team. Figure 1.1 defines the key terms used in the CCSS and identifies the domains that are presented in grades 3–5.

Standards define what students should understand and be able to do.

Clusters summarize groups of related standards. Note that standards from different clusters may sometimes be closely related because mathematics is a connected subject.

Domains are larger groups of related standards. Standards from different domains may sometimes be closely related. The domains for grades 3–5 are Operations and Algebraic Thinking, Number and Operations in Base Ten, Number and Operations—Fractions, Measurement and Data, and Geometry.

Domain

Number and Operations in Base Ten 3.NBT

Use place-value understanding and properties of operations to perform multidigit arithmetic.

1. Use place-value understanding to round whole numbers to the nearest 10 or 100.
2. Fluently add and subtract within 1,000 using strategies and algorithms based on place value, properties of operations, or the relationship between addition and subtraction.
3. Multiply one-digit whole numbers by multiples of 10 in the range 10–90 (for example, 9 × 80, 5 × 60) using strategies based on place value and properties of operations.

Standard

Cluster

Source: Adapted from NGA & CCSSO, 2010, p. 5.

Figure 1.1: How to read the grade-level standards.

Visit **go.solution-tree.com/commoncore** for a reproducible version of this figure.

The focused nature of the CCSS, and the careful attention paid to students' developmental learning progressions, means that some of the topics you traditionally taught in certain grades have been moved to other grades, and some topics have simply been eliminated from the elementary school curriculum. For example, the CCSS emphasize fractions beginning at the third-grade level and delay probability until the middle grades. Traditionally, both of these topics were introduced in the primary grades and remained topics in each elementary school grade. The purpose of this more focused curriculum is to provide you more time to teach fewer critical topics in greater depth.

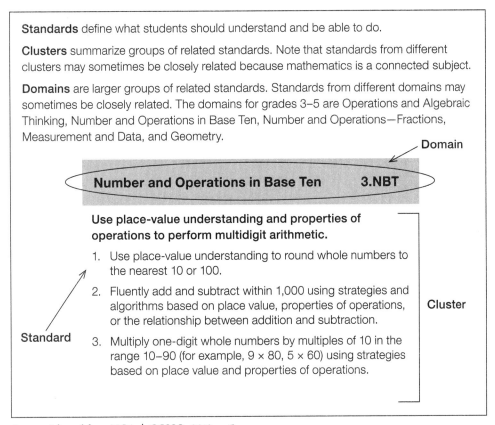

You need to spend time in your collaborative team reviewing and reaching agreement on the grade-level scope and sequence you will use to ensure the alignment of the mathematics content with your district's expectations as well as the CCSS. You should also spend some collaborative team time in vertical discussions. For example, if you are a fourth-grade teacher, you should meet with the third- and fifth-grade teachers to ensure appropriate articulation across grade levels.

One of the primary purposes for taking time to discuss the CCSS content standards in grade-level collaborative teams is to develop *shared teacher ownership* of the CCSS content standards and Mathematical Practices. This means discussing each domain and standard cluster as a team to develop a common understanding of what each standard means and what student understanding and proficiency with each standard looks like. For example, in third grade, one of the CCSS content standards for the domain Number and Operations—Fractions states that students will "Understand a fraction $1/b$ as the quantity formed by 1 part when a whole is partitioned into b equal parts; understand a fraction a/b as the quantity formed by a parts of size $1/b$" (NGA & CCSSO, 2010, p. 24). Simply reading this standard might be a language issue, as you or your teammates may not have typically used this exact phrasing of the standard. It is crucial that every third-grade teacher understands what the standard means, what mathematics content he or she should expect students to learn about the standard, and what it will look like when students have learned it. It is one thing to be handed a set of written standards—even if the standards are clear, concise, coherent, focused, and individually understood. It is quite another to ensure that everyone on your team has a shared understanding of what those standards mean and what student demonstrations of that understanding, fluency, or proficiency look like.

It is most important that your collaborative team spends significant time discussing the CCSS critical areas for instructional emphasis at your grade level. It should be noted that these critical areas are directly connected to the *Curriculum Focal Points* (NCTM, 2006), so they may present a common ground for discussing grade-level priorities and focus. Consider the following three critical areas for instructional emphasis in grade 4:

1. Developing understanding and fluency with multi-digit multiplication, and developing understanding of dividing to find quotients involving multi-digit dividends.
2. Developing an understanding of fraction equivalence, addition and subtraction of fractions with like denominators, and multiplication of fractions by whole numbers.
3. Understanding that geometric figures can be analyzed and classified based on their properties, such as having parallel sides, perpendicular sides, particular angle measures, and symmetry. (NGA & CCSSO, 2010, p. 27)

Your collaborative team needs to ensure that the mathematics content you teach students, as reflected in your pacing documents, lessons, assessments, judicious review activities, and intervention time, are all consistent with the CCSS emphasis on these three critical areas. The *Teaching With Curriculum Focal Points* (NCTM, 2008–2011) series and *Developing Essential Understanding* (NCTM, 2010–2012) series are excellent resources to support you as you work with your colleagues to develop highly effective lessons aligned with the identified critical areas of CCSS.

Resources for Developing Highly Effective Lessons

Developing Essential Understanding **(NCTM, 2010–2012):** This sixteen-book series addresses topics in preK–12 mathematics that are often difficult to teach but critical to student development. Each book gives an overview of the topics, highlights the differences between what students and teachers need to know, examines the big idea and related essential understandings, reconsiders the ideas presented in light of connections with other ideas, and includes questions for reflection.

Teaching With Curriculum Focal Points **(NCTM, 2008–2011):** This series supplements the *Curriculum Focal Points* with detailed guidance on instructional progressions, ways to introduce topics, and suggestions to build deeper understanding of essential topics. It includes grade-level volumes for preK–8 and grade-band volumes for preK–2, 3–5, and 6–8.

Considering the unprecedented clarity of the CCSS for mathematics, DuFour et al. (2010) verify why it is essential to take *action* in your collaborative team to develop a shared understanding of the content to be taught, because doing so:

- Promotes clarity among your colleagues
- Ensures consistent curricular priorities among teachers
- Is critical to the development of common pacing required for effective common assessments
- Ensures that the curriculum is viable—that it can be taught in the allotted time
- Creates ownership among all teachers required to teach the intended curriculum

Change in Instructional Emphasis

The Common Core State Standards for mathematics call for a different, and in some cases radically different, way of approaching the content as embodied in the Mathematical Practices. This significant change in instructional emphasis implies an increased need for pedagogical decision making and consistency as you work with your colleagues in your collaborative team to create equitable environments for students in which you use the Mathematical Practices as a vehicle to promote student learning with understanding.

A 2011 review of the Common Core State Standards for mathematics found that the standards represent an instructional shift toward higher levels of cognitive demand than traditionally represented in many state standards (Porter, McMaken, Hwang, & Yang, 2011). The cognitive demand of mathematical tasks matters. Higher student achievement is associated with more challenging mathematical tasks (Schmidt, Cogan, Houang, & McKnight, 2011). Traditional mathematics instruction is often characterized by low-level cognitive-demand tasks that do not support students in developing a deep understanding of mathematics (Silver, 2010). Consequently, it will be critical for you to work within your collaborative team to carefully design your mathematics instruction to engage students with the Mathematical Practices. This will be critical during initial planning, and especially after analyzing student learning, in order to increase the cognitive demand and effectiveness of the selected instructional tasks. *How* the mathematics content is approached to engage students in doing mathematics, as articulated in the Mathematical Practices, is as important—if not more important—than *what* is taught (Schmoker, 2011). Teachers working within grade-level collaborative teams are uniquely positioned to support one another in meeting the challenges associated with implementing the CCSS Mathematical Practices.

Mathematics education in the United States has a long history of confidence in standards and curriculum programs as the primary means to improve student achievement (Larson, 2009). But reliance on standards and materials alone to improve student achievement has not resulted in dramatic improvements in student learning over time. If implementation of the CCSS is to be more than merely superficial (little more than a content-standards mapping), and instead is to result in real improvements in student learning, then implementation efforts need to be more about *how* you approach the Mathematical Practices and not solely the curriculum or content standards.

Ultimately, how you teach the curriculum has a greater influence on student learning than the curriculum itself (Stein & Kaufman, 2010). As Wiliam (2011) contends, "Pedagogy trumps curriculum. Or more precisely, pedagogy *is* curriculum, because what matters is how things are taught, rather than what is taught" (p. 13). As school districts work to interpret and implement the CCSS, there will be a rush to adopt new textbooks, supplemental materials, intervention programs, and online materials as *the* solution to the transition and implementation challenges of the CCSS. Textbook publishers will be poised to offer their latest digital or text-based solutions. However, no matter what publishers promise, innovative materials alone will not—nor will they ever—improve mathematics instruction (Cohen & Ball, 2001). Student achievement is not solely a function of the agreed-on curriculum and the adopted commercial program.

Student achievement is more highly correlated with the nature of classroom instruction—how mathematics is taught rather than what program or materials are used (Slavin & Lake, 2008). An instructional approach that emphasizes high-cognitive-demand tasks that provide opportunities to reason, justify, analyze, and model mathematics—which are expectations in the CCSS Mathematical Practices and NCTM's Process Standards (NCTM, 2000)—is associated with higher student achievement (Stein & Smith, 2010). The CCSS Standards for Mathematical Practice are (NGA & CCSSO, 2010):

1. Make sense of problems and persevere in solving them.
2. Reason abstractly and quantitatively.
3. Construct viable arguments and critique the reasoning of others.
4. Model with mathematics.

5. Use appropriate tools strategically.
6. Attend to precision.
7. Look for and make use of structure.
8. Look for and express regularity in repeated reasoning. (pp. 6–8)

For the full descriptions of the Standards for Mathematical Practice, refer to appendix A (page 159).

Figure 1.2 outlines some high-leverage processes linked to the CCSS Mathematical Practices (Franke, Kazemi, & Battey, 2007; Hiebert & Grouws, 2007; Leinwand, 2009; NCTM, 2007; Stein, Remillard, & Smith, 2007; Stein & Smith, 2010; Teacher Education Initiative Curriculum Group, 2008; Weiss, Heck, & Shimkus, 2004).

- An instructional emphasis that approaches mathematics learning as problem solving (Mathematical Practice 1)
- An instructional emphasis on cognitively demanding conceptual tasks that encourage all students to remain engaged in the task without watering down the expectation level (maintaining cognitive demand) (Mathematical Practice 1)
- Instruction that places the highest value on student understanding (Mathematical Practices 1 and 2)
- Instruction that emphasizes the discussion of alternative strategies (Mathematical Practice 3)
- Instruction that includes extensive mathematics discussion (math talk) generated through effective teacher questioning (Mathematical Practices 2, 3, 6, 7, and 8)
- Teacher and student explanations to support strategies and conjectures (Mathematical Practices 2 and 3)
- The use of multiple representations (Mathematical Practices 4 and 5)

Figure 1.2: High-leverage mathematics instructional practices linked to CCSS Mathematical Practices.

Visit **go.solution-tree.com/commoncore** for a reproducible version of this figure.

The implementation of new standards—in this instance, the CCSS content standards—cannot once again be used as a distraction from a needed laser-like focus on *instruction* (that is, instruction that results in developing students who are proficient with the Standards for Mathematical Practice) if the goal is improved student learning (Noguera, 2004; Schmoker, 2006, 2011). Traditionally, mathematics educators have focused on standards and curriculum because they are easier to address than instruction. Make no mistake, standards, curriculum, textbooks, and related instructional materials are crucial tools for teaching and learning, but to truly improve student learning, the quality of mathematics instruction must improve, and that quality must become consistent across all grade levels.

To effectively implement the CCSS Mathematical Practices, you will need to acquire knowledge and ways of reasoning that enable you to analyze and make sense of your teaching, curricula, and students' mathematical thinking in new or more intense ways than you likely have previously done. In order to adopt the high-leverage instructional practices outlined in figure 1.2 (page 15), you also have to align your beliefs with this vision for instruction and decide that the change in your practice is worth the effort (Gresalfi & Cobb, 2011). Collaborative teams are perfectly structured to support you as you work to analyze and make sense of your teaching, come to identify with this new vision of teaching, determine that the change is worthwhile, and find the support necessary to change. This is only possible if the *how* of mathematics instruction—how students do mathematics, embodied in part by the Standards for Mathematical Practice—becomes a significant focus of the collaborative work accomplished in your collaborative team.

Research indicates that effective instruction rests in part on careful planning and that you should consider investing more of your work time in intentionally and systematically planning mathematics lessons with your grade-level colleagues (Morris, Hiebert, & Spitzer, 2009). One of the most effective strategies within collaborative teams to support your adoption of the high-leverage instructional practices (figure 1.2, page 15) is the use of a modified form of Japanese lesson study. Japanese lesson study is a highly structured process for designing and improving mathematics lessons (Fernandez & Yoshida, 2004) first introduced on a wide scale in the United States by Stigler and Hiebert (1999). Teachers collaboratively examine *problems of practice* and design lessons to address those problems (Little & Horn, 2007). Describing the process of formal lesson study in detail is beyond the scope of this book, but using some of the concepts of lesson study within your collaborative team is an effective way for you and your colleagues to begin to analyze how you will teach critical grade-level topics. Consider the following scenario, which describes a fifth-grade collaborative team engaged in much of the work this book recommends you undertake in your collaborative team as you work to implement the CCSS.

A collaborative team of fifth-grade teachers is meeting during its common plan time. The teachers know from work they have previously conducted this year that one of the CCSS fifth-grade critical areas for instructional emphasis is developing fluency with adding and subtracting fractions. The team also knows, based on its review of last year's assessment results, that this is an area in which students have traditionally struggled to demonstrate fluency. Even more concerning to the team is its belief that students don't understand the underlying concepts but rather rely on rote procedures, and this lack of understanding contributes to students' lack of fluency. The team recognizes that in order to develop deeper student understanding of adding and subtracting fractions, teachers need to improve the lessons they use to teach this concept, and this means they too need to develop a deeper understanding of the concepts.

So, the team members begin by discussing some reading they have done outside of their learning team on the topic using the book *Developing Essential Understanding of Rational Numbers for Teaching Mathematics in Grades 3–5* (Barnett-Clarke, Fisher, Marks, & Ross, 2010) and the report "Developing Effective Fractions Instruction for Kindergarten Through 8th Grade: A Practice Guide" (Siegler et al., 2010). This background reading has deepened the teachers' understanding of fractions and sparks a productive discussion of new instructional tasks, representations, and questions they can use with students to engage them in the concept and to check to make sure students understand the concept as the lesson unfolds. By the time the collaborative team is done, team members have written detailed lesson plans to introduce these concepts, which include detailed lesson notes, tasks and examples, key questions, anticipated student responses and their planned responses, guided practice tasks, summary questions, adaptations for English learners (ELs) or students with disabilities, and formative assessment strategies to determine if students have accomplished the instructional objective.

Each member of the team commits to using the lesson with his or her students, and the team has agreed to watch a video together of one team member teaching the lesson in order to evaluate the lesson's effectiveness. The team plans to focus its next collaborative team session on discussing the effectiveness of the designed lesson based on student performance, so teachers can both plan necessary responses to student learning and make modifications to the lesson so that they can further improve on the lesson prior to teaching it next year.

Intensive lesson planning as described in the preceding example is not only a high-leverage strategy to support you as you work to change your practice but is also an effective strategy to prevent the degradation of collaborative team discussions into mere story and material swapping or activity sharing (Perry & Lewis, 2010; Stein, Russell, & Smith, 2011). This type of intense collaborative lesson planning is time consuming and difficult to do for each lesson that is taught annually; unfortunately, you do not have that kind of planning time. However, the lack of time to devote to carefully planning and reflecting on all lessons cannot be used as an excuse to *never* collaboratively learn, plan, and reflect on the effectiveness of certain key lessons per standard cluster. Your goal must be to collaboratively design and refine more and more lessons over time. Effective planning is so important that Wiliam (2011) believes that "sometimes a teacher does her best teaching before the students arrive in the classroom" (p. 49). In order to begin the process of improving instruction, your collaborative team should determine the two to three most critical lessons that will be your focus in each unit and commit yourselves to collaboratively planning these key lessons, designing necessary interventions based on student learning, and revising these critical lessons for future use. Which lessons should be selected? The lessons selected for intensive planning and reflection should be focused on those standards students have struggled with most in the past, based on your analysis of prior student assessment results, and the CCSS critical areas for instructional emphasis.

Gradually, year after year, your collaborative team creates and revises more and more highly effective lessons, thereby continuously improving your instruction in small manageable chunks with shared energies rather than in isolation. Simultaneously, as your collaborative team works on lessons—hopefully side by side with other grade-level teams—and uses the refined lessons, you reduce the variation in instructional quality among teachers in your school by following a process that is similar to how other professions in the United States continually improve and develop consistency

(Morris & Hiebert, 2011). This process involves collaborative sharing of the same problem for which a product offers a solution, making adjustments to improve the product, and continuously improving the product with contributions from everyone in the system. This collegial approach is comparable to that of the PLC process as well as lesson study.

Over the course of a decade, a team of fifth-grade teachers might amass nearly one hundred highly effective lessons, in addition to more effective interventions for students who struggle and challenges for gifted students. The potential cumulative impact of this work on instructional effectiveness and student learning would be truly remarkable. Now imagine each collaborative teacher team within your school district carrying out this process. The powerful cumulative effect of students receiving more and more effective instruction, which can only be accomplished through this system of continuous improvement, has the potential to substantially eliminate the differences in student achievement due to inconsistencies in the quality of instruction and differences in socioeconomic status (Rivkin, Hanushek, & Kain, 2005).

Assessing What Students Should Learn

Once your collaborative team has agreed on the content you intend to teach students and the Mathematical Practices you intend to develop, you must next collaboratively create assessments and scoring rubrics that will indicate whether or not your students have learned the agreed-on content standards. The National Mathematics Advisory Panel recommends using weekly formative assessments with elementary students as a key strategy to support struggling students, provided the assessment results are used to adapt instruction based on student progress (NMAP, 2008).

This recommendation is based on a wealth of research on effective instructional interventions in mathematics; research on the power of formative assessment to impact student achievement; and research on the practices that are in place at schools that are successfully raising the achievement of all students while simultaneously closing the achievement gap (Baker, Gersten, & Lee, 2002; Hanley, 2005; McCall, Hauser, Cronin, Kingsbury, & Houser, 2006; Popham, 2008; Wiliam, 2007b, 2011; Wiliam & Thompson, 2007; Williams, 2003). Researchers have found that the use of formative assessment processes (described fully in chapter 4) as a component of mathematics instruction is one of the most effective educational interventions (Black & Wiliam, 1998).

It is important to recognize that every assessment used in grades 3–5 can and should serve a formative function because the results can be used to provide students with targeted additional support. But before your collaborative team can modify instruction and provide students with targeted additional support, it is necessary to clearly identify the specific mathematics weaknesses and strengths of individual students (Hanley, 2005). Chapter 4 discusses the use of summative assessment instruments as formative tools. Chapter 5 provides in-depth guidance on structuring intervention. The focus now is to explain why it is important for you to spend time collaboratively developing assessments and scoring rubrics within your collaborative team.

When you meet in your collaborative team to discuss and plan a phase of instruction, you need to begin your planning with the end in mind (Wiggins & McTighe, 2000). Once your collaborative team has identified what you want your students to learn, and before you begin to collaboratively plan the first lesson of a *unit* (a period of instructional time, not content), it is crucial your team works together to build the common formative and summative assessments you will use during that unit.

During that time, your team will determine if your students are making progress learning the agreed-on curriculum (by using formative assessment for regularly monitoring and improving understanding) and acquiring the agreed-on curriculum at the end of the instructional unit (by using summative assessment to provide an indication of understanding, proficiency, fluency, and problem-solving skill).

It is essential that these assessments be collaboratively created *and* that each member of the collaborative team agrees to use these assessments and scoring rubrics. During the process of creating these common classroom assessments and scoring rubrics, each member of your collaborative team clearly defines and solidifies his or her own expectations for student performance and, more important, each team member develops a shared expectation for student performance, how it will be measured, and how it will be recorded—removing one of the instructional inconsistencies that plagues teaching and learning.

Consider an example. One of the critical areas for instructional emphasis in the grade 3 CCSS is that students will develop an "understanding of multiplication and division and strategies for multiplication and division within 100" (NGA & CCSSO, 2010, p. 21). Unless you work together as a team to develop and use common assessments, one teacher may plan to administer a series of timed procedural multiplication and division basic fact tests, while another teacher may require students to write a series of related facts and explain how the different equations are related, emphasizing the conceptual relationship between multiplication and division. The qualitative difference in depth of knowledge expectations between these two approaches is significant and has a tremendous impact (from an equity perspective) on what students will learn.

If your team collaboratively writes the assessments and scoring rubrics with agreed-on depth of knowledge expectations, then each member of the team shares an understanding of what is expected of students and, more important, *the same performance level is expected of all third-grade students* no matter which teacher the students are assigned. Equally important—by starting with the development of the assessments—all members of your team from the beginning know how students will be assessed. This in turn affects how you will teach. The assessment must focus on conceptual understanding, as CCSS require, and each teacher must know this in advance of teaching the lessons. The collaborative team commitment to using the common assessments and scoring rubrics in turn demands that daily mathematics instruction must also focus on conceptual understanding.

Student performance on these common assessments will be shared with everyone in the collaborative team in order to plan appropriate and targeted intervention. The common unit assessments provide a powerful incentive to make sure that the same content is taught and the same high level of student performance is expected of all students—procedural *and* conceptual learning goals. In this sense, assessment not only informs instruction but actually directs instruction.

The type of formal formative assessment suggested here is to be relatively short in duration—ten minutes, at most, and only covering material taught in the previous two to three lessons—and its use does not result in a significant loss of instructional time. This use of formative assessment as an instructional tool should not be distinguished from the act of effective instruction; in fact, the evidence suggests that the use of formative assessment actually leads to increased precision in how instructional time is used (NMAP, 2008). It is important to keep in mind that formative assessment is a continuous process and not characterized by the use of any specific pencil-and-paper assessment instrument (see chapter 4 for details).

Response to Intervention

An assessment is only formative if you use the results to inform and improve your instruction; effective assessment requires you to take action (respond) when it is determined that students have not learned some component of the agreed-on curriculum. The response also has to be directive; all students who need additional support must be provided the additional support they need (Buffum et al., 2009). DuFour et al. (2008) outline four practices that a school must do to truly ensure learning for all:

1. Implement intervention plans that provide students with additional time and support for learning as soon as they experience difficulty
2. Implement systematic processes to ensure students' learning needs are addressed schoolwide rather than according to the discretion of individual teachers
3. Implement timely procedures to identify and respond to students who need additional time and support
4. Implement directive interventions, meaning students are not *invited* to receive additional support but rather are *required* to receive additional support

This collaborative team process, with its grade-level sessions focused on mathematics lesson planning and the development and analysis of common assessments, is designed to support you in implementing a systematic and timely system of intervention for all students in need of such assistance.

RTI should not be viewed as a program "but rather [as] a system for meeting all students' needs" (Buffum et al., 2009, p. 23). One of the most effective interventions in mathematics at the K–8 level is an approach to instruction that carefully monitors student acquisition of the agreed-on curriculum based on collaboratively designed formative assessments. Ideally, the "formal" formative assessments (recall that formative assessment is a continual process) should be administered at least once a week, with the results of those formative assessments used to form smaller groups of students who should receive *additional* instruction in the skills and concepts with which they are struggling (Baker et al., 2002).

Much of the required targeted additional instructional support will occur during Tier 1 core instructional time (see chapter 5). However, the evidence is clear concerning the positive impact of providing students with an additional period of well-targeted mathematics instruction at the elementary level when it is necessary at Tier 2 and Tier 3 (Slavin & Lake, 2008). But this is the important point: the well-targeted supplemental instruction must take place *in addition to* whole-class instruction instead of *in place of it.* Interventions need to be supplementary in nature and not replace the core program but instead provide additional, more targeted instruction in the core concepts (Buffum et al., 2009). In too many cases, traditional elementary school interventions have failed because they are not done *in addition to* whole-class instruction but *instead of it.* The RTI-tiered preventative approach is designed to minimize the number of students who require Tier 2 or Tier 3 intervention in your PLC.

When students struggle in mathematics, as teachers we traditionally respond in one of two ways:

1. We slow the pace of instruction for all students until each student has enough time to master content—"going as fast as the slowest student."
2. We "cover" the content—racing through it and ignoring the fact that some students "get it" while others do not.

Given the accountability requirements of No Child Left Behind (NCLB), racing through the curriculum without ensuring that students have demonstrated mastery of essential content is no longer an option. This is one of the positive consequences of NCLB. But slowing down the pace of instruction is not a viable alternative. All too often, schools that serve large numbers of struggling students emphasize slowing down the pace of instruction and end up teaching less mathematics content to the very students who most need more instruction in order to learn more content (Walker, 2007).

Strategic efforts must be made to ensure that all students have an opportunity to learn the agreed-on grade-level curriculum and simultaneously guarantee each student the instructional time and support he or she needs to learn it well. Intervention time must be allocated from within the regular school day. There are as many different ways to find the additional instructional time needed for Tier 2 or Tier 3 interventions during the school day as there are schools. Compacting the curriculum can provide the additional mathematics instructional time recommended in the models in figure 1.3 (page 22). The same focus and coherence applied to the CCSS for mathematics curriculum need to be applied to all subjects in the elementary curricula.

There is simply too much content in the elementary school curriculum, both within subjects and across subjects. Selecting and focusing on fewer essential standards can free up the time necessary for a daily differentiated instruction block in mathematics (Schmoker, 2011). The bottom line is that in instrumental subjects—reading, writing, and mathematics—instructional time must expand so that the learning becomes constant for all students (Buffum et al., 2009). Figure 1.3 describes four successful models for finding additional instructional time for mathematics intervention in grades 3–5.

Model One: Additional Total Mathematics Time That Individual Teachers Administer

Some schools dedicate additional total time to mathematics instruction. For example, they allot only the equivalent of seventy-five minutes of daily math instruction in grades 3–5. However, teachers spend sixty minutes daily on new instruction and collect the "left-over time" to have a thirty- to forty-five-minute differentiated math block of time twice a week in which they address individual student needs based on weekly formative assessments. Individual teachers work with their own students.

Model Two: Additional Total Mathematics Time That Grade-Level Teams Collaboratively Administer

Other schools allocate time as in model one, but the teachers work as a team to regroup students so each teacher is not trying to teach as many topics to as many different small groups of students. The teachers meet in their grade-level collaborative teams to determine which students need additional instruction and support in what topics and then regroup the students during the differentiated instruction block. Teachers can then focus their reteaching on fewer targeted topics, and many of the students have the opportunity to learn the concept or skill from a different teacher.

Model Three: Curriculum Compacting to Gain a Weekly Intervention Day

Some schools compact the social studies and science curriculum in grades 3–5 by focusing only on the essential objectives, eliminating up to 20 percent of the curriculum. They then use this time to provide all students with a weekly period of additional mathematics instruction to meet individual needs.

Model Four: Compacting Curriculum to Gain a Daily Intervention Time

Some schools have left the traditional sixty-minute daily allocation for mathematics instruction intact but compacted other parts of the day to create a daily thirty-minute differentiated instruction block of time. In the most successful implementations, teachers meet in grade-level collaborative teams to identify student needs based on weekly formative assessments and regroup students so each teacher is teaching a smaller set of skills or concepts.

Figure 1.3: Intervention time models in grades 3–5.

Visit **go.solution-tree.com/commoncore** for a reproducible version of this figure.

An advantage of the last model is that it allows one teacher in your collaborative team to use the differentiated instruction block to work with those students who have demonstrated high levels of proficiency with the content, permitting these students to study topics in more depth as well as to explore additional but connected concepts. When you work as a collaborative team to regroup students for targeted additional instruction and support (or extended learning), you also ensure every team member carries out interventions and that every student receives either necessary intervention or extended learning time, thereby removing all perceptions that intervention is a punishment. An additional benefit of the collaborative team approach to intervention is that you have the opportunity to brainstorm, share, discuss, and develop alternate instructional strategies to meet the needs of individual students. As Buffum et al. (2009) argue, "The vast majority of educators teach the very best way they know how. . . . Most teachers re-teach using the same instructional practices that failed to work the first time" (p. 68). Collaborative teams are uniquely structured to provide you the support and opportunity you need to expand and improve your instructional practices.

The Future of Mathematics in Your School

Transitioning to and implementing the Common Core State Standards is a one-time opportunity for you and your students. If the implementation of the CCSS is to move beyond the typical superficial implementation of previous reforms (Reys & Reys, 2011), then the implementation effort will require you to engage with your colleagues in an ongoing process of professional development and learning as a PLC. Well supported by research, this book outlines deliberate steps that you can take as you work with your colleagues to improve your own mathematics instruction, improve the quality of mathematics education in your school, and help all students develop a deep understanding and proficiency with Common Core mathematics. Your collaborative team functioning within the designed culture of a PLC is the most effective way to successfully improve mathematics instruction in grades 3–5 and meet the challenges of transitioning to and implementing the Common Core State Standards for mathematics.

As you begin to work together with your grade-level colleagues to plan more effective mathematics instruction, it will be critical that you focus on the CCSS Mathematical Practices. The Mathematical Practices (see appendix A, page 159) provide the overarching habits of doing mathematics that all learners at every grade level should experience. In the chapters that follow, we will unpack the Mathematical Practices and the CCSS content standards—and explore the role collaborative teams play in implementing and supporting all students' successful acquisition of these new standards through highly effective instruction, assessment, and intervention practices. In addition, you will discover tools you can use in your collaborative team as you work to make the vision of the Common Core State Standards a reality for your students.

Chapter 1 Extending My Understanding

1. Compare the current model of collaborative professional development used in your school or district with Darling-Hammond's (2010) definition of effective professional development (page 6).
    - How much time and during what time of day (before, during, or after school; late start or early release) is devoted to effective professional development each school year? Each month? Is this time spent in grade-level or vertical collaborative teams?

  - What evidence exists to support or improve your existing model?

2. Discuss what an instructional shift toward higher levels of cognitive demand looks like in terms of mathematical tasks and measures of formative assessment. What is the relationship between higher levels of cognitive demand and the Mathematical Practices?
3. Examine the high-leverage instructional practices linked to the CCSS Mathematics Practices in figure 1.2 (page 15). How do these practices compare with the individual and group philosophies of staff in your collaborative team? How might you use this information to identify a starting point for your work with the Mathematical Practices?
4. Using figure 1.3 (page 22), discuss the advantages and disadvantages of each intervention time model. Which model for finding and using additional instructional time might work best in grades 3–5 in your school? What modifications in scheduling might be needed to implement these changes?

Online Resources

Visit **go.solution-tree.com/commoncore** for links to these resources.

- **"A Professional Collaboration Model" (Jenkins, 2010; www.nctm.org/publications/article.aspx?id=27410):** This article describes a well-defined structure to guide the efforts of grade-level collaborative teams as they work to promote positive changes to instructional practices.
- **The Center for Comprehensive School Reform and Improvement (2009; www.centerforcsri.org/plc/websites.html):** Here you can peruse a collection of resources to support an in-depth examination of professional learning communities.
- **Inside Mathematics (2010b; www.insidemathematics.org/index.php/tools-for-teachers/tools-for-coaches):** This portion of the Inside Mathematics website helps mathematics coaches and specialists support the professional learning teams they lead. Tools to support lesson study and teacher learning, including video vignettes that model coaching conversation, are available.
- **Inside Mathematics (2010c; www.insidemathematics.org/index.php/tools-for-teachers/tools-for-principals-and-administrators):** This portion of the Inside Mathematics website supports school-based administrators and district mathematics supervisors who are responsible for establishing the structure and vision for the professional development work of grade-level and cross-grade-level learning teams or in a PLC.
- **Learning Forward (2011; www.learningforward.org/standards/standards.cfm):** Learning Forward is an international association of learning educators focused on increasing student achievement through more effective professional learning. This website provides a wealth of resources, including an online annotated bibliography of articles and websites, to support the work of professional learning teams.

CHAPTER 2

Implementing the Common Core Standards for Mathematical Practice

The Common Core State Standards for mathematics include standards for mathematics content as well as standards describing expectations for mathematical practice. According to the CCSS, "The Standards for Mathematical Practice describe varieties of expertise that mathematics educators at all levels should seek to develop in their students" (NGA & CCSSO, 2010, p. 6). Implementation of the Standards for Mathematical Practice address the second required paradigm shift: a shift to include within daily lesson plans intentional strategies to teach mathematics in different ways—in ways that focus on the process of learning and developing deep student understanding of the mathematical content. Your goal will be to develop in students conceptual understanding *and* procedural fluency of the CCSS content through the collaborative selection of high-cognitive-demand mathematical tasks with a focus on student engagement with the Mathematical Practices. (See appendix A, page 159, for the Standards for Mathematical Practice.)

Your ultimate goal is to equip students with particular expertise that will help them be successful across the mathematics curriculum and at every level of their mathematics learning. In this chapter, we interpret the CCSS Mathematical Practices to provide you guidance as you work in your collaborative team. This chapter will help you develop understanding for each of the eight Mathematical Practices as you work collaboratively to design lessons that embed these practices into your daily instruction and make the pedagogical decisions necessary to create environments in which the practices enhance instruction focused on student learning.

The CCSS Mathematical Practices are based on the National Council of Teachers of Mathematics' (2000) Process Standards (problem solving, reasoning and proof, communication, connections, and representation) and the National Research Council's (2001) Strands of Mathematical Proficiency (adaptive reasoning, strategic competence, conceptual understanding, procedural fluency, and productive disposition). NCTM's and NRC's groundwork is reinforced and further refined in the CCSS Mathematical Practices.

The CCSS Mathematical Practices describe what *students* should be *doing* as they learn the CCSS for mathematics content standards. How should students engage with that mathematics and interact with their fellow students? By creating a classroom culture that extends beyond traditional, teacher-centered instruction, you can successfully facilitate students' engagement in mathematics learning that leads to proficiency in the Standards for Mathematical Practice. The Standards for Mathematical Practice are not a checklist of teacher to-dos, but rather, they support an environment in which the CCSS for mathematics content standards are enacted and are framed by specific expertise that you can use to help students develop to support their understanding and application of mathematics.

The CCSS Mathematical Practices

By first defining each CCSS Mathematical Practice through exposure to its meaning and examples and then addressing each of the questions in figure 2.1 by working in the collaborative team, you can make sense of a particular CCSS Mathematical Practice, generate ideas for how to support the CCSS Mathematical Practice, and analyze ways to assess students' success with the CCSS Mathematical Practice. The questions in figure 2.1 are designed to guide the work of the collaborative team as you explore the eight CCSS Mathematical Practices.

1. What is the intent of this CCSS Mathematical Practice?
2. What teacher actions facilitate this CCSS Mathematical Practice?
3. What evidence is there that students are demonstrating this CCSS Mathematical Practice?

Figure 2.1: Key questions used to understand the CCSS Mathematical Practices.

Tasks for collaborative teams are provided for each CCSS Mathematical Practice. The purpose of these tasks is to facilitate the work of the collaborative teams by suggesting activities you can complete within classroom settings or between collaborative team meetings. Your collaborative team can choose to complete the tasks in the order they are provided, address one at each team meeting, group tasks together, or pick and choose tasks that best meet the goals of your team.

Mathematical Practice 1: Make Sense of Problems and Persevere in Solving Them

The first step in exploring CCSS Mathematical Practice 1, "Make sense of problems and persevere in solving them," is to provide a clear definition of what a problem is as it specifically relates to mathematics instruction (NGA & CCSSO, 2010, p. 6). A *problem* is defined as a *situation,* be it real or contrived, in which a challenge (question or unknown) that requires an appropriate response (such as an answer, solution, explanation, or counterexample) is presented and for which the person facing the challenge does not have a readily accessible appropriate response (Kantowski, 1980). That is:

> To solve a problem is to find a way where no way is known, to find a way out of a difficulty, to find a way around an obstacle, and to attain a desired end that is not immediately attainable, by appropriate means. (Hatfield, Edwards, Bitter, & Morrow, 2008, p. 100)

Students do not always initially see a viable solution pathway and sometimes will need multiple attempts to successfully solve the problem. This inherently means that problems can vary regarding topics, contexts, structure, and so on, and it means that teaching problem solving is not about teaching specific problems but about teaching students how to use their knowledge, skills, attitudes, and resources to successfully respond to problems (Pölya, 1957).

A subsequent notion is this: *problem solving is one of the hallmarks of mathematics.* What allows problem solving to earn such a grand title is that problem solving is the essence of doing mathematics (NCTM, 1980). When students are engaged in problem solving, this means that students are drawing on their understanding of mathematical concepts and procedures with the goal to reach a successful response to the problem.

Although problem solving is a critical element of school mathematics, you may sometimes find that problem solving is a source of frustration for your students. For example, Reys, Lindquist, Lambdin, and Smith (2012) report that "children who think they should always be able to solve problems immediately and easily are likely to view as impossible any problem where the solution is not immediately apparent, and they are unlikely to persist in working toward a solution" (p. 110). Additionally, according to the results of the *TIMSS Videotape Classroom Study* (Stigler, Gonzales, Kawanaka, Knoll, & Serrano, 1999), teachers are often likely to "design lessons that remove obstacles and minimize confusion. Procedures for solving problems would be clearly demonstrated so students would not flounder or struggle" (p. 137). Lessons planned from the perspective that students need protection from struggle do not support the perseverance aspect of this CCSS Mathematical Practice, and they deny students the opportunity to develop meaningful mathematical understandings (Stein et al., 2007).

There are two problem-solving issues that students must deal with: (1) the ability to make sense of problems and (2) the fortitude to participate or persevere in the problem-solving process toward a successful end. The latter is an important component of a *productive disposition,* which is addressed as one of the strands of mathematical proficiency defined in *Adding It Up* (NRC, 2001).

The Teacher's Role in Developing Mathematical Practice 1

You are instrumental in helping students develop skills and attitudes that build their ability to solve problems effectively. The tasks presented and the guidance provided enable students to gain confidence as they encounter a variety of problems that require them to employ a range of mathematical skills. To learn how to persevere in solving problems, students must be given opportunities to meet challenges but not be overwhelmed by them.

Provide Good Problems

You play a critical role supporting students' ability to make sense of problems and persevere in solving them. The first of these roles is the presentation of appropriate problems or tasks for students to solve. While it seems that *appropriate* is subjective, there are six questions you might discuss within your collaborative team when planning lessons to assess the quality of a problem or mathematical task.

1. **Is the problem interesting to students?** With information about students' lives (for example, their social and creative interests), you can create or select problems that will engage students by inviting them to be personally invested in the problem.
2. **Does the problem involve meaningful mathematics?** Meaningful mathematics is mathematics that will propel students forward in their mathematical knowledge at an appropriate level. Consider the problem in figure 2.2 related to the CCSS for mathematics grade 5 domain Number and Operations in Base Ten. (Refer to figure 1.1 in chapter 1, page 11, for an explanation of CCSS terminology.)

   This very common problem is distorted by the use of mathematics that does not contribute to students' understanding of the problem context. While this problem meets the intent of the standard in which students are multiplying decimals to hundredths, it involves unreasonable dimensions and makes the problem nonsensical.

Randy has a rectangular yard within which he wishes to build a rectangular pool. The pool will be surrounded by a walkway that is the same width all the way around.

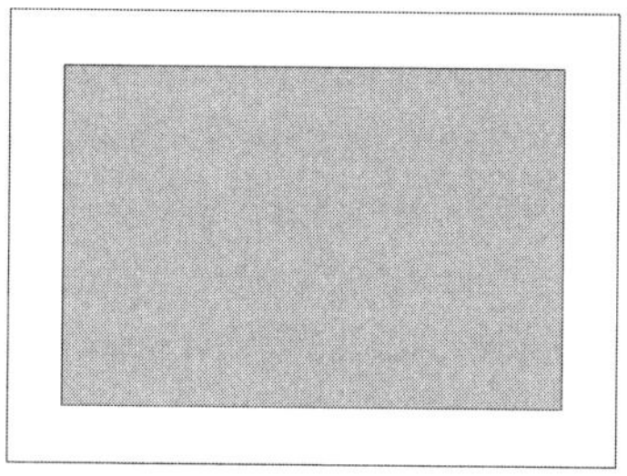

If the yard's dimensions are 36.34 ft. by 25.65 ft., and the pool's dimensions are 28.14 ft. by 19.35 ft., how much of the yard will be used for the walkway?

Figure 2.2: Sample mathematics task.

3. **Does the problem provide an opportunity for students to apply and extend mathematics?** Problems that support students in applying and extending the mathematics they are learning or have learned help students understand the purpose of the problems and give students a starting point for solving the problem.
4. **Is the problem challenging for students?** The purpose of this challenge is not to frustrate students but to build within students the kind of attitudes and perseverance necessary to be a successful problem solver and to exercise students' mental mathematical thought. This is a good exercise for the collaborative team to engage in as well.

5. **Does the problem support the use of multiple strategies?** Two students can read the same problem and have two different ways of perceiving and approaching the problem. Consider the following example in figure 2.3 from the fifth-grade CCSS for mathematics domain Number and Operations in Base Ten (see 5.NBT.5).

> Students who have not been taught the standard algorithm for dividing multidigit numbers are presented with the following problem:
>
> *There are 228 players in the softball league. How many 12-member teams can be formed if each player is placed on exactly one team?*
>
> **Solution one:** Students might repeatedly subtract 12 from the number of available players until there are no players left.
>
> **Solution two:** Students might use a guess-and-check strategy in which they multiply 12 by different factors until they reach a product of 228.

Figure 2.3: Sample mathematics task.

6. **Will students' interactions with the problem reveal information about students' mathematics understanding?** Examining students' interactions with a problem (for example, students' work, discussions, and processes) should provide information about how students' thinking is hindered or advanced by interaction with the problem.

This is not an exhaustive list of questions, but it is a beginning step toward examining problems that will potentially benefit students' mathematical learning.

Facilitate Student Engagement in the Problem-Solving Process

Successful problem solving does not mean that students will always conclude with the correct response to a problem but rather that students will undertake a genuine effort to engage in the problem-solving process, drawing on resources such as appropriate tools, prior knowledge, discussion with others, and questions to aid in the process. Successful problem solvers also recognize that powerful learning can be experienced even when an appropriate answer to a problem cannot be found. Successful problem solvers exhibit a willingness to persevere.

Support Students to Unpack Problems, Check Reasonableness of Solutions, and Make Connections

To unpack a problem means to dissect it for the components (the information given, information needed, context, mathematical content, and so on) that might lead to an understanding of the problem and an appropriate response. This is where teachers should be cautioned against an overreliance on *key words* (such as *how many left* and *in each*) and instead incorporate something more closely related to reading comprehension strategies (Clements, 2011). To comprehend problems effectively, students have to employ strategies they have learned during reading instruction. These cognitive strategies include identifying relevant details, noting relationships, predicting, making inferences, synthesizing, visualizing, and distinguishing between mathematics terms and general vocabulary, as well as activating prior knowledge. You may need to remind students that the comprehension strategies they have learned during reading instruction can also be used to understand mathematics problems.

The thinking that is involved in unpacking a problem involves the student seeking information that gives insight on what strategies or ways of thinking might be helpful for solving the problem. It also requires students to flip through their mental files to determine if they have been previously confronted with a similar problem or with a problem that is in some way connected to the present problem. Unpacking a problem also entails gathering data about the mathematics of the problem to determine what mathematical concepts are meaningful to the problem. Consider the following problem from the CCSS for mathematics grade 5 domain Number and Operations—Fractions (5.NF.7).

> Ms. Fox's class has 24 lbs. of jellybeans to sell to raise money for the class garden. If the class packages the jellybeans in bags with ¼ lb. of jellybeans each, how many packages of jellybeans can students make in all?

In this problem, focusing on the key words *in all* does not help the students; what is meaningful is that students need to determine how many groups of one-fourth pounds are in twenty-four pounds. This is the mathematics of the problem; the key words are not the mathematics. The mathematical concept is division of a whole number by a fraction and, more generally, measurement division, which is supported by several solution paths including using repeated subtraction, pictorial models, or an algorithm.

You can help students develop strengths of several processes that are important for the problem-solving experience. For instance, students benefit from knowing that as problem solvers, they have the responsibility of organizing their thoughts for tackling the problem. These thoughts include a comparison of ways to represent the problem—Should it be with manipulatives? Should it be with drawings? Should it be with an algebraic expression? Students could use figure 2.4 to organize their thoughts about the problem.

The Problem in My Own Words	Information Given	Information Needed	Constraints (In What Unit Should the Answer Be?)

Figure 2.4: Problem-solving organizer.

Visit **go.solution-tree.com/commoncore** for a reproducible version of this figure.

Even after organizing thoughts about a problem and asking questions, students still might struggle with the problem-solving experience. However, healthy struggle is invaluable because it builds students' perseverance for long-term engagement with mathematics. Through perseverance, students come to expect that doing mathematics will often lead to a need to try different routes of thinking.

You can also help students understand that the answer is not the final step in problem solving. A great deal of mathematical learning can happen when students are guided to explain and justify processes and check the reasonableness of the solution. In many instances, students can learn about other solutions for the problem and other ways of solving the problem, and mathematical connections can be made to other problems and content. Students can examine and change variables in the problem and hypothesize what might change in the process of solving the new problem and how the answer might change.

The Understanding Questions for Mathematical Practice 1

Discussions within the collaborative team are intended to extend your understanding of the Mathematical Practices and ways in which to plan instruction to provide learning experiences that will enable students to become successful in solving problems. Use these questions to guide the discussion.

1. **What is the intent of this CCSS Mathematical Practice?** A goal of CCSS Mathematical Practice 1 is for students to become successful problem solvers.
2. **What teacher actions facilitate this CCSS Mathematical Practice?** To facilitate CCSS Mathematical Practice 1, you select appropriate problems and guide students in the problem-solving process (for example, engage students in discussions about problems, and ask questions that promote students' thinking about problems).
3. **What evidence is there that students are demonstrating this CCSS Mathematical Practice?** When students are demonstrating CCSS Mathematical Practice 1, they are actively pursuing solutions to a variety of problems. They make decisions about strategies to use, showcase their thinking (show their work, respond to questions, and ask questions), and explain the outcomes of problem-solving experiences.

This Collaborative Team Task is designed to guide the team to consider factors in developing instructional experiences that will contribute to students' skill in solving problems. This discussion will provide additional insight into what constitutes a *good* problem.

Collaborative Team Task: Mathematical Practice 1

Students' problem-solving experiences are grounded in the problems you provide them to discuss, explore, or solve. Your role in selecting good problems is very important because sometimes students work on "exercises" that do not extend their

continued →

learning and only reinforce what they already know. Your task is to select a good problem and submit it to the collaborative team for exploration and discussion. The following questions will support this discussion.

1. What is the source of this problem? What are other fruitful sources for problems?
2. What is the grade level for this problem? (This is a valuable discussion for vertical collaborative teams.)
3. What CCSS for mathematics content is reflected in this problem?
4. Is the context of the problem generally familiar to students?
5. What piqued your interest in this problem when you first read it? Do you think it will capture students' attention in the same way?
6. What characteristic of this problem promotes mathematical discussion?
7. What type of learner will benefit from this problem?
8. Is there only one or more than one way to solve the problem?
9. Is there only one or more than one answer for the problem?
10. Can this problem be used flexibly for assessment (formative or summative)?
11. How might you differentiate the problem (make it more or less challenging) to adjust to individual student learning needs?
12. How does engagement with the problem extend students' learning?
13. What is most challenging about selecting good problems for students?

Visit **go.solution-tree.com/commoncore** for a reproducible version of this feature box.

Mathematical Practice 2: Reason Abstractly and Quantitatively

Reasoning in mathematics is the means by which students try to make sense (by thinking through ideas carefully; considering examples, counterexamples, and alternatives; asking questions; hypothesizing; pondering; and so on) of mathematics so it is usable and useful (NCTM, 2000). Hence, the role of CCSS Mathematical Practice 2, "Reason abstractly and quantitatively," is critical to students' engagement in every area and at every level of the mathematics curriculum (NGA & CCSSO, 2010, p. 6). According to Ball and Bass (2003), "Mathematical reasoning is something that students can learn to do" (p. 33). In fact, these authors suggest two very important benefits of reasoning: it (1) aids students' mathematical understanding and ability to use concepts and procedures in meaningful ways and (2) helps students reconstruct *faded knowledge*—that is, knowledge that is forgotten but can be restored through reasoning with content.

Of course, students can reason about many things, including definitions, examples, and counterexamples. However, paramount in learning mathematics is the need for students to specifically reason about quantities, that is, the need to make sense of quantities and their meanings. Making sense of quantities and understanding their meaning involve addressing the numerical representation—either abstractly (25 ÷ 4) or supported by context. (For example, there are twenty-five students, and four students can ride in each car. How many cars are needed to transport the students?). On the surface, the concept of number may seem trivial, but actually, the concept of number is very complex. For example, dividing 25 by 4 can be completed using an algorithm. However, determining the number of cars needed to transport the students requires an interpretation of the remainder. As Perry and Dockett (2002) state, "Almost all the mathematics that children encounter in elementary school, and much of what they encounter beyond that level, is firmly based in number, [so] the importance of sound number sense cannot be overstated" (p. 93).

The Teacher's Role in Developing Mathematical Practice 2

Although students may have the ability to use reasoning to address everyday occurrences, they are not likely to have had frequent opportunities to reason in the context of mathematics. Students' strategic use of reasoning is fostered through activities centered on numbers and their applications, along with conversations about the mathematical thinking involved.

Provide Distinct Opportunities for Students to Develop a Deep Number Sense

Students need to develop a deep number sense so they will have a strong foundation for reasoning. With a clear articulation of number sense, you can provide students with a variety of instructional supports to help develop theirs. Number sense can be viewed as an understanding of number that empowers students mathematically in at least six ways.

1. **Express interpretations about number:** Consider these numbers—5, 17, 32, 9, and 3—and what would be involved in students making sense of them and their meanings. For example, the knowledge of *five-ness* affords students the ability to describe sets as equal to, greater than, or less than five. Students can also recognize when a set has five objects and when it does not. However, these same numbers can be considered further, but in context: page 5, 17-inch monitor, age 32, 9 lb. box, and 3rd place.
2. **Apply relationships between numbers:** Knowing how two or more numbers relate to each other supports students' engagement in mathematics in many ways. For example, in the CCSS for mathematics fifth-grade content domain Number and Operations—Fractions (5.NF.1), when students add $\frac{1}{3} + \frac{4}{9}$, knowing that 9 is a multiple of 3 allows them to replace $\frac{1}{3}$ with $\frac{3}{9}$ to find the sum.
3. **Recognize the magnitude of numbers:** Age ninety-three is pretty old. The sun being approximately ninety-three million miles from Earth is a very large distance. Ninety-three dollars might even be a lot of money, but ninety-three blades of grass isn't enough to crank up the mower! Students' understanding of the magnitude of numbers, including comparing quantities and sizes, is important for helping students make sense of their world. Students also need to

understand that although magnitude may be abstract, it is also contingent on context. Simply asking students, "Is 775 a big number?" is not enough to support students' reasoning about the magnitude of number because 775 may be big in one context but not very big at all in another context.

4. **Compute:** Computation using the basic operations depends on students' number sense, and the stronger students' number sense, the more they are able to use strategies such as estimation and alternate representations of numbers—for example, viewing *thirty-two* as $32 = 8 \times 4$, 4×8, or $4 \times 4 \times 2$ (see third-grade CCSS domain Operations and Algebraic Thinking in appendix B, pages 164–166)—to facilitate computation. Moreover, in the realm of computation, students need to reason to make sense of operations. For instance, it is through reasoning, not mere memorization, that students come to truly understand that "multiplication doesn't always make bigger" or that multiplying a number by two is the same as adding the number to itself or doubling the number. Flexibility in computation is also supported when students can reason about numbers by doing mathematical actions, such as breaking them apart and restructuring the computation request. For example, when multiplying 4×28, students might approach this from a place-value perspective and multiply in this manner: $(4 \times 20) + (4 \times 8)$.
5. **Make decisions involving numbers:** One thing that makes the ability to reason abstractly and quantitatively critical is that it is a very important life skill useful for making daily decisions. For example, consider a mathematical task from the CCSS for mathematics third-grade domain Measurement and Data (see 3.MD.1 in appendix B, page 167). Suppose students know that the bus arrives at their home at 6:45 a.m. Students need to develop reasoning (and their parents would be grateful!) about how much time is needed for the student to awake and be ready for the bus pickup. Is fifteen minutes enough time? Is forty-five minutes enough time? By exploring various real-life examples that involve decision making around real-life quantities, students come to realize the importance of being able to make sense of numbers in their own lives.
6. **Solve problems:** For students to be successful solving word problems, they need to be able to translate given information into an algebraic representation. Reasoning through given information in a word problem is what affords students with the numbers, variables, structures, and so on needed to develop algebraic representations that support efficient manipulations of numerals and symbols. Consider the following task from the fifth-grade CCSS for mathematics domain Operations and Algebraic Thinking (see 5.OA.2).

   > At his father's dry-cleaning business, Charlie evenly divides the number of pants he needs to fold. He folds the same number of pants each day of the week. On Saturday, he only has time to fold 8 pairs of pants. For one six-day workweek last month, Charlie folded 83 pairs of pants. How many pairs of pants did Charlie fold on each day Monday through Friday?

   Translated into an algebraic equation, this might be written as $(n \times 5) + 8 = 83$.

Draw Students' Attention to Numbers and Their Applications

There are several ways teachers can help students reason about numbers. First, it is helpful to consider numbers to be a source of exploration for learners. Numbers are found everywhere, including on signs, license plates, room numbers, street addresses, and so on. Secondly, as the National Council of Teachers of Mathematics (2000) recommends, "regularly encourage students to demonstrate and deepen their understanding of numbers and operations by solving interesting, contextualized problems and by discussing the representations and strategies they [students] use" (p. 79). The benefit of problem solving can be strengthened by further supporting students' understanding and reasoning about responses to and extensions of the problem. Another way to help students develop reasoning skills is to require students to justify their responses—whether numerical or otherwise—and to consider examples and counterexamples of their thinking. How might the dry-cleaning problem be extended? Inequalities could be incorporated by asking the students to determine the number of pants Charlie would need to fold each day if the total were changed to "*at least* 83 pants" or "*at most* 83 pants." This also leads to discussions of reasonableness of responses. For example, it would not be reasonable to fold a fraction of a pair of pants.

Encourage Discussion That Promotes Reasoning

Classroom discussion that promotes reasoning is dialogue that involves teacher-to-student communication as well as student-to-student communication. Teacher-to-student communication might include questions from the teacher that probe students' thinking beyond the suggestion of an answer. You consider students' answers, whether right or wrong, as opportunities to stretch students' thinking beyond the answer realized. In addition, teacher-to-student communication can and should involve discussions emerging from students' hypotheses about a mathematical concept or procedure and students' conjectures on how mathematics works. This discussion can even stem from the presentation of student work samples, even work samples from fictitious students. Student-to-student communication is supported by peer-to-peer explanations and debates when students are required to provide justification for their thinking. Students working collaboratively to engage in mathematics can fuel student-to-student dialogue by sharing their mathematical thought and decision making about the routes their thinking should take in order to arrive at sensible conclusions. Inferences about students' ability to reason can also be determined through the careful analysis of student work and performance in mathematics.

The Understanding Questions for Mathematical Practice 2

Being able to reason is central to students' success in learning mathematics as well as in other areas of the curriculum. These questions provide a framework for collaborative team discussions of Mathematical Practice 2.

1. **What is the intent of this CCSS Mathematical Practice?** A goal of CCSS Mathematical Practice 2 is for students to learn how to reason with and about mathematics.
2. **What teacher actions facilitate this CCSS Mathematical Practice?** To support students' development of reasoning, teachers must give students space to think and reflect on mathematical content and support students in communicating and refining their thinking.
3. **What evidence is there that students are demonstrating this CCSS Mathematical Practice?** When students are demonstrating CCSS Mathematical Practice 2, they are sharing and justifying their mathematical conceptions and adjusting their thinking based on mathematical information gathered through discussions and responses to questions.

The following Collaborative Team Task is designed to focus the team's discussion on activities that promote the development of students' reasoning. The discussion, based on two articles from *Teaching Children Mathematics,* will allow you to compare your practices with those the authors recommend.

Collaborative Team Task: Mathematical Practice 2

Articles from professional journals can be used to promote constructive discussions within the collaborative team. In the following example, two articles from *Teaching Children Mathematics* are used to support discussion and comparison of instructional practices within the collaborative team. If you do not have access to this journal, the team can select two other readings related to reasoning about number.

One-half of the collaborative team could read the following article:

Rathouz, M. (2011). 3 ways that promote student reasoning. *Teaching Children Mathematics, 18*(3), 182–189.

The other half of the collaborative team could read the following article:

Olson, J. (2007). Developing students' mathematical reasoning through games. *Teaching Children Mathematics, 13*(9), 464–471.

For the collaborative team meeting, each subteam should prepare to present a summary of the article and engage the other subteam in a discussion regarding the primary points of the article.

For example, Rathouz's article addresses the role of justifying solution methods in students' mathematics learning. What norms does your team have in place to ensure that students are learning how to justify their solution methods and how to determine whether others' solution methods are valid?

Olson's article presents a variety of games that support students' mathematics learning and encourages the development of students' reasoning skills. What games are best for this role? What games do the collaborative team members currently use that support students' reasoning skills?

Visit **go.solution-tree.com/commoncore** for a reproducible version of this feature box.

Mathematical Practice 3: Construct Viable Arguments and Critique the Reasoning of Others

Students engaged in CCSS Mathematical Practice 3, "Construct viable arguments and critique the reasoning of others," are making conjectures based on their analysis of given situations (NGA & CCSSO, 2010, pp. 6–7). Students explain and justify their thinking as they communicate to other classmates and to you. Classmates listen to explanations and justifications and judge the reasonableness of the claims. The successful facilitation of this standard is based on the social learning environment of the classroom. As Rasmussen, Yackel, and King (2003) state:

> Every class, from the most traditional to the most reform-oriented, has social norms that are operative for that particular class. What distinguishes one class from another is not the presence or absence of social norms but, rather, the nature of the norms that differ from class to class. (pp. 147–148)

Does your class have a norm that requires students to provide an explanation with their solution? This norm, if present, places importance on *how* students solved a problem rather than just *if* they solved the problem.

In a classroom in which students are expected to construct arguments and critique others' reasoning, students should:

1. Provide explanations and justifications as part of their solution processes
2. Attempt to make sense of their classmates' solutions by asking questions for clarification
3. Communicate when they don't understand or don't agree with solutions others present, spurring discussion between and among students

Eventually, these discussions become a natural part of the classroom discourse and can occur in an organized way without teacher direction. These norms are established through a process of negotiation that makes expectations clear but that also involves students in the process of implementing the norms (Cobb, 2000). These negotiations often emerge when establishing classroom rules, such as "be respectful" and "listen when others are speaking." You need to discuss the importance of classroom rules, and the class can generate a reasonable number of rules and create a list that it agrees to follow at all times. These sorts of rules help to support what effective mathematics learners do. Mathematics learners make conjectures, test those conjectures, and discuss their implications within a community that is receptive to such discussions.

Dixon, Egendoerfer, and Clements (2009) describe a study in which an elementary school teacher encouraged students to participate in whole-class discussion during mathematics instruction without raising their hands to speak. While this was intimidating for the teacher at first, ultimately the students in this class provided more rich verbal and written mathematical explanations and justifications; students who were unsure of their solutions were more comfortable sharing them, and "students began to exhibit understanding that could be defined as more conceptual than procedural in nature" (Dixon et al., 2009, p. 1074). The expectation isn't that all teachers should now eliminate the rule that students must raise their hands and be acknowledged before speaking, but rather, you should think about what sorts of expectations and behaviors support desired engagement during mathematics instruction and what might detract from it.

The Teacher's Role in Developing Mathematical Practice 3

A learning-centered classroom affords students opportunities to engage in conversations with their teacher and peers about their thoughts and actions as they solve problems. Such a classroom embodies a positive environment in which mutual respect flourishes because everyone is aware of the social norms and expectations. Teaching practices should foster a communicative atmosphere in which student voices are evident as students explore mathematics concepts, use mathematics vocabulary, and demonstrate their ability to use mathematical processes (Kinzer, Virag, & Morales, 2011).

Establish Supportive Social Norms

Once you determine desirable characteristics of classroom engagement that will support students making and testing conjectures and evaluating the reasoning of others, you will likely need to model these sorts of behaviors for the students. One way to do this is to share several correct solutions to the same problem. The solutions should vary in terms of the included explanations and justifications. You can share the solutions with the class as a whole-class discussion or have small groups evaluate the acceptability of the solutions (Smith & Stein, 2011). Discussion should focus on the completeness of the solutions and whether or not the explanations are limited to a list of steps followed to solve a problem or the *mathematical reasoning* involved. Emphasis should be placed on the need to include mathematical reasoning with solutions.

Similarly, you should share solutions that include adequate explanations and justifications and facilitate students to work in groups to critique the reasoning itself. This is different from determining if enough information was included. The focus here is on the mathematics. Think-aloud techniques can be used with students to make sense of the reasoning shared in the problem as a way to model what it means to critique the reasoning of others. In these instances, sample work that reflects common misconceptions provides a useful means for generating discussion around common errors.

Provide Opportunities for Students to Make and Evaluate Conjectures

Consider the following scenario in a fifth-grade classroom from the domain Number and Operations—Fractions (see 5.NF.3) in which students interpret a fraction as dividing the numerator by the denominator. Students have been asked to describe how six granola bars could be shared equally among four people. A student quickly explains that each person could get one whole granola bar and then half of another granola bar. The students are then challenged to find another way to equally share the granola bars. Two groups of students divide each granola bar into two equal pieces and *give* three of those pieces to each of the four people. One group says that each person would get $3/2$ granola bars. The second group agrees with the reasoning of the first group but says it solved the problem differently, so each person will get 3⁄12 of a granola bar. Members of the first group indicate they do not agree but ask the second group to explain. A member of the second group goes to the board and draws the solution and says, "We shared the pieces so each person got 3 pieces. There were 12 pieces all together, so that is 3⁄12 of a granola bar." (See figure 2.5.)

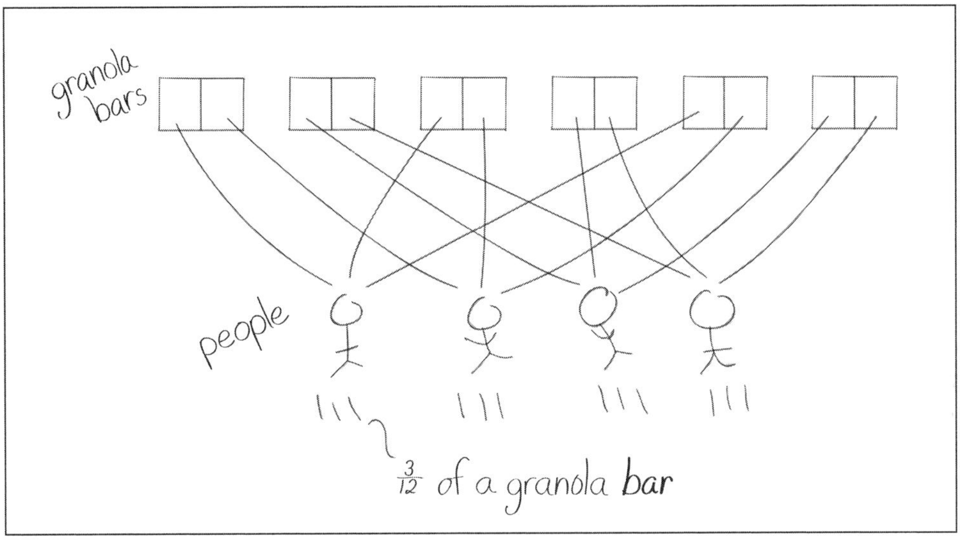

Figure 2.5: Sample student work.

A member of the first group says, "I see how you got 3⁄12, because each person has three of twelve pieces, but that is not 3⁄12 of the granola bar. It doesn't make sense because we know that each person gets more than one whole granola bar, and 3⁄12 is less than one whole. You are showing 3⁄12 of *all* the granola bars." The student in the second group who shared the solution strategy 3⁄12 looks at her drawing and solution. Then she looks at the solution 3⁄2 from the other group and indicates her agreement. This generates a needed discussion about the importance of the unit in naming fractions.

Facilitate Meaningful Discussions of the Mathematics

During the discussion of solutions to the granola bar problem, the students were able to share their solutions with rich explanations and justifications so that others could make sense of their reasoning. Additionally, a member of the class was able to identify and address the misconception the second group held. If students did not provide enough information for a good discussion or were not able to identify the misconception, it would be necessary for the teacher to facilitate this process. This can often be facilitated by asking challenging and probing questions ("What does the 3⁄12 represent? What is one whole in your representation?"). These advancing or assessing questions guide the sharing of information and the critiquing of arguments or solutions. To do this effectively, develop a deep understanding of the mathematics you teach so student engagement in this practice can be supported. Hill, Ball, and Schilling (2008) call this type of mathematics knowledge *specialized content knowledge.* In the granola bar problem, the teacher would need to know that an important aspect of the problem is to make sense of the whole when describing the solution. Her questions would then be based on bringing this concept to the foreground during the discussion. Collaborative teams are uniquely positioned to support teachers in collaboratively developing this specialized content knowledge.

The Understanding Questions for Mathematical Practice 3

Purposeful talk is an essential component of an effective mathematics class. As students present their approaches to solving problems and listen to the comments of their peers, they acquire skills in engaging with ideas, thinking out loud with others, and working to co-construct those ideas. Similarly, as students work to make sense of the reasoning of others, they learn the very important skill of critical analysis.

1. **What is the intent of this CCSS Mathematical Practice?** A goal of CCSS Mathematical Practice 3 is for students to make and test conjectures and to communicate their mathematical thinking.
2. **What teacher actions facilitate this CCSS Mathematical Practice?** You establish social norms in the classroom that support communicating mathematical ideas and questioning the thinking of others. Your level of specialized content knowledge is such that you are able to provide rich problems to elicit conjectures and arguments, to identify common misconceptions, and to guide discussions around important mathematical ideas.
3. **What evidence is there that students are demonstrating this CCSS Mathematical Practice?** Students are presenting their solutions along with the justifications for their choices. When there is disagreement regarding a solution, the student making the claim explains her thinking. The student critiquing the claim makes sense of the argument and then provides clarification including examples or counterexamples and another justification.

Individually assessing interactions with students is not an easy task, even though it is likely that you routinely reflect on what happens to make some lessons successful and others not so successful. This Collaborative Team Task provides a framework for observing whole-class instruction with a colleague.

Collaborative Team Task: Mathematical Practice 3

Collaboration can support reflection on one's own practice. Work with a partner to set up a time to observe one another teaching a mathematics lesson. The purpose of the observation will be to collect data regarding teacher-to-student and student-to-student interactions during whole-class instruction. Keep track of the following throughout the lesson.

1. What types of questions does the teacher ask students? Are they higher-order thinking questions, or are they questions that elicit rote responses?

2. How do students respond to questions? Do they just give solutions, or is there an expectation that they will also explain their solution strategies?
3. How does the teacher react to the students' responses? Does the teacher ask for additional justifications and clarifications? Does the teacher ask other students to explain classmates' reasoning?
4. Do the students in the class listen to one another's contributions to the class discussion? If so, what data support this?
5. To whom does the teacher direct questions? Are only students who raise their hands called on? Does the teacher tend to call on students known to have the correct answers or students who will likely share misconceptions?

Discussion Questions

1. What trends do you notice in questioning techniques and social norms across the observed lessons of teachers within the collaborative team?
2. How might questioning help to improve the level of mathematics conversation in the classroom?
3. What action items are needed to establish social norms conducive to implementing CCSS Mathematical Practice 3?

Visit **go.solution-tree.com/commoncore** for a reproducible version of this feature box.

Mathematical Practice 4: Model With Mathematics

Students engaged in CCSS Mathematical Practice 4, "Model with mathematics," solve real-world problems by applying known mathematics (NGA & CCSSO, 2010, p. 7). This practice is often misinterpreted as representing mathematical concepts by using physical or pictorial manipulatives, or other renderings, because of the word *model.* While manipulatives and other representations can be used as instructional tools to make sense of real-world problems, that is just one element of this Mathematical Practice. Students might also use tools such as diagrams, tables, graphs, and formulas to make sense of the mathematics. More generally, students use symbols and tools to represent real-world situations and move fluidly between different representations based on what questions they are trying to answer. The ways students model and represent situations will evolve as students learn more mathematics. For example, a grade K–2 student might model a situation in which a student and two friends each have four friendship bracelets by writing 4 + 4 + 4 to determine how many bracelets they have in all, whereas a third-grade student might model the same situation with the expression 3 × 4. Both students have modeled the situation with mathematics using representations appropriate to their grade levels. A goal is for students to model mathematics to become more mathematically proficient. As students move through the content domains for grades 3–5, there will be increasing opportunities for them to model their responses to mathematics learning opportunities. Such modeling will include expressions, equations, diagrams, tables, graphs, and formulas.

The Teacher's Role in Developing Mathematical Practice 4

Students' learning in mathematics is enhanced when they have opportunities to use various modes to express their ideas. Although verbal communication is an important feature of mathematics instruction, students also need opportunities to use nonlinguistic representations including diagrams or mathematical models. Both verbal and nonverbal presentations can be used to facilitate students' ability to determine whether their thinking makes sense or is reasonable.

Provide Opportunities for Students to Solve Real-World Problems

This standard serves to connect CCSS Mathematical Practices 1 and 2 with its focus on mathematizing real-world problems. Students must first be given the opportunity to explore real-world problems or situations, and then they must be encouraged to represent those problems mathematically. Once students represent the problems with mathematics, they should solve the problems and interpret their results within the context of the problem. All of this depends on the students being provided the opportunity to solve problems that arise from everyday life.

Consider a mathematical task related to the CCSS for mathematics fifth-grade domain Number and Operations in Base Ten (see 5.NBT.6). Suppose students are asked to explore how they might collect the amount of money needed for the fifth-grade end-of-year party that will cost $360. Some students might decide that because there are ninety-six students in fifth grade, they would just need to represent the problem as $360 ÷ 96. Other students might assume that not all students will be able to or choose to contribute, so they might model this situation by trying to see how many students would need to bring $5 in order to meet the goal of $360 by dividing $360 by $5. Another group might determine the number of students who would need to contribute just $2 to make the goal by finding $360 ÷ $2. Another group might even propose a fundraiser to raise part of the money. The list of ideas could go on and on. Most importantly, your role is to provide opportunities for students to explore and share solutions to real-world situations that present themselves in and out of daily school life. The classroom environment must be conducive to the sorts of discussions that are described in CCSS Mathematical Practice 3.

Focus Students' Attention on Sense Making and Reasonableness of Results

The answers to each of the problems in the preceding example would be different. The students would then need to determine if their solutions were *reasonable* based on the context of the problem. Would it be reasonable for each student to bring in $3.75? Would it be reasonable to expect to receive $5 from 72 students in the fifth grade? What if each student brought just $2? Would it be reasonable to expect that 180 fifth graders would each contribute $2 toward the party? While the first two solutions are reasonable, the third solution is not. Because there are only 96 fifth-grade students, it is unreasonable to have 180 fifth graders donate money. The mathematical expression is correct, and the computation is accurate; however, the solution is not reasonable in this context. This student focus on reasonableness of results is often lacking in mathematics discussions. Students engaged in this Mathematical Practice will not only check for reasonableness of the computation but will extend this sense making to determine if the solution is appropriate given the original problem context. You will need to support this practice by asking students if their answers are reasonable, facilitating classroom dialogue that allows students to learn from each other, and ensuring that students make sense of their answers according to the context of the problem.

Have Students Develop Real-Life Contexts to Support Mathematical Expressions

A useful strategy to help students make sense of modeling real-world contexts with mathematics is to provide students with expressions and challenge them to develop a corresponding real-world context. Consider a task from the fifth-grade CCSS for mathematics domain Number and Operations—Fractions (see 5.NF.2) in which students are presented with the expression $4/5 - 1/2$. Developing a context to accurately represent this expression is actually somewhat difficult. It is often surprising how easy it is to represent this particular problem using a real-world situation incorrectly. Because this is something that elicits errors, it is actually a useful task for uncovering misconceptions. Suppose you were to develop a context that uses cake. Many people write something like this:

> There is $4/5$ of a cake left over in the refrigerator. Marc eats $1/2$ of the leftover cake. How much cake remains?

Does this context make sense? On one level, it does. You can imagine $4/5$ of a cake, and you can imagine someone eating half. However, it does not accurately represent $4/5 - 1/2$. If Marc were to eat $1/2$ of the leftover cake, he would actually be eating $1/2$ of $4/5$ of the cake. Modeling this scenario would require a student to first find $1/2$ of $4/5$ then subtract that from $4/5$. This would be modeled using mathematics: $4/5 - (1/2 \times 4/5)$. Instead, a correct context involving cake would be:

> There is $4/5$ of a cake left over. Marc eats $1/2$ of an entire cake from what's left. How much cake remains?

One aspect that makes this particular word problem so difficult to write is the context for the problem. By making the unit a cake, the language sort of gets in the way. If the context were something with a more clearly identifiable unit—like say, a pound—this issue would be somewhat resolved. A problem using this unit could be:

> There is $4/5$ of a pound of chocolate left after Valentine's Day. Marc eats $1/2$ of a pound of chocolate from the leftovers. How much chocolate is there now?

By affording opportunities for students to develop real-world contexts to correspond to mathematics expressions and then checking to make sure the correspondence is accurate, you are facilitating students' sense making relative to modeling mathematics. In order for you to be comfortable in this role, you should spend time exploring such representations with your colleagues in your collaborative team.

The Understanding Questions for Mathematical Practice 4

Many situations that students encounter in their daily lives involve the use of mathematics—counting change from a purchase, sharing pieces of birthday cake, figuring out how much material is needed to make a puppet, choosing menu items that match the money they have in hand, and so on. Presenting students with problems that reflect everyday experiences ensures that students recognize the practicality and value of learning mathematics.

1. **What is the intent of this CCSS Mathematical Practice?** A goal of CCSS Mathematical Practice 4 is for students to model real-world situations with mathematics in order to solve problems in everyday life in reasonable ways.
2. **What teacher actions facilitate this CCSS Mathematical Practice?** You can focus students' attention on mathematizing real-life situations and then question students to remind them to be sure that the solutions to these problems are reasonable relative to the context in which they arose.
3. **What evidence is there that students are demonstrating this CCSS Mathematical Practice?** Students are active participants in using mathematics to make sense of daily life. They use symbols and tools to help them make sense of and solve naturally arising problems in reasonable ways.

Are you in the habit of thinking about everyday experiences in terms of mathematics? Or is that something you do only when absolutely necessary, such as making sure that the discount received on a purchase is correct? In this Collaborative Team Task, you are invited to track everyday scenarios that lend themselves to thinking in mathematical ways.

Collaborative Team Task: Mathematical Practice 4

Thinking about the world in mathematical ways may take effort for some. Spend a week or two making this a priority, with the goal of making it a habit. Appropriate mathematical problems to explore can present themselves in unexpected situations. Consider this scenario. A family was at a restaurant, and the children were given *CrayAngles™* crayons in triangular-prism-shaped boxes. The crayons also resembled triangular prisms. The family, who enjoyed thinking of the world mathematically, began posing questions. One question was, "There are four crayons in this box; how many crayons would be in the next-size-larger box?" The family began looking for a pattern to describe the number of crayons in each box. This problem corresponds to CCSS for mathematics domain Operations and Algebraic Thinking (see 5.OA.3). What other questions could relate to this crayon box? What standards would they address?

Keep a list of the real-world mathematics problems you identify. Share and explore the problems with your collaborative team. Work in your collaborative team to come up with (and solve) additional problems related to the scenarios that are shared.

Visit **go.solution-tree.com/commoncore** for a reproducible version of this feature box.

Mathematical Practice 5: Use Appropriate Tools Strategically

The nature of mathematics facilitates the use of a variety of tools for teaching and learning. Every mathematics classroom should be equipped to accommodate CCSS Mathematical Practice 5, "Use appropriate tools strategically" (NGA & CCSSO, 2010, p. 7). Hands-on, active, and concrete learning support this CCSS Mathematical Practice. For students, this standard is *not* about watching the teacher demonstrate various tools. Specifically, this practice is about students *experiencing* the opportunity to develop an understanding by engaging in applications involving mathematics. In fact, some mathematics content domains, such as Measurement and Data, cannot be sufficiently explored unless students have access to appropriate tools.

The Teacher's Role in Developing Mathematical Practice 5

In far too many classrooms, the teacher does most of the talking and demonstrating while students play a spectator role. The CCSS for mathematics have established conditions for instructional practice that require students' active participation in the learning tasks. Consequently, classrooms need to be equipped with resources that enable students to use various sensory modes as they explore solutions to mathematical problems.

Provide Students With Access to Appropriate Tools

In order for students to select appropriate tools, those tools first have to be made available to them. You should have an effective plan for acquiring or providing access to tools and an effective system for students to use those tools. In a nutshell, a variety of tools should be readily available to students to support their mathematical explorations. These explorations may occur with concrete manipulatives or virtual manipulatives. Table 2.1 lists ten common mathematics teaching and learning manipulatives for grades 3–5 and the corresponding CCSS for mathematics content domain (though the manipulatives may be used for other domains as well). Make sure that a variety of other practical tools (for example, scissors, rulers, tape, and grid or graph paper) are available to students.

Table 2.1: Common Mathematics Teaching and Learning Manipulatives

Manipulative	CCSS Content Domain
Base ten blocks	Number and Operations in Base Ten
Cuisenaire® rods	Number and Operations—Fractions
Square color tiles	Measurement and Data
Pattern blocks	Operations and Algebraic Thinking
Tangrams	Geometry
Cubes	Geometry

continued →

Manipulative	CCSS Content Domain
Fraction tiles	Number and Operations—Fractions
Two-color counters	Number and Operations—Fractions
Fraction circles	Number and Operations—Fractions
Number cubes	Measurement and Data

Facilitate Students' Selection of Tools

Once you have ensured that a variety of tools is available to students, you can provide them with support in selecting appropriate tools for a particular mathematics exploration. It is important to keep in mind that often a mathematical tool (manipulative) can be used instructionally in multiple areas of mathematics. For instance, a set of pattern blocks is useful for studying numerical and visual patterns but also for studying fractions and geometry (models for plane figures and symmetry). Sometimes, students may be uncertain about which tool to select for a particular mathematical task. By providing students with options, you can gather information about students' learning preferences, their thinking as related to a particular tool, and which tools work most effectively for which students. In addition, by providing guidance instead of selecting tools for students, you provide space for students to make hypotheses, try new ways of studying mathematics, and have a context for comparing how different tools can either be useful or a hindrance for studying the specific mathematics. Here are five questions for use in the collection of tools made available to students:

1. Does the tool provide a meaningful model to support the mathematics?
2. Does the tool extend students' thinking and support their learning of the given mathematical topic?
3. Is the tool necessary?
4. Is the tool easy to use?
5. Does the tool provide support for students to engage in and solve a problem?

Help Students Become Aware of the Power of Tools

You may find that it is very engaging (and even enjoyable) to teach mathematics with a variety of tools. However, the real issue is whether student learning is supported by the use of tools—tools should not be used for the sake of using tools. If students use tools to engage in mathematics and walk away from the experience with little or no understanding of the mathematics, then the use of the tools was ineffective. You will continually want to ask challenging questions and probe students' thinking before, during, and after students use tools to study mathematics. Figure 2.6 has useful questions for probing students' thinking with respect to tool usage.

Questions Before Tool Usage

What tool is needed for this task?

Why did you select this tool?

Questions During Tool Usage

Show me how you are using the tool. Is it helpful?

How is using the tool supporting your understanding?

Questions After Tool Usage

What did you learn by using this tool?

Would a different tool lead to the same response, or could another tool have been better?

How did using the tool connect with what you already knew?

Figure 2.6: Tool-usage questions.

The Understanding Questions for Mathematical Practice 5

Effective instruction achieves the goal of successful learning and achievement for all students. Such instruction takes into account activities that appeal to the visual, auditory, and tactile kinesthetic learning modes (Erwin, 2004). Appropriately using tools in mathematics lessons is another component in ensuring that all students are successful.

1. **What is the intent of this CCSS Mathematical Practice?** A goal of CCSS Mathematical Practice 5 is for students to make proper decisions about the tools (if any) they will use to learn the mathematics.
2. **What teacher actions facilitate this CCSS Mathematical Practice?** You can facilitate this practice by making appropriate tools accessible to students and guiding students in their selection and use of these tools.
3. **What evidence is there that students are demonstrating this CCSS Mathematical Practice?** Students engaged in this CCSS Mathematical Practice are actively using manipulatives and other practical learning tools, when needed, to develop their mathematics understanding.

Access to a cumulative list of learning tools is a great time-saver for busy teachers. In this Collaborative Team Task, you have the opportunity to assemble a catalog of learning tools.

Collaborative Team Task: Mathematical Practice 5

Each member of the collaborative team has access to a variety of learning tools to support students' mathematics learning. The results of this task will be team members' catalog of learning tools that may be shared for students' benefit.

Create a chart similar to the following, and provide it to each team member to complete. The information on this chart can be collapsed into one chart to be shared with and discussed by all team members.

continued →

	Manipulative Tool	General Tool	Technology Tool
Pattern blocks	✓		
Calculator			✓
Ruler		✓	

Visit **go.solution-tree.com/commoncore** for a reproducible version of this feature box.

Mathematical Practice 6: Attend to Precision

CCSS Mathematical Practice 6, "Attend to precision," refers to the need for students (and teachers) to communicate precisely and correctly (NGA & CCSSO, 2010, p. 7). Student communication might involve developing and using definitions properly; using symbols appropriately, including the equal sign; specifying units, along with the associated quantities; and including clear and concise explanations when describing solutions. Additionally, an expectation of CCSS Mathematical Practice 6 is that students will be accurate and appropriate with procedures and calculations. Accuracy is self-explanatory, but appropriateness as it relates to precision is a bit more elusive. Part of solving problems provided in context involves determining the level of precision that is necessary. Sometimes an estimate is sufficient. If that is the case, how close of an estimate is warranted or acceptable? The same is true with measurement. The level of accuracy for measurements is often determined by the context of the problem. Consider, for example, the following mathematical task for the fourth-grade CCSS for mathematics domain Operations and Algebraic Thinking (see 4.OA.3), including problems in which remainders must be interpreted.

> Maria's father gave her a piece of rope 16.5 meters long and told her she could cut it to make jump ropes for herself and her friends. Maria and her friends are in fourth grade. How many jump ropes do you think Maria can make?

In this problem, the problem solver is faced with several unknowns: the total number of people (Maria and her friends) who might receive jump ropes and the length of those jump ropes. Questions such as the following arise: What is the reasonable height for a fourth grader? What might be the average height of a fourth grader? Based on a person's height, what is a reasonable length for a jump rope for this person? Also, the problem solver must consider if jump-rope lengths will be whole-number lengths (2 meters) or lengths including fractional parts (1.5 meters). Students engaged in solving this problem might develop justifications that support variation in acceptable accuracy. These aspects of solving problems and making sense of mathematics are explicated through CCSS Mathematical Practice 6.

The Teacher's Role in Developing Mathematical Practice 6

Acquiring, using, and understanding the language of mathematics is essential to students' success in the subjects and in applications of mathematics within other subject areas. This means that students must be exposed to mathematical vocabulary and symbols in meaningful contexts and given tasks that enable them to use the terms purposefully in both oral and written activities. Because many words in English have more than one meaning, students need experiences that help them recognize that familiar words have specialized meanings when used in mathematics.

Model Appropriate Use of Mathematics Vocabulary, Symbols, and Explanations

Students often emulate their teachers when they are not precise with definitions, general language, and ideas related to mathematics. For example, when teaching the third-grade CCSS for mathematics domain Geometry (see 3.G.1), if teachers describe a rhombus as a *squished* or *slanted* square in order to develop the definition of rhombus, they are often doing so to help provide students with an accessible visual representation. However, in the process, they are also inadvertently excluding the square as a special case of the rhombus. Similarly, a rectangle might be described as having two long sides and two short sides. While *some* rectangles can be described in this manner, the *definition* of a rectangle must not be so limiting as, once again, to exclude the square. Be careful concerning the messages you send to students at all times through mathematics instruction. Reaching agreement on the use of mathematics language is an appropriate use of your time during lesson planning in the collaborative team.

The CCSS for mathematics promote the use of strategies based on place value and properties to multiply multidigit numbers (NGA & CCSSO, 2010). When you model such practices or record the thinking of students, be careful to honor the meaning of the equal sign. Consider 4 × 28. As suggested in the fourth-grade Number and Operations in Base Ten domain (see 4.NBT.5), a student might use the distributive property to solve this task using mental math by first multiplying 4 × 25 and then adding 4 × 3 to that product. The student might think and say, "I multiplied 4 × 25 to get 100, then I added 4 × 3, which is 12, to get 112." When recording this student's thinking, be careful to not "string" the equal signs together and write $4 \times 25 = 100 + (4 \times 3) = 112$. While this represents the student's spoken explanation, it also indicates that $4 \times 25 = 112$. That is not a precise or accurate use of the equal sign in the recorded solution of the task and must be avoided. Instead, represent the student's explanation in stages or steps as follows.

$4 \times 25 = 100$

$4 \times 3 = 12$

$100 + 12 = 112$

This representation models the appropriate use of symbols while simultaneously representing the student's thinking related to the problem. You want to attend to precision with the vocabulary, symbols, and explanations you use in the classroom so that students do not learn unintended and inaccurate mathematics but rather are provided a model of attending to precision.

Provide Opportunities for Students to Share Their Thinking

When students are given opportunities to explain and justify their mathematical ideas, they become engaged in Mathematical Practice 6. For example, when students are asked to describe how they solved a multidigit multiplication problem, they should be expected to perform the calculations accurately and to use language to describe the procedures they used precisely. Revisiting 4 × 28, a student might describe how he or she used a standard algorithm to find the product. The student might say, "I multiplied 4 × 8 to get 32. I put down the 2 and carried the 3, I multiplied the 4 × 2 to get 8, and then I added 3 to get 11. The answer is 112." This student has not used proper place-value language in his explanation. By providing the opportunity for the student to share his thinking, you can now ask this student and the class questions to develop the proper language to describe the multiplication process. For example, ask, "When you multiplied the 4 × 2 to get 8, were you actually multiplying 4 and 2, and is the product 8?" In this way, the students focus on the precision of the vocabulary used and the explanations provided. The students will be led to see that what they were actually doing is multiplying 4 times 2 tens. Similarly, expect students to include appropriate units with quantities when sharing solutions to problems involving linear, area, and volume measurements as well as other solutions to problems provided in context.

Preparing Students for Further Study

How often is a phrase like "multiplication makes bigger and division makes smaller" heard in elementary school classrooms? While this is true for whole-number computation, it does not necessarily hold true when multiplying fractions, particularly fractions less than one. By using language that does not support the mathematics to come later in the curriculum, teachers often unintentionally set students up for confusion as they encounter mathematics in later grades. This confusion is avoidable when you model Mathematical Practice 6.

The Understanding Questions for Mathematical Practice 6

To think and act like a mathematician, students need to be able to use the language of mathematics accurately and appropriately. Helping students become lovers of words—logophiles—should not be limited to reading and writing instruction. Many opportunities exist in mathematics class to help students become word conscious and, at the same time, build their knowledge of mathematics.

1. **What is the intent of this CCSS Mathematical Practice?** A goal of CCSS Mathematical Practice 6 is for students to attend to precision in all aspects of communication related to mathematics.
2. **What teacher actions facilitate this CCSS Mathematical Practice?** When you model the appropriate use of vocabulary, symbols, and explanations for current grade-level content, you also prepare students for the mathematics to come in future grades. It is important to provide opportunities for students to share their mathematical ideas to attend to what they share for accuracy.

3. **What evidence is there that students are demonstrating this CCSS Mathematical Practice?** Evidence of this CCSS Mathematical Practice must be grounded in communication, whether written or oral. Students engaged in this CCSS Mathematical Practice are using careful, accurate definitions; they are including units with quantities as necessary; and they are performing calculations carefully and appropriately and accurately describing the procedures they used. Sharing of ideas for this aspect of student learning should be an ongoing part of collaborative team time.

The following Collaborative Team Task centers on precision in using mathematical language. Through discussion of the activity, you may discover that occasionally you need to be more precise in how you use mathematics vocabulary, as well as general terms that have specialized meanings in mathematics. If you have videos of lessons from the observations accompanying the Collaborative Team Task for CCSS Mathematics Practice 3 (page 40), use them to examine how precisely language is used in those lessons.

Collaborative Team Task: Mathematical Practice 6

Work as a collaborative team to brainstorm ways in which students might be using imprecise language in their mathematics talk. Topics might include language associated with place value, fractions, geometry, measurement, and so on. Identify a topic that is closely related with the students' current focus of instruction. Keep a journal of students' imprecise use of the identified terms during mathematics instruction over the next one to two weeks. Share the journals with the team and discuss ways of supporting students' attention to precision. Use a chart similar to the following.

Topic:		
Term	**Use of Term**	**Description of Inaccuracy**
Carry	Regrouping during multiplication	Treating the tens digit without regard to place value

Visit **go.solution-tree.com/commoncore** for a reproducible version of this feature box.

Mathematical Practice 7: Look For and Make Use of Structure

A major contribution to the beauty of mathematics is its structure. There's structure all across the mathematics curriculum. Consider structure in geometry (every square is a rhombus), basic operations (an even number plus an even number always results in a sum that is an even number), place value (the place to the left of a given digit is ten times greater than that given place), and numerical patterns (1, 4, 9, 16, and so on). Structure helps students determine what to expect in mathematics. If students learn how and why mathematics works, they then begin to notice, look for, and even anticipate how to make use of the structure within mathematics to solve problems—they become engaged in what it means to do mathematics. There are several ways to support students in their development of looking for and making use of structure in mathematics.

The Teacher's Role in Developing Mathematical Practice 7

Students are familiar with school and classroom routines, which provide structure for the time and activities they experience. Consequently, they develop an understanding of structure in their lives. But they have also learned about structure in the subjects they learn. For example, they may be familiar with the narrative patterns of stories from reading instruction and relationship patterns in science or social studies. They will also learn that structure is an important component of mathematics learning.

Draw Students' Attention to Structure in Mathematics

Students may or may not recognize structure in mathematics. For those students who do not readily recognize structure in mathematics, it is important that they be encouraged to attend to structure. You can do this by presenting examples that are conducive for exploring structure (see figure 2.7) and then providing students with opportunities to create their own examples of structure to share and discuss with one another.

Engage Students in Exploring Patterns in Numbers

Patterns provide a very productive context for helping students recognize and use structure in mathematics. A point of flexibility that makes patterns important for the mathematics curriculum is that a pattern can be represented numerically and visually. Consider the following pattern and its representations in figure 2.8.

The more students have an opportunity to explore structure and the more frequently you point out and discuss structure, the more confident students will become in looking for and recognizing structure on their own.

Help Students Make Use of Structure

Students can benefit from acknowledging structure when studying it across the mathematics curriculum. As students gain confidence in recognizing structure, you can model for students the mathematical power that comes from using structure in mathematics. For example, there are many instances in which students can learn through a problem and develop an understanding that no matter the context, problems of a certain structure are worked similarly. Consider the following tasks related to arrays from the third-grade CCSS for the mathematics domain Operations and Algebra (see 3.OA.3).

> There are 7 rows of students in the marching band with 5 students in each row. How many students are in the marching band?
>
> Sharon went to the ice-cream parlor to get dessert. There were so many flavors to choose from! There were 4 rows of ice-cream flavors on the menu board with 9 ice-cream flavors listed in each row. How many ice-cream flavors were there?

1

1 + 1 = 2

1 + 1 + 1 = 3

1 + 1 + 1 + 1 = 4

1 + 1 + 1 + 1 + 1 = 5

---

1 x 0 = 0

2 x 0 = 0

3 x 0 = 0

4 x 0 = 0

5 x 0 = 0

6 x 0 = 0

5-sided polygon = pentagon

6-sided polygon = hexagon

7-sided polygon = heptagon (or septagon)

8-sided polygon = octagon

9-sided polygon = nonagon

10-sided polygon = decagon

Figure 2.7: Three mathematical structure examples.

1, 3, 6, 10, . . .

The same pattern can be represented visually:

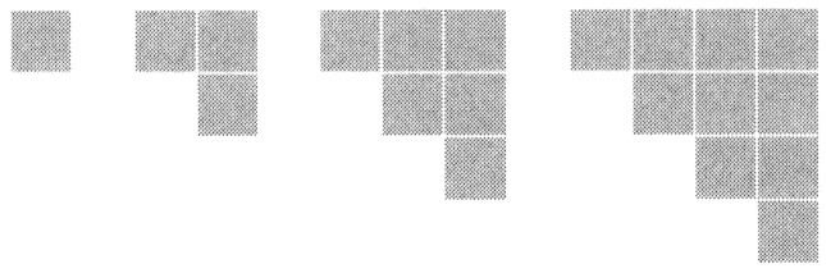

Figure 2.8: Sample patterns and structure.

If students understand the structure of the problem, represented by arrays, they can be successful with this problem type. Students can determine the solution by determining the number of rows and the number of objects in each row and then multiplying the two quantities to find the product, regardless of what the rows and objects represent.

The Understanding Questions for Mathematical Practice 7

Understanding the structure within mathematics enables students to discern relationships. The various experiences you provide will help them recognize familiar patterns or structure in problems, which may include, but certainly aren't limited to, patterns inherent when working with the commutative, associative, and distributive properties.

1. **What is the intent of this CCSS Mathematical Practice?** A goal of CCSS Mathematical Practice 7 is for students to recognize structure and to use mathematical structure to learn mathematics with understanding.
2. **What teacher actions facilitate this CCSS Mathematical Practice?** You can facilitate CCSS Mathematical Practice 7 by showcasing various patterns for students to explore and providing students the opportunity to describe the structure they see.
3. **What evidence is there that students are demonstrating this CCSS Mathematical Practice?** Students engaged in this CCSS Mathematical Practice demonstrate awareness of structure in mathematics by identifying instances of structure, discussing structure, and using structure in advantageous ways to solve problems and learn other mathematics. For example, in exploring strategies for multiplication, if students are aware that if a factor is even, half that factor can be multiplied by the other factor, and then the product can be doubled to determine the solution, such as in 6 × 7 by finding 3 × 7 and doubling 21.

Teachers can represent structure in mathematics using visuals, as well as words, models, symbols, or instructional tools (Mathematical Practice 5). In the following Collaborative Team Task, you are invited to examine a visual pattern and form a generalization related to expansion of the pattern. As you compare team members' responses to the task, you will gain further insight into application of Mathematical Practice 7.

Collaborative Team Task: Mathematical Practice 7

Structure adds beauty to mathematics because it helps learners determine what is predictable or generalizable about mathematics. However, structure does not necessarily dictate learners' points of view on mathematics. Consider the following visual pattern. The first term has six segments. The second term has eleven segments. The third term has sixteen segments.

What is a generalization for how many segments are needed for the *n*th term? Different learners might have different ways of seeing the structure in this problem.

Two generalization possibilities for this pattern are:

1. $6n - n + 1$
2. $4n + n + 1$

Visit **go.solution-tree.com/commoncore** for a reproducible version of this feature box.

Mathematical Practice 8: Look For and Express Regularity in Repeated Reasoning

When engaged in CCSS Mathematical Practice 8, "Look for and express regularity in repeated reasoning," students move beyond simply solving problems to finding ways to generalize the methods they use and to determine shortcuts for those procedures (NGA & CCSSO, 2010, p. 8). Consider the following task of finding equivalent fractions that extends understanding of fraction equivalence and supports the fourth-grade CCSS for mathematics domain Number and Operations—Fractions (see 4.NF.1). Students can quickly make sense of how to determine equivalent fractions when provided with an appropriate context. For example, imagine three-fourths of a pizza. Students can imagine cutting each of the four pieces of pizza into two equal pieces. That process would result in eight slices of pizza with the original three slices representing sixth-eighths of the pizza. Now imagine cutting each of those eight slices into two equal pieces. Three-fourths of the pizza could be renamed as twelve-sixteenths of the pizza, and so on. Students look for and express regularity in repeated reasoning when they make conjectures regarding general methods for processes like these. Students might notice that each time they cut each slice into two equal pieces, the number of slices representing the part of the pizza doubles, as did the number of slices in the whole pizza. They develop shortcuts when they realize they can get the same numeric result by multiplying the numerator and the denominator of the fraction by 2. These intermediate results are then checked to determine if they make sense. Students ask themselves, "Why can we multiply the numerator and denominator by 2?" Students see that this is reasonable because when the total number of pieces is multiplied by 2, so are the pieces in the part, because the numerator is part of the denominator.

Eventually, students generalize this result to finding equivalent fractions by multiplying the numerator and denominator of any fraction by the same number. This process of first noticing repeated calculations (seeking regularity) and making sense of them to determine general methods and ultimately shortcuts for computing is the intent of CCSS Mathematical Practice 8.

The Teacher's Role in Developing Mathematical Practice 8

Being able to acknowledge regularity in reasoning is important in mathematics, as it is in everyday life. Think how complicated life would be if every individual experience had to be recalled in isolation without the benefit of appreciating similarities and differences. The skills of understanding relationships and forming generalizations in mathematics develop over time as students learn to identify regularity in reasoned responses and recognize the value of structure in their learning.

Avoid Teaching Shortcuts Before Students Develop Understanding of Important Concepts

With their desire to simplify students' learning pathways and minimize confusion (Stigler et al., 1999), teachers are often tempted to provide students with efficient computational procedures too early. When this occurs, students miss the opportunity to look for and express regularity in repeated reasoning. Instead, you should provide students with opportunities to make sense of problems and to look for the regularity in the calculations. This practice interacts with CCSS Mathematical Practice 1 (see appendix A, page 159), as this will require that students develop perseverance to make sense of the repeated reasoning.

Scaffold Examples to Highlight Regularity in Repeated Reasoning

The examples you provide and the questioning techniques you employ help students notice if calculations repeat. Asking students to describe the processes they use and look for repetition in those processes provides the scaffolding necessary for grades 3–5 students to begin to make sense of the process of determining general methods for calculations. You will need to consider multiple examples—as well as their progression—to help students move from seeing the repeated reasoning of a single example to being able to build a general method.

Establish Expectations for Students, and Share Conjectures About General Methods

The classroom environment and expectations established that relate to classroom mathematics interactions set the stage for students to engage in this practice. If there is an expectation that students will make conjectures related to what they notice in the mathematics they experience, students are more likely to look for and make sense of such generalizations. Your role is to create and maintain these norms in the classroom. In classrooms, in which teachers expect students to create generalizations and then defend them and consider potential counterexamples, students will have the opportunity to create general methods for repeated reasoning. In a classroom such as this, students might explore computations and record those computations in a table. The whole class might then discuss the generalizations that can be made from the table to form and test conjectures. Thus, CCSS Mathematical Practice 8 is closely linked to CCSS Mathematical Practice 3 (see appendix A, page 160).

The Understanding Questions for Mathematical Practice 8

Developing proficiency with this CCSS Mathematical Practice might be considered in the context of these adages: *haste makes waste* and *slow and steady wins the race.* You can help students learn to appreciate that slowing down, having patience, and persevering are valuable behaviors in achieving success in mathematics.

1. **What is the intent of this CCSS Mathematical Practice?** A goal of CCSS Mathematical Practice 8 is for students to look for repetition in the calculations they complete with the goal of determining general methods and related shortcuts.
2. **What teacher actions facilitate this CCSS Mathematical Practice?** Be careful to avoid oversimplifying instruction or using shortcuts in computational

procedures for students. Instead, provide examples for students to complete, highlighting regularity for students to identify by questioning students regarding the processes they use. For example, when dividing whole numbers by unit fractions (such as with $3 \div \frac{1}{7}$), first allow students to solve problems with models and then ask them to look for shortcuts in determining similar quotients rather than just telling them to invert and multiply, which is often heard too early in many classrooms. This will require instructional time to develop. Additionally, create an environment that supports students' making and sharing conjectures about the general methods they notice.

3. **What evidence is there that students are demonstrating this CCSS Mathematical Practice?** Evidence that students are demonstrating this practice takes the form of classroom discussions or written descriptions in which students describe the conjectures they make regarding what they notice about repeated calculations as well as define their general methods.

Repetition is a key element in determining patterns and in allowing one to develop conjectures. The following Collaborative Team Task provides an opportunity for you to examine mathematics content that is suitable for repeated reasoning and to consider the instructional strategies you will use to teach such concepts.

Collaborative Team Task: Mathematical Practice 8

As you begin to make plans to engage students in this CCSS Mathematical Practice, it is helpful to think of opportunities for students to use repeated reasoning. This sort of reasoning can be promoted with a variety of mathematical tasks, such as when using the *doubling strategy* (useful when exploring products for basic facts in which both factors are equal), when finding equivalent fractions, when finding areas of rectangles or volumes of rectangular prisms, and when dividing whole numbers by unit fractions.

Work as a collaborative team to examine mathematics concepts and related skills that lend themselves to an emphasis on looking for and making sense of repeated reasoning. Make plans to engage students in this practice during instruction of those concepts and in writing reflections on the results. Discuss the reflections at the next collaborative team meeting.

Visit **go.solution-tree.com/commoncore** for a reproducible version of this feature box.

Mathematical Practices Implementation

As discussed in chapter 1, effective mathematics instruction rests in part on careful planning (Morris et al., 2009). Ensuring that the CCSS Mathematical Practices are an important component of each day's mathematics lesson will require significant and careful planning by the collaborative team. The lesson-planning tool in figure 2.9 (page 58) will support your collaborative development of daily lessons to embed the Standards for Mathematical Practice. This tool is intended to support the vision of instruction for your school or district, and teams can use it to discuss daily lesson construction that will include the Standards for Mathematical Practice.

<table>
<tr><td colspan="3">Unit: Date: Lesson:</td></tr>
<tr><td colspan="3">Learning target: As a result of today's class, students will be able to ______</td></tr>
<tr><td colspan="3">Formative assessment: How will students be expected to demonstrate mastery of the learning target during in-class checks for understanding?</td></tr>
<tr><th colspan="3">Probing Questions for Differentiation on Mathematical Tasks</th></tr>
<tr><td colspan="2">Assessing Questions
(Create questions to scaffold instruction for students who are "stuck" during the lesson or the lesson tasks.)</td><td>Advancing Questions
(Create questions to further learning for students who are ready to advance beyond the learning target.)</td></tr>
<tr><td colspan="3">Targeted Standard for Mathematical Practice:
(Describe the intent of this Mathematical Practice and how it relates to the learning target.)</td></tr>
<tr><th>Tasks
(The number of tasks may vary from lesson to lesson.)</th><th>What Will the Teacher Be Doing?</th><th>What Will the Students Be Doing?
(How will students be actively engaged in each part of the lesson?)</th></tr>
<tr><td>Beginning-of-Class Routines
How does the warm-up activity connect to students' prior knowledge?</td><td></td><td></td></tr>
<tr><td>Task 1
How will the learning target be introduced?</td><td></td><td></td></tr>
<tr><td>Task 2
How will the task develop student sense making and reasoning?</td><td></td><td></td></tr>
<tr><td>Task 3
How will the task require student conjectures and communication?</td><td></td><td></td></tr>
<tr><td>Closure
How will student questions and reflections be elicited in the summary of the lesson? How will students' understanding of the learning target be determined?</td><td></td><td></td></tr>
</table>

Figure 2.9: CCSS Mathematical Practices lesson-planning tool.

Visit **go.solution-tree.com/commoncore** for a reproducible version of this figure.

It might be useful to categorize the CCSS Mathematical Practices in ways that are meaningful to the team. The conversation regarding best ways to group the practices will likely lead to useful discussions related to ways to engage students meaningfully in mathematics. Collaborative teams are uniquely structured to provide you the time and support you need to interpret the CCSS Mathematical Practices, focus on their intent for students, embed the Mathematical Practices in daily mathematics lessons and plans for assessment, and reflect together on the effectiveness of implementation. The questions provided and the unpacking or understanding for these practices in this chapter can serve as a guide to your collaborative team as you work together to develop a shared understanding of the CCSS Mathematical Practices. Use table 2.2 to support your efforts to develop shared understanding in the collaborative team.

Table 2.2: Developing Shared Understanding of the Mathematical Practices

	Describe the Intent of This CCSS Mathematical Practice	Describe One Teacher Action That Might Facilitate This CCSS Mathematical Practice	Describe Evidence of Students Engaged in This CCSS Mathematical Practice
CCSS Mathematical Practice 1			
CCSS Mathematical Practice 2			
CCSS Mathematical Practice 3			
CCSS Mathematical Practice 4			
CCSS Mathematical Practice 5			
CCSS Mathematical Practice 6			
CCSS Mathematical Practice 7			
CCSS Mathematical Practice 8			

Visit **go.solution-tree.com/commoncore** for a reproducible version of this table.

Although the CCSS Mathematical Practices are not content per se but rather ways of interacting with the content, they cannot exist without the CCSS for mathematics content standards (see appendices B, C, and D, pages 163, 169, and 175). Planning for instruction, therefore, must simultaneously involve careful consideration of the mathematical content goals and of how the CCSS Mathematical Practices can be implemented during instruction to aid students in developing deep understanding of the content standards. Chapter 3 will examine the unique characteristics and essential features of the CCSS for mathematics content standards.

Chapter 2 Extending My Understanding

1. Examine the Process Standards (NCTM, 2000) and the Strands of Mathematics Proficiency in *Adding It Up* (NRC, 2001) in detail. How are each related to the CCSS Mathematical Practices? How might you and your collaborative team explain these relationships to other stakeholders, including parents and guardians?
2. Design a plan for building student awareness (or deepening student understanding) of the Mathematical Practices. What initial tasks or activities will you use? How do you plan to continue to reinforce these practices? What is your plan for developing parent, guardian, and family awareness of the practices? Initial tasks? Ongoing reinforcement?
3. Develop a list of student behaviors as defined in the Mathematical Practices. Record the teacher actions that might promote student implementation of the practices. Then schedule informal peer observations or video mathematics classes in action. Spend time as a collaborative team debriefing these observations.
    - Did collaborative teams observe these dispositions? How, when, and under what conditions did they see students exhibit the Mathematical Practices?
    - What surprised you?

Online Resources

Visit **go.solution-tree.com/commoncore** for links to these resources.

- **Common Core Implementation Videos (NGA & CCSSO, 2011; www.ccsso.org/Resources/Digital_Resources/Common_Core_Implementation_Video_Series.html):** To assist states with CCSS implementation, this series of video vignettes examines the standards in greater depth. Be sure to check out "Mathematical Practices, Focus and Coherence in the Classroom" and "The Importance of Mathematical Practices." You can also visit the Hunt Institute's YouTube channel (www.youtube.com/user/TheHuntInstitute#g/u) to access these videos.

- **Common Core Look-Fors (CCL4s) (http://splaysoft.com/CCL4s/Welcome.html):** CCL4s is a comprehensive tool designed to help teacher learning teams deepen their awareness and understanding of the actions and conditions that promote student engagement with the CCSS Mathematical Practices, with connections to the content standards. An exciting blend of creativity, innovation, and strategic technology use, the iPad and iPhone apps support purposeful classroom observation though effective staff collaboration.
- **Mathematical Practices Learning Community Templates (http://schools.utah.gov/CURR/mathsec/Common-Core/MathematicalPracticesLearningCommunityTemplates.aspx):** These resources include nine templates for teacher learning teams seeking to understand the Mathematical Practices and their connections to the NCTM Process Standards and Standards of Mathematics Proficiency.
- **Video Illustrations of the Common Core Standards for Mathematical Practice (Inside Mathematics, 2010a; http://insidemathematics.org/index.php/common-core-standards):** This site provides classroom videos and lesson samples designed to illustrate the Mathematical Practices in action.
- **Standards for Mathematical Practice (Common Core State Standards Initiative, 2011; www.corestandards.org/the-standards/mathematics/introduction/standards-for-mathematical-practice):** This site links the text of the eight Mathematical Practices and the selection on "Connecting the Standards for Mathematical Practice to the Standards for Mathematical Content."
- **Common Core State Standards Resources (NCSM, 2011; www.mathedleadership.org/ccss/materials.html):** These professional development files are ready to use and designed to help teachers understand how to implement the Mathematical Practices in their classrooms.

CHAPTER 3

Implementing the Common Core Mathematics Content in Your Curriculum

Chapter 2 presented a strong argument for designing the transition to the CCSS through the window of teacher and student engagement in the Mathematical Practices (see appendix A, page 159). This makes a lot of sense as you consider the mathematics content of the CCSS. What's the content? How does this content differ from what you are now teaching or have previously taught? Are there particular learning standards that require additional focus? What about topics that appeared to be a struggle for your students last year or throughout your career? These "in my room with my kids" concerns are legitimate at every grade level.

This chapter provides a number of analysis tools for examining your classroom, school, or district implementation of the content domains and expectations of the Common Core State Standards. As you work collaboratively with colleagues, you will be able to address and become conversant with the paradigm shift *less is more.* The Common Core standards require you to shift to *less* (fewer standards) is *more* (opportunity to dig deeper with understanding) at each grade level in your school.

The CCSS at the elementary level (K–5) outline a clearly defined and coherent set of grade-level standards calling for a deep student understanding of those standards. Knowing how to read the CCSS grade-level standards is an important first step in developing a common vocabulary within the collaborative team. Recall figure 1.1 (page 11) and the key terms for the common core standards for grades 3 through 5. Three key terms from figure 1.1 are used throughout this chapter—*standards, clusters,* and *domains.*

The focused nature of the CCSS, and the careful attention paid to students' developmental learning progressions, means that some of the topics you traditionally taught in certain grades have been moved to other grade levels, and some topics have simply been eliminated from the elementary school curriculum. The purpose of the more focused CCSS curriculum is to provide you more time to teach fewer critical topics with greater depth and student understanding. As you use the analysis tools in this chapter, be sure to also plan for the amount of time (days) you will need for teaching the various content standards and subsequent mathematics units.

One of the primary purposes for taking time to discuss the CCSS content standards in your grade-level collaborative team is to develop shared teacher ownership and understanding of the CCSS content standards and the Mathematical Practices. By discussing each domain and the corresponding content standard cluster, your team will better understand the meaning of each standard. Your collaborative team discussions will also allow your team to design expectations for student demonstrations of understanding and proficiency for each standard.

But first, your team should spend some time exploring the historical and policy-related underpinnings of the mathematics curriculum for the CCSS.

Collaborative Content Analysis

Helping students use their prior knowledge to enable them to recognize what is new and different in their learning is a key element of scaffolding instruction. Similarly, as you explore the CCSS for mathematics, it will be helpful to compare aspects of the different mathematics standards that have framed your prior knowledge for the grade-level curriculum you teach. Taking a look at the historical documents that have influenced the CCSS content allows you and your colleagues to identify what is familiar, what is new, and what is challenging. And, it will allow for team discussions about the changes required in the CCSS you will deliver to your students.

Before you examine the CCSS for mathematics for your grade level, you may find it helpful to use appendix E (page 183) and refer to the history of mathematics curriculum standards development that framed previous standards and provides the foundation for the CCSS. In all likelihood, standards you have been using were based on three landmark documents that have influenced preK–8 mathematics instruction since 1989, when the National Council of Teachers of Mathematics published *Curriculum and Evaluation Standards for School Mathematics* (NCTM, 1989).

1. In 2000, NCTM updated the curriculum standards in *Principles and Standards for School Mathematics* (PSSM), which has served as the blueprint for revised state standards throughout 2000–2010.
2. In 2006, NCTM released the *Curriculum Focal Points.* The *Curriculum Focal Points* were intended to serve as a discussion document for states and school districts as they began a conversation around the more important or *focus* topics at particular grades for preK–8. The CCSS *critical areas* presented at the beginning of each grade level's discussion (see appendix B, page 163, for example) are, in essence, the *Curriculum Focal Points.*
3. In 2008, the National Mathematics Advisory Panel identified the Critical Foundations of Algebra. These clusters of concepts and skills are considered essentials for all students prior to formal coursework in algebra and include major content topics, with suggested grade-level benchmarks for grades 3–5, as outlined in appendix E.

The CCSS provides a second-level professional development opportunity for your collaborative team on the important mathematics for grades 3–5. By reading through appendix E and responding to the questions provided, your collaborative team will be better prepared to engage in meaningful discussions about what's mathematically important across each of these three grade levels. Additionally, the documents described in appendix E provide a resource that eliminates any major surprises regarding actual content topics as experienced teachers review the CCSS domains, standards, and clusters for grades 3–5.

You and your team can use the following Collaborative Team Task to help you summarize your observations about the changes in mathematics standards and what you can look forward to as you learn more about the CCSS content expectations. Use appendix E as needed to help you respond to these questions.

Collaborative Team Task: What Do the Changes in Mathematics Standards Mean for Our Grade Level and Our School?

Your team needs to focus on changes that will be required with implementation of the CCSS for mathematics at your grade level. The following questions will help your team expand on your thinking about the impact of the CCSS for your work and planning.

1. Which aspect of the CCSS content is of most concern to you?
2. What kind of support do you anticipate you will need to make the transition from what you do now to what you will be required to do with implementation of the CCSS?
3. In what ways has the information about the CCSS Mathematical Practices (chapter 2) helped to provide you with new insights relative to how you will approach your instruction with the expectations of the CCSS content standards?
4. What do you think should be the priorities for your team during the school year as you reflect on the changes in mathematics standards for your grade level?

As discussed in chapter 1, it is critical that you develop a shared understanding with your colleagues of the content to be taught because it helps develop consistent curricular expectations, serves equity goals, and creates ownership among all teachers (DuFour et al., 2010). As you examine the content domains within grades 3–5 to develop this shared understanding, you can use these understanding questions for the content standard clusters in each of the five domains to guide your work.

1. What's familiar in the CCSS for each grade level?
2. What appears to be new content to this particular grade level based on prior standards (*Principles and Standards for School Mathematics* [NCTM, 2000], state standards, and so on)? What's challenging for students and teachers (this may include common misconceptions)?
3. What needs unpacking? What topics need emphasizing?

Additional considerations will include how your team may want to unpack the standards within a content standard cluster in order to highlight areas of emphasis, which may be distributed throughout the year or emphasized at a particular time: for example, a two- to four-day lesson on the content standard cluster and where this mathematics may occur within the instructional year—first half of the year, early in the year, and so on—and how this standard might be revisited throughout the year. Your role in implementing the standards is developed through the collaborative team task, a model of which comes at the end of the first domain section for each grade level. This task provides an opportunity for your team to participate in an in-depth examination of selected standards, those that present the greatest challenge for you and your students. This activity will enable your team to think about what needs to be unpacked and what topic needs to be emphasized. The task also asks you to identify relevant Mathematical Practices and resources and to identify indicators for the student demonstrations of learning the standard.

The following sections provide an in-depth view of each content domain and standard within grades 3–5 based on the teacher's role for implementing the standards. You should view this analysis as a beginning point for the ongoing discussions in your collaborative team. This analysis and related discussion with your team is critical to developing mutual understanding of and support for consistent curricular priorities, pacing, lesson design, and the development of grade-level common assessments (see chapter 4). This analysis, because of its depth, should follow the *Curriculum Focal Points'* (NCTM, 2006) connection to the critical areas of the CCSS (see table E.1 in appendix E, page 184).

As you participate in the professional development linked to this analysis, you and your collaborative team members should continuously examine and discuss your grade-level content reactions as a grade-level team. However, from time to time, you should also examine the other grade-level content expectations for the grades 3–5 cluster in order to discuss transition issues noted across grades.

Finally, you and your colleagues at each grade level should use tables 3.1 through 3.3 (pages 67, 79, and 93) as you review a particular grade's standards and provide your own response to the analysis questions for each standard. The activities in tables 3.1 through 3.3 are designed to help you analyze the CCSS for mathematics in relation to your experience in working with other standards. The understanding questions in the tables represent a continuum from known (What's familiar?) to the unfamiliar (What's new? What's challenging?) to accommodation (What needs unpacking? What topics need emphasizing?). These understanding questions for the content standard clusters can be used to frame your team's discussion of the standards.

This chapter provides a sequenced response to these questions for the content standard clusters in each domain for each grade level. You can use the responses as benchmarks against which to compare those that result from your team discussions.

Grade 3: What's the Mathematics?

The CCSS content at the third-grade level is similar to what you may already know, but there are far fewer topics; remember that preCCSS state standards typically had many more standards and expectations for each grade level. That said, having fewer standards does not mean less mathematics in this less-is-more paradigm shift. The language of the CCSS content domains, clusters, and standards with its emphasis on *understanding and the consistent use of a variety of representations* (for example, number lines, drawings, and so on) requires a depth of student demonstrations of understanding far deeper than the bulleted statements of prior standards at the state or district level.

The CCSS for mathematics specify four critical areas for the third-grade level:

> (1) developing understanding of multiplication and division and strategies for multiplication and division within 100; (2) developing understanding of fractions, especially unit fractions (fractions with numerator 1); (3) developing understanding of the structure of rectangular arrays and of area; and (4) describing and analyzing two-dimensional shapes. (NGA & CCSSO, 2010, p. 21)

Table 3.1 provides an analysis tool you can use as you think about the understanding questions for the content standard clusters in each domain for grade 3. The CCSS Mathematics Content Domain and Standards for Grade 3 are provided in appendix B (page 163).

Table 3.1: Grade-by-Grade Analysis Tool—Grade 3

Content Standard Cluster	Which Standards in the Cluster Are Familiar?	What's New or Challenging in These Standards?	Which Standards in the Cluster Need Unpacking or Emphasizing?
Operations and Algebraic Thinking (3.OA)			
Represent and solve problems involving multiplication and division.			
Understand properties of multiplication and the relationship between multiplication and division.			
Multiply and divide within 100.			
Solve problems involving the four operations, and identify and explain patterns in arithmetic.			

continued →

Content Standard Cluster	Which Standards in the Cluster Are Familiar?	What's New or Challenging in These Standards?	Which Standards in the Cluster Need Unpacking or Emphasizing?
Number and Operations in Base Ten (3.NBT)			
Use place-value understanding and properties of operations to perform multidigit arithmetic.			
Number and Operations—Fractions (3.NF)			
Develop understanding of fractions as numbers.			
Measurement and Data (3.MD)			
Solve problems involving measurement and estimation of intervals of time, liquid volumes, and masses of objects.			
Represent and interpret data.			
Geometric measurement: Understand concepts of area, and relate area to multiplication and to addition.			
Geometric measurement: Recognize perimeter as an attribute of plane figures and distinguish between linear and area measures.			
Geometry (3.G)			
Reason with shapes and their attributes.			
General Comments			

Visit **go.solution-tree.com/commoncore** for a reproducible version of this table.

Operations and Algebraic Thinking (3.OA)

The Operations and Algebraic Thinking domain (see appendix B, pages 164–166) emphasizes the conceptual understanding of operations, including the importance of properties (like the distributive property), in understanding operations and problem solving involving the operations and the foundations of algebra (for example, patterns, expressions, and equations).

The 3.OA Content Standard Clusters

The Operations and Algebraic Thinking (3.OA) domain has four content standard clusters, which contain nine standards (see appendix B, page 164-166).

1. Represent and solve problems involving multiplication and division.
2. Understand properties of multiplication and the relationship between multiplication and division.
3. Multiply and divide within 100.
4. Solve problems involving the four operations, and identify and explain patterns in arithmetic.

The Understanding Questions for the 3.OA Content Standard Clusters

The three questions in table 3.1 (page 67) provide a framework for you and your team to use to develop a greater understanding of the intent of each content standard cluster for the Operations and Algebraic Thinking domain (3.OA).

Represent and solve problems involving multiplication and division is the first content standard cluster for the 3.OA domain. In general, this cluster of standards is very consistent with current expectations for third-grade mathematics learning standards but does require additional time to ensure student understanding. This content standard cluster connects well to many of the Mathematical Practices (see appendix A, page 159) because it strongly suggests that your students have regular opportunities through much of the third-grade year to make sense of problems and persevere in solving them.

- **What's familiar?** You should notice the emphasis on understanding and contexts for interpreting products and quotients. For example, "Basketball teams were being formed. If there were 5 players on each team and 7 teams, how many players were there?" (multiplication). "If we have 56 chairs for Mia's party with 8 people seated at each table, how many tables will I need for the party?" (division). The language and emphasis for the four standards in this cluster (appendix B, pages 164–166) are all about understanding multiplication and division, which have long been third-grade topics for emphasis.
- **What's new? What's challenging?** The challenge for you will be to continually develop lessons that require student demonstrations of understanding multiplication concepts throughout the school year. So your suggestions for continuously presenting multiplication and division in the context of meaningful problems will be very important.

- **What needs unpacking? What topics need emphasizing?** To develop understanding within this content standard cluster, your students will also need opportunities to reason abstractly and quantitatively, construct viable arguments, and critique the reasoning of others—all the Mathematical Practices—as they model with the mathematics content of this cluster.

Understand properties of multiplication and the relationship between multiplication and division is the second content standard cluster for the 3.OA domain. It requires an emphasis on the development of student understanding and use of the commutative, associative, and distributive properties.

- **What's familiar?** While the understanding and use of the commutative, associative, and distributive properties should be familiar, important topics, previous treatment of these properties with students has most likely been through a one- to two-day lesson. These lessons are often not extended to the use of properties more flexibly to break apart facts, as noted in the 8 × 7 example presented in the CCSS standard 3.OA.5 (see appendix B, page 165). This type of student learning experience now becomes increasingly more important at this grade level and will require additional days of instruction in your unit planning calendar.
- **What's new? What's challenging?** Students at this grade level should be able to literally view the connections between multiplication and division as they create 7 jumps of 3 on a number line, which lands them on 21, and then recognize that 21 ÷ 7 shows the number of hops from 21, with each hop being a hop of 3. (See figure 3.1.) Connecting multiplication to division will be an expected learning outcome for students leaving third grade and is a very important link to student understanding of multiplication and division. It will also be very important for your third graders to demonstrate an understanding of how and when to use the commutative, associative, and distributive properties.

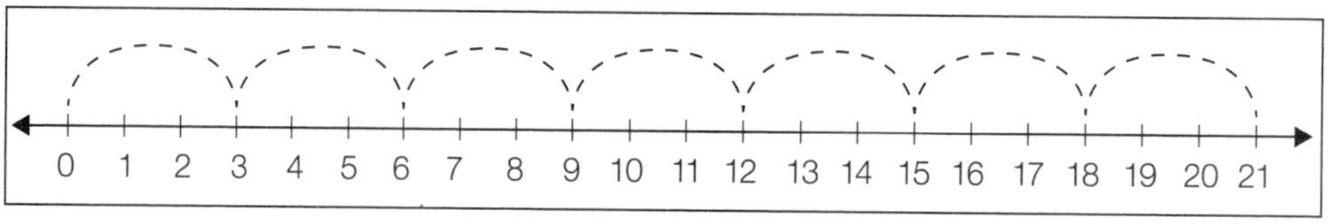

Figure 3.1: Sample number line.

- **What needs unpacking? What topics need emphasizing?** Actual lessons on use of the commutative, associative, and distributive properties are foundational to work with multiplication and division. This may be a one- to three-day lesson. However, opportunities to use the properties and subsequently think about division as the unknown factor with a multiplication problem (for example, "7 × ? = 28. If I know 28 ÷ 7 = 4, then I can solve 7 × ? = 28") must occur as a student proficiency during the instructional year.

Multiply and divide within 100 is the third content standard cluster for the 3.OA domain. It is a historically important element of mathematics content within the third grade, as this work is foundational for multiplication and division at this grade level and beyond.

- **What's familiar?** This should be very familiar content for you as a third-grade teacher. Student fact acquisition and fluency with the basic multiplication and related division facts through 10 × 10 have always been must-have critical foundations (NMAP, 2008). Students' fluency should be developed at this grade level, with an emphasis on fact strategies and an emphasis on connecting the relationship between multiplication and division.
- **What's new? What's challenging?** As indicated, although this standard expectation is not new for third grade, the importance of relating multiplication to division and then division back to multiplication (for example, a student will think, "If I know 8 × 7 = 56, I should know that 56 ÷ 7 = 8 and that 7 × 8 = 56; and if I know that 48 ÷ 6 = 8, then I should be able to connect that with 6 × 8 = 8 × 6 = 48") becomes a foundational element of number-sense development and understanding for the student.
- **What needs unpacking? What topics need emphasizing?** This is one of those standards that you will need to develop and maintain regularly throughout the year. Exiting third graders should be fluent when multiplying and dividing within 100. However, reaching student fluency will require a significant time emphasis and commitment from your team's lesson design and planning efforts.

Solve problems involving the four operations, and identify and explain patterns in arithmetic is the fourth content standard cluster for the 3.OA domain. This is, once again, a foundational element of the curriculum at the grade level and, as noted earlier, will engage your students in opportunities for proficiencies in several of the Mathematical Practices (see appendix A, page 159).

- **What's familiar?** In addition to regularly engaging students in solving problems, what may also be familiar for you is the more essential algebra readiness connection established by the two standards in this cluster—3.OA.8 and 3.OA.9 (see appendix B, pages 165–166)—involving the use of a variable and identification of patterns within the addition or multiplication table.
- **What's new? What's challenging?** What could be new and challenging for your instruction time will be the emphasis on solving two-step word problems and on the student use of mental mathematics and estimation as part of how they attend to precision. For many of your students at this grade level, this content standard cluster will require careful development over time.
- **What needs unpacking? What topics need emphasizing?** Students will need opportunities throughout the year to solve problems moving from one-step to two-step problems. Actual lessons involving the use of rounding as an estimation strategy and mental math techniques may be one- to two-day lessons but will need to be maintained and extended by you and your team into additional lessons throughout the school year. You can do this through regular

review activities and problem situations or tasks that engage students in mental math or ask them to consider providing an estimated response to a problem's solution.

The three-part analysis of each standard cluster will enable your team to build understanding and extend insights into how to most effectively teach the CCSS for mathematics. The following Collaborative Team Task is a model that you can use to plan implementation of the selected domain standards. The template for the model is shown for the 3.OA domain. This template is available as a reproducible for each of the five content domains in third grade. You can use these guides to support your team's discussion and planning for the CCSS implementation at your school.

Collaborative Team Task: Planning Implementation of Domain 3.OA

Based on your analysis of the content standard clusters for Operations and Algebraic Thinking, select a content standard cluster that you know will be challenging for your students (and possibly for you, too). Use the questions in the table to guide development of your unit design plans. Ask one of your team members to be video recorded while teaching the lesson you design. You could also share a digital version of your notes in an interactive document, such as a pencast (see page 111 for more information), of the mathematics within the lesson that is developed in this activity. Use your video or pencast for discussion in a subsequent team meeting as you provide formative feedback to your team about student progress toward mastery of the chosen content standard cluster and the 3.OA standards in that cluster.

Content standard cluster (see appendix B, pages 164–166): ______________________

Reason for selecting the content standard cluster: ______________________

What Content Needs to Be Unpacked for Lesson Design Around This Cluster?	Which Topics Need to Be Emphasized?	How Will Students Be Engaged in the Mathematical Practices as They Learn This Content?	What Resources Will Be Needed?	How Will Students Demonstrate Learning of This Content Standard Cluster?

Visit **go.solution-tree.com/commoncore** for a reproducible version of this feature box.

Number and Operations in Base Ten (3.NBT)

The focus on Number and Operations in Base Ten is on place value, properties (once again) of the operations, and performing whole-number operations (addition, subtraction, multiplication, and division). Place value, operations involving decimals, and rounding involving both whole numbers and decimals are also an integral aspect of the content standard clusters in this domain (see appendix B, page 166).

The 3.NBT Content Standard Cluster

The Number and Operations in Base Ten (3.NBT) domain has one content standard cluster, which contains three standards (see appendix B, page 166).

1. Use place-value understanding and properties of operations to perform multi-digit arithmetic.

The Understanding Questions for the 3.NBT Content Standard Cluster

The three questions in table 3.1 (page 67) provide a framework for you and your team to use to develop a greater understanding of the intent of the content standard cluster for the Number and Operations in Base Ten domain (3.NBT).

Use place-value understanding and properties of operations to perform multidigit arithmetic is the single content standard cluster for the 3.NBT domain. This cluster will, in general, be familiar content from your current and previous curriculum standards.

- **What's familiar?** At this grade level, your students are expected to be fluent when adding and subtracting whole numbers through three-digit numbers. *Fluency*, by the nature of its definition, means to *speak or write with ease and accuracy*. Computational fluency is defined as having and using efficient and accurate methods for computation (NCTM, 2000). Using the standard algorithm for addition and subtraction will also be expected at this level, but your emphasis will be on student demonstrations of understanding regarding how addition and subtraction *work*, the relationship between addition and subtraction, and the ability of the student to add and subtract numbers with ease (fluently). In addition, multiplying single-digit numbers by multiples of ten are part of this content standard cluster in third grade.
- **What's new? What's challenging?** The newness, for some third-grade teachers, will be the expectation that your students *understand* what they are doing as they progress with addition, subtraction, and multiplication. That is, can your students use strategies that are based on place value, properties of operations, and, in the case of addition and subtraction, the relationship between adding and subtracting? As importantly, the standards for multiplying by multiples of ten will be new third-grade expectations for student learning and must be addressed in your unit lesson-plan development for this grade level.
- **What needs unpacking? What topics need emphasizing?** The work with addition and subtraction is largely an extension of prior work at the second-grade level and will occur earlier in the instructional year, and will be linked, as noted earlier in this analysis, to solving problems. The content expectations

for multiplication extend to student work involving multiplication and related division facts and will need at least a two- to three-day lesson on the standard.

Number and Operations—Fractions (3.NF)

Number and Operations—Fractions (see appendix B, pages 166–167) is solely a grades 3–5 content domain and stresses foundational work with fractions, including understanding fractions as numbers, fraction equivalence, comparing and ordering fractions, and the operations of addition, subtraction, multiplication, and division with fractions. This domain also includes work with decimal notation and comparing decimals.

The 3.NF Content Standard Cluster

The Number and Operations—Fractions (3.NF) has one content standard cluster, which contains three standards (see appendix B, pages 166–167).

1. Develop understanding of fractions as numbers.

The Understanding Questions for the 3.NF Content Standard Cluster

The three questions in table 3.1 (page 67) provide a framework for you and your team to use to develop a greater understanding of the intent of the content standard cluster for the Number Operations—Fractions domain (3.NF).

Develop understanding of fractions as numbers is the single content standard cluster for the 3.NF domain. Establishing fractions as numbers will be an important foundational topic at this grade level.

- **What's familiar?** This cluster will be familiar yet at the same time challenging due to the points of content emphasis for developing student understanding based on the three standards in this cluster.
- **What's new? What's challenging?** The emphasis on fractions at the third-grade level will be different and challenging for you and your third-grade students. The CCSS approach to this standard places an emphasis on developing student understanding by using *unit fractions*. You are also expected to use the number line as a representational tool for demonstrating the magnitude of fractions and to help teach with an emphasis on fraction equivalence. For example, your students should be able to compare fractions by being able to reason about their size. Students will need to be able to demonstrate that two fractions are equivalent if they are the same size or represent the same point on the number line.
- **What needs unpacking? What topics need emphasizing?** Emphasizing fractions in third grade and developing deeper student understanding of fractions as numbers will be one of the biggest curricular differences and challenges you face as you transition to the CCSS expectations. The 3.NF content standard cluster for fractions will require extensive and dedicated instruction and lesson-plan design spread over two to three weeks. This

pacing is necessary in order to include work with modeling, representing, and comparing fractions as you help students to connect those activities to their work on fraction equivalence. Your team will need to dedicate significant student time to this content standard cluster and design lesson tasks and assessment that demonstrate a student understanding of fraction equivalence.

Measurement and Data (3.MD)

The Measurement and Data domain (see appendix B, pages 167–168) for grade 3 provides the opportunity for your students to represent and interpret data, develop estimation skills, and continue developmental work in geometric measurement.

The 3.MD Content Standard Clusters

The Measurement and Data (3.MD) domain has four content standard clusters, which contain eight standards (see appendix B, pages 167–168).

1. Solve problems involving measurement and estimation of intervals of time, liquid volumes, and masses of objects.
2. Represent and interpret data.
3. Geometric measurement: Understand concepts of area and relate area to multiplication and to addition.
4. Geometric measurement: Recognize perimeter as an attribute of plane figures and distinguish between linear and area measures.

The Understanding Questions for the 3.MD Content Standard Clusters

The three questions in table 3.1 (page 67) provide a framework for you and your team to use to develop a greater understanding of the intent of the four content standard clusters and the eight standards for the Measurement and Data domain (3.MD).

Solve problems involving measurement and estimation of intervals of time, liquid volumes, and masses of objects is the first content standard cluster for the 3.MD domain. It presents many opportunities for your students to do and use mathematics.

- **What's familiar?** This standard presents an aspect of mathematics—time—that people, be they parents or the community at large, expect students to know and know well. So, this is certainly familiar and expected as a standard. While involving your students with metric measurement is typically a grade 3–5 expectation, the depth of understanding expected by the standards within this content standard cluster needs to be closely examined by your team. They present a new challenge for your unit lesson planning and design for this domain.
- **What's new? What's challenging?** Expecting third-grade students to solve problems involving time with time intervals in minutes while engaging in

addition and subtraction of timed amounts may be a challenge for some of your students. In addition, using a number-line diagram to solve problems involving time may be challenging. Careful lesson design by your collaborative team for these standards will be important. Finally, the suggested applications involving grams, kilograms, and liters involving all four operations are new content for this grade level.

- **What needs unpacking? What topics need emphasizing?** Actual lessons involving telling time to the nearest minute and involving addition and subtraction of time intervals may take you two to three days but should be maintained in problem-solving situations throughout the year. Similarly, estimating and measuring to the nearest gram (g), liter (L), and kilogram (kg) will take one to two days, but the problems involving these applications may be spread across the instructional year.

Represent and interpret data is the second content standard cluster for the 3.MD domain. It expects students to draw and interpret bar and picture graphs and construct a line plot.

- **What's familiar?** These standards in this cluster are typically taught in third grade, so it is likely you and your team will be familiar with teaching students how to interpret bar and picture graphs. Interpreting line plots has generally been part of the current third-grade curriculum in most states as well.
- **What's new? What's challenging?** What will be new and challenging for you will be teaching students to draw appropriately scaled picture and bar graphs. For some of your colleagues, showing measurement using a line plot may be a new content standard as well.
- **What needs unpacking? What topics need emphasizing?** Measurement and Data provide an opportunity to connect to Mathematical Practice 4—Model with mathematics. Instructional time needed for student understanding related to actually drawing scaled bar and picture graphs and line plots should last two to four days. Applications that involve analyzing the graphs and connecting this work to measurement should spread throughout the instructional year. Such problems connect mathematics to real-life activities.

Geometric measurement: Understand concepts of area and relate area to multiplication and to addition is the third content standard cluster for the 3.MD domain. It involves applications of area concepts and builds on prior student experiences with geometry, particularly with rectangles.

- **What's familiar?** These measurement geometry experiences are a current expectation within your third-grade curriculum.
- **What's new? What's challenging?** What's new for this standard is typical of almost all the third-grade standards. Teaching for *depth* is important with this standard. There is a depth of understanding expected as students encounter

tasks for learning about area. Participating in activities involving tiling, solving problems involving area, and using area models representing the distributive property are all important area-related understandings.

- **What needs unpacking? What topics need emphasizing?** Activities designed to address student understandings related to area may take at least portions of two to four instructional days. Problems or mathematical tasks that involve area should continue to be an emphasis of your team throughout the instructional year. Using area models to represent the distributive property should be an integral component of work with multiplication algorithms throughout the year as well.

Geometric measurement: Recognize perimeter as an attribute of plane figures and distinguish between linear and area measures is the fourth content standard cluster for the 3.MD domain. It connects linear measure to area measure.

- **What's familiar?** The most familiar aspect of this content standard cluster is student demonstration of skill in finding the perimeter of polygons.
- **What's new? What's challenging?** Once again, the depth of understanding expected may be a challenge, but the links between geometry and area are an important emphasis of your content development and lesson design at this grade level.
- **What needs unpacking? What topics need emphasizing?** Your instruction for this content standard cluster will parallel your work with area, as related to rectangles, and then expand to include perimeter of a variety of polygons. While there may only be one to two dedicated perimeter lessons as part of your unit design, applications involving the solving of real-world problems should occur throughout the year.

Geometry (3.G)

At third grade, the Geometry domain (see appendix B, page 168) focuses on reasoning with shapes and the subsequent connection of partitioning shapes with equal areas.

The 3.G Content Standard Cluster

The Geometry (3.G) domain has one content standard cluster, which contains two standards (see appendix B, page 168).

1. Reason with shapes and their attributes.

The Understanding Questions for the 3.G Content Standard Cluster

The three questions in table 3.1 (page 67) provide a framework for you and your team to develop a greater understanding of the intent of the third-grade content standard cluster for the Geometry (3.G) domain.

Reason with shapes and their attributes is the single content standard cluster for the 3.G domain. The two standards in this cluster address recognizing shapes in different categories and partitioning shapes into parts with equal areas.

- **What's familiar?** This standard is a learning target that is likely familiar to you at this grade level. Students in third grade typically work with shapes in different categories, including shared attributes (for example, the number of sides). They generally categorize quadrilaterals by their properties.
- **What's new? What's challenging?** Partitioning of shapes into parts with equal areas will be a natural link to fractions but may be a new experience for you as a third-grade teacher.
- **What needs unpacking? What topics need emphasizing?** Consider two to four instructional days (lessons) for activities involving categorization of shapes. Partitioning shapes would be a viable lesson and provide a way to continue application of student work within Number and Operations—Fractions.

Grade 3 Analysis: Concluding Comment

Third grade is an important year for students' mathematics learning. At the third-grade level, students are expected to become fluent with addition and subtraction of whole numbers and develop important understandings related to multiplication and division. However, as noted in the previous analyses of the content standard clusters, the major content change for you, your colleagues, and your students at this level will be the emphasis on fractions. You and your team should give special consideration to a professional development initiative dedicated to the examination and discussion around current expectations for fractions at the third-grade level. The grade 3 CCSS expectations for the domain Number and Operations—Fractions (3.NF), with its particular emphasis on equivalent fractions and the use of the number line as an instructional tool to develop student understanding of the content standards, will require special planning by you and your team.

Decisions and subsequent adjustments about the number of teaching days and lessons that will be dedicated to student demonstrations of understanding for each of these content standard clusters will be important as well.

Grade 4: What's the Mathematics?

The CCSS content at the fourth-grade level includes several important additions to your current fourth-grade-level curriculum expectations. Like the third grade, the expectations regarding fractions are more than what has typically been the case for past state standard requirements. This increased standard expectation occurs as you are also working on important standards related to multiplication and division involving whole numbers. Other new content in fourth grade includes angles, line plots for data display, and overall student *depth of understanding* of particular concepts within all of the domains at this grade level. As noted previously, the language of the CCSS content domains, clusters, and standards with its emphasis on understanding and the regular use of a variety of representations (like number lines, drawings, and so on) requires students to develop a depth of understanding that depends on time—time to teach, time to learn, and time to truly understand. This is where the Mathematical Practices enter as guideposts and opportunities for engaging and understanding fourth-grade mathematics content standards that, although fewer in number, will require more attention and depth.

According to the CCSS, three critical areas should be the focus of your instructional time at this grade level:

> (1) developing understanding and fluency with multi-digit multiplication, and developing understanding of dividing to find quotients involving multi-digit dividends; (2) developing an understanding of fraction equivalence, addition and subtraction of fractions with like denominators, and multiplication of fractions by whole numbers; (3) understanding that geometric figures can be analyzed and classified based on their properties, such as having parallel sides, perpendicular sides, particular angle measures, and symmetry. (NGA & CCSSO, 2010, p. 27)

The content standard clusters for this domain are listed in appendix C (page 169).

The questions in table 3.2 are organized for you to consider the impact of the Common Core standards for this grade level. As noted previously on page 66, use table 3.2 as an analysis tool to consider what's familiar, what's new or challenging, and what needs unpacking or emphasizing in each content standard cluster. The understanding questions are designed to help you analyze the CCSS for mathematics in relation to your experience in working with other standards. We've provided answers to these questions for the standards in each domain. (See appendix C, page 169, for the CCSS Mathematics Content Domains and Standards for Grade 4.)

Table 3.2: Grade-by-Grade Analysis Tool—Grade 4

Content Standard Cluster	Which Standards in the Cluster Are Familiar?	What's New or Challenging in These Standards?	Which Standards in the Cluster Need Unpacking or Emphasizing?
Operations and Algebraic Thinking (4.OA)			
Use the four operations with whole numbers to solve problems.			
Gain familiarity with factors and multiples.			
Generate and analyze patterns.			
Generalize place-value understanding for multidigit whole numbers.			

continued →

Content Standard Cluster	Which Standards in the Cluster Are Familiar?	What's New or Challenging in These Standards?	Which Standards in the Cluster Need Unpacking or Emphasizing?
Number and Operations in Base Ten (4.NBT)			
Use place-value understanding and properties of operations to perform multidigit arithmetic.			
Number and Operations—Fractions (4.NF)			
Extend understanding of fraction equivalence and ordering.			
Build fractions from unit fractions by applying and extending previous understandings of operations on whole numbers.			
Understand decimal notation for fractions, and compare decimal fractions.			
Measurement and Data (4.MD)			
Solve problems involving measurement and conversion of measurements from a larger unit to a smaller unit.			
Represent and interpret data.			
Geometric measurement: Understand concepts of angle and measure angles.			

Content Standard Cluster	Which Standards in the Cluster Are Familiar?	What's New or Challenging in These Standards?	Which Standards in the Cluster Need Unpacking or Emphasizing?
Geometry (4.G)			
Draw and identify lines and angles, and classify shapes by properties of their lines and angles.			
General Comments			

Visit **go.solution-tree.com/commoncore** for a reproducible version of this table.

Operations and Algebraic Thinking (4.OA)

The Operations and Algebraic Thinking domain (see appendix C, pages 170–171) emphasizes conceptual understanding and problem solving with whole-number operations, early work with factors and multiples, and generating and analyzing number and shape patterns.

The 4.OA Content Standard Clusters

The Operations and Algebraic Thinking (4.OA) domain has three content standard clusters, which contain five standards (see appendix C, pages 170–171).

1. Use the four operations with whole numbers to solve problems.
2. Gain familiarity with factors and multiples.
3. Generate and analyze problems.

The Understanding Questions for the 4.OA Content Standard Clusters

The three questions in table 3.2 (page 79) provide a framework for you and your team to use to develop a greater understanding of the intent of each content standard cluster for the Operations and Algebraic Thinking (4.OA) domain.

Use the four operations with whole numbers to solve problems is the first content standard cluster for the 4.OA domain. The three standards address multiplication and division.

- **What's familiar?** Your lessons with multiplication and division at this grade level should deepen student conceptual understanding of these operations through connections to equations as a prealgebra experience and should align with your current lessons for this standard cluster.

- **What's new? What's challenging?** Use of the phrases *multiplicative* and *additive comparison* could be new and different for you and your students. For ways to express common addition and subtraction as well as multiplication and division situations related to this 4.OA cluster, refer to appendix C (pages 170–171). Additional examples are provided in chapter 5 (see table 5.2, page 150, and table 5.3, page 151).

  Addition and subtraction and related multiplication and division situations are discussed in *Mathematics Learning in Early Childhood: Paths Toward Excellence and Equity* (NRC, 2009). You will benefit from discussing these conceptual representations of whole-number operations with your collaborative team members and considering how you might use them as part of your lesson development for this domain.

- **What needs unpacking? What topics need emphasizing?** One or more of your lessons for this content standard cluster will need to connect prior student learning experiences with multiplication and division to the modeling with mathematics link for equations in these standards. Note there is a clear prealgebra emphasis with this content standard cluster. You will need to focus on lesson elements that connect using a letter (variable) to represent an unknown quantity. In addition, your instructional attention will be needed for designing lessons that interpret the remainder—when is the remainder used in solving a problem, or when may the remainder become critical to the problem's solution? Your emphasis on using the four operations to solve problems should be a consistent effort throughout the instructional year. Repeated student opportunities to solve problems and construct viable arguments that also critique the reasoning of others (an intentional pursuit of the Mathematical Practices) will help your students develop and demonstrate proficiency toward the related abilities of using estimation and mental mathematics with determining the reasonableness of responses.

Gain familiarity with factors and multiples is the second content standard cluster for the 4.OA domain. It is readily recognized as part of the fourth-grade curriculum by most fourth-grade teachers.

- **What's familiar?** Fourth-grade teachers and students have engaged in student experiences with factors and multiples as part of the curriculum for some time. Activities involving *number theory*—typically, understanding factors and multiples and determining whether numbers are prime or composite—are frequent extensions of student work with multiplication and division of whole numbers, which have historically bridged to student work with fractions (for example, using multiples and the least common multiple to help determine the least common denominator, and using factoring and the greatest common factor to create fractions in lowest or simplest terms).

- **What's new? What's challenging?** What you may find different within this cluster for the 4.OA domain is the relative lack of attention to factors and multiples and the absence of the phrase *number theory* as a descriptor of such work. Your new lesson-design focus and emphasis will be on the actual use of factors and multiples as students develop their understanding of multiplication and division.
- **What needs unpacking? What topics need emphasizing?** Your lesson plans with factors and multiples and connections of this work to prime and composite numbers may be one- to two-day lessons, followed by subsequent applications throughout the year. Such opportunities for students to easily recognize, for example, all the factors of 24 will help them throughout the year in the short term in working with fractions and in the long term for developing their sense of number.

Generate and analyze patterns is the third and final content standard cluster for the 4.OA domain. Patterns are often thought of as an early algebra learning opportunity for students.

- **What's familiar?** This standard will be familiar to you as an early-algebra opportunity as students consider shape and number patterns and early work with expressions, all precursors to formal work with algebra.
- **What's new? What's challenging?** This content standard cluster provides an opportunity for your students to examine patterns in counting sequences, with multiples, and so on. The opportunity for exploring patterns with shapes provides an extension of your work with the geometry standards from grade 3. Student learning experiences involving patterns related to number and shape provide an opportunity for your students to extend their understandings related to operations and shape.
- **What needs unpacking? What topics need emphasizing?** Consider your instruction involving patterns related to number and shape as an opportunity for your students to engage in looking for and expressing regularity in repeated reasoning (Mathematical Practice 8).

The three-part analysis of each content standard cluster will enable your team to build understanding and extend insights into how to most effectively teach the CCSS for mathematics. The Collaborative Team Task (page 84) is a model that you can use to plan implementation of the selected domain standards. The template for the model is shown for the 4.OA domain. This template is available as a reproducible for each of the five content domains in fourth grade. You can use these guides to support your team's discussion and planning for the CCSS implementation at your school.

Collaborative Team Task: Planning Implementation of Domain 4.OA

Based on your analysis of the content standard clusters for Operations and Algebraic Thinking, select a content standard cluster that you know will be challenging for your students (and possibly for you, too). Use the questions in the table to guide development of your unit design plans. Ask one of your team members to be video recorded while teaching the lesson you design. You could also share a digital version of your notes in an interactive document, such as a pencast (see page 111 for more information), of the mathematics within the lesson that is developed in this activity. Use your video or pencast for discussion in a subsequent team meeting as you provide formative feedback to your team about student progress toward mastery of the chosen content standard cluster and the 4.OA standards in that cluster.

Content standard cluster (see appendix C, pages 170–171): ______________________

Reason for selecting the content standard cluster: ______________________

What Content Needs to Be Unpacked for Lesson Design Around This Cluster?	Which Topics Need to Be Emphasized?	How Will Students Be Engaged in the Mathematical Practices as They Learn This Content?	What Resources Will Be Needed?	How Will Students Demonstrate Learning of This Content Standard Cluster?

Visit **go.solution-tree.com/commoncore** for a reproducible version of this feature box.

Number and Operations in Base Ten (4.NBT)

The Number and Operations in Base Ten domain (see appendix C, pages 171–172) focuses on place value, properties (once again) of the operations, and performing whole-number operations (addition, subtraction, multiplication, and division). Place value, operations involving decimals, and rounding involving both whole numbers and decimals are also an integral aspect of the content standard clusters in this domain.

The 4.NBT Content Standard Clusters

The Number and Operations in Base Ten (4.NBT) domain has two content standard clusters, which contain six standards (see appendix C, pages 171–172).

1. Generalize place value understanding for multidigit whole numbers.
2. Use place-value understanding and properties of operations to perform multidigit arithmetic.

The Understanding Questions for the 4.NBT Content Standard Cluster

The three questions in table 3.2 (page 79) provide a framework for you and your team to use to develop a greater understanding of the intent of each content standard cluster for the Number and Operations in Base Ten domain.

Generalize place-value understanding for multidigit whole numbers is the first content standard cluster for the 4.NBT domain. In general, it will be a familiar set of student learning standards at the fourth-grade level.

- **What's familiar?** The place-value focus and expectations in this cluster and the connection to rounding as an estimation strategy are typical learning outcomes for students in fourth grade.
- **What's new? What's challenging?** As indicated, the emphasis of this content standard cluster is familiar content. However, this does not diminish its importance and the challenge the standards in this cluster create for some, if not many, learners. Understanding the place and value of numbers and being able to read and write numbers, including determining the value of each digit within a multidigit number, is not a trivial expectation. Additionally, rounding as an estimation strategy is often not well understood by fourth-grade students.
- **What needs unpacking? What topics need emphasizing?** Sufficient instructional time is needed for developing student proficiency in this content standard cluster. Your work with place value will typically occur early in the instructional year and will need to be maintained as your students work with operations involving whole numbers during the school year. Students should be provided opportunities to use base-ten materials and related representations (such as pictured renderings) as tools for developing and demonstrating understanding of these standards.

Use place-value understanding and properties of operations to perform multidigit arithmetic is the second content standard cluster for the 4.NBT domain. It consists of three standards that provide typical student learning expectations in the fourth-grade curriculum for your students.

- **What's familiar?** While multiplication and division of whole numbers are familiar at this level, extending the work to include multiplication and division with larger numbers must be developed with an increased level of student understanding. This will be your lesson-design and lesson-implementation challenge.
- **What's new? What's challenging?** While the topics and learning expectations are not particularly new for your teaching, the suggested size of the dividends (up to four digits) may be beyond prior expectations for fourth grade. The challenge for your lesson design is related to the amount of time needed on the

topics in this cluster during a year when student work with fractions will be expanded. Consequently, developing student understanding for this cluster is the lesson-design challenge for your team (see table 3.4, page 105, for one view of number emphasis at this grade level).

- **What needs unpacking? What topics need emphasizing?** While not a new learning standard for you, the standard regarding fluency with addition and subtraction, using the standard algorithm, represents a *capstone for student work* with these two early operations. This fluency should be assessed for student mastery early in the year and supported through problem-solving activities throughout the year. The work with multiplication and division will need to be distributed across the first half of your instructional year, with the goal to have most, not necessarily all, of this completed prior to your lessons involving fractions.

Number and Operations—Fractions (4.NF)

The Number and Operations—Fractions domain (see appendix C, pages 172–173) is solely a grades 3–5 content domain and stresses foundational work with fractions, including understanding fractions as numbers, fraction equivalence, comparing and ordering fractions, and the operations of addition, subtraction, and multiplication with fractions. This domain also includes decimal notation and comparing decimal fractions at this grade level.

The 4.NF Content Standard Clusters

The Number and Operations—Fractions (4.NF) domain has three content standard clusters, which contain seven standards (see appendix C, pages 172–173).

1. Extend understanding of fraction equivalence and ordering.
2. Build fractions from unit fractions by applying and extending previous understandings of operations on whole numbers.
3. Understand decimal notation for fractions, and compare decimal fractions.

The Understanding Questions for the 4.NF Content Standard Cluster

The three questions in table 3.2 (page 79) provide a framework for you and your team to use to develop a greater understanding of the intent of each content standard cluster for the Number and Operations—Fractions domain.

Extend understanding of fraction equivalence and ordering is the first content standard cluster for the 4.NF domain. It consists of two student learning standards and extends students' prior experiences with fractions from the third-grade standards (see domain 3.NF, appendix B, pages 166–167).

- **What's familiar?** Student work with fractions at this level extends prior learning experiences with fraction equivalence and ordering, and the addition and subtraction of fractions.
- **What's new? What's challenging?** Your teaching challenge will be to attend to lesson development that requires a level of student understanding expected with fraction equivalence and comparing (and ordering) fractions. This work is foundational and represents the place-value equivalent to your students' early work with whole numbers.
- **What needs unpacking? What topics need emphasizing?** You will need to spend significant instructional time using tools such as visual fraction models (particularly tools described in Mathematical Practice 5; see appendix A, pages 160–161). This could be a full week of instruction, with your lesson designs focused on equivalence and comparing, which are subsequently applied through your additional student work with fractions throughout the year.

Build fractions from unit fractions by applying and extending previous understandings of operations on whole numbers is the second content standard cluster for the 4.NF domain. It consists of two standards with multiple parts and is a familiar and expected topic for fourth grade.

- **What's familiar?** Student learning experiences with addition and subtraction of fractions in fourth grade involve fractions with like denominators. This is a current standard at the fourth-grade level for most teachers.
- **What's new? What's challenging?** Beginning work with multiplication of fractions will be new at this grade level. Assuming instructional attention to the prior work of extending fraction equivalence—comparison and ordering—your major lesson-design challenge will be providing the time needed to ensure students can demonstrate *conceptual understanding* of these important fraction topics. You should note that the operations of addition, subtraction, and multiplication developed in this cluster are based on your students' prior experience with whole numbers. This connection of prior student work with whole-number-operations fluency to fraction operations is important.
- **What needs unpacking? What topics need emphasizing?** Your instructional lesson designs for this standard cluster involving fraction operations will need to be based on your student success with fraction equivalence, comparing, and ordering. Again, you and your team will need to provide the time necessary to present and fully engage your students in working with addition and subtraction of fractions. Your use of visual models and relating these fraction operations back to addition and subtraction of whole numbers will be important foci of your instructional planning. Multiplication of fractions extends the work with factors, multiples, and whole-number multiplication,

which would occur earlier in the year. What will be most important is to ensure the time necessary to develop student links between whole numbers and fraction operations and to develop student understanding of how and why these operations work. Your major unpacking emphasis issue in this standard is the level of importance and the amount of time spent developing proficiency with multiplying and dividing whole numbers—this is an instructional planning load from both a time- and a concept-development perspective. It is also important for you to provide content tasks for student problem-solving opportunities with fractions as you foster student problem solving throughout the year.

Understand decimal notation for fractions, and compare decimal fractions is the third and final content standard cluster for domain 4.NF. This cluster consists of three standards (see appendix C, page 173) and will be very familiar student content for some fourth-grade teachers.

- **What's familiar?** While decimals are like old friends for many teachers and, hopefully, their students, for others, the standard could appear to be a new topic. It should be noted that while decimals appear as a standard within the Number and Operations—Fractions domain at this grade level, they are not mentioned in grade 3. They appear within the Number and Operations in Base Ten domain in grade 5 (see appendix D, pages 177–178).
- **What's new? What's challenging?** Consider the popularity and use of decimals in our culture. For example, adults use decimals far more frequently than fractions when adding distances or solving problems involving money. Decimals show up in lots of other places in daily life as well. Every gas pump shows two sets of decimal numbers: the amount of gas you bought as a decimal and the amount of money you owe. Your gas mileage in miles per gallon is always shown as a decimal number. Look at the car's odometer; the miles on it are always shown with decimal notation too.

  Given this fact, decimals are, far too often, forgotten as important fractions (the ones with denominators of 10, 100, and so on). Your teaching challenge will be to ensure student understanding of decimals not as whole numbers with an add-on (the decimal point) but as ways to connect fractions to the place-value system. Again, you and your team will need time to teach this content cluster standard well—with deep student understanding and making sure students can use appropriate tools like number lines, rulers, and other visual models strategically, as they develop such understanding (see Mathematical Practice 5, appendix A, pages 160–161).
- **What needs unpacking? What topics need emphasizing?** Some teachers like to teach decimals as extensions of their work with whole numbers. This is probably due to the fact that the procedures for adding, subtracting, multiplying, and dividing are the same, with one major exception: placement of the decimal point in the sum, difference, product, or quotient. However,

you should note that decimals are intentionally placed with fractions at this level so you can develop student understanding along with or following the student learning experiences with fractions. The learning standard emphasis for this cluster is not so much about student work with operations as it is with expressing, comparing, and writing decimals. This is an important standard at this grade level and clearly connects to your work with those other fractions—the a/b type.

Your team should consider a vertical professional development discussion with your colleagues in grades 3 and 5, analyzing the activities and tasks used for teaching and representing fractions and decimals. Pay particular attention to the similarities and differences in your approaches when writing and comparing fractions and decimals.

Measurement and Data (4.MD)

The Measurement and Data domain (see appendix C, pages 173–174) consists of seven standards and provides opportunities for your students to represent and interpret data, solve problems involving measurement and the conversion of measurement units, and continue developmental work in geometric measurement with specific attention to work with angles.

The 4.MD Content Standard Cluster

The Measurement and Data (4.MD) domain has three content standard clusters, which contain seven standards (see appendix C, pages 173–174).

1. Solve problems involving measurement and conversion of measurements from a larger unit to a smaller unit.
2. Represent and interpret data.
3. Geometric measurement: Understand concepts of angle and measure angles.

The Understanding Questions for the 4.MD Content Standard Clusters

The three questions in table 3.2 (page 79) provide a framework for you and your team to use to develop a greater understanding of the intent of each content standard cluster for the Measurement and Data (4.MD) domain.

Solve problems involving measurement and conversion of measurements from a larger unit to a smaller unit is the first content standard cluster for the 4.MD domain. It consists of three standards and contains a typical set of student learning expectations for the fourth grade.

- **What's familiar?** While solving problems involving measurement and converting within a measurement system is familiar for students, student demonstration of proficiency with measurement often receives a very shallow treatment instructionally. Far too often, students depart fourth grade with minimal experience actually using measurement—a content domain they will use throughout their lives.

- **What's new? What's challenging?** Perhaps your greatest teaching and lesson planning challenge will be to determine when measurement will occur within your fourth-grade curricular sequence. The preceding standards suggest relating measurement to preratio and proportion activities involving fractions as an early student learning expectation in fourth grade. Linking perimeter to area may be a challenge for some students and implies an opportunity for you to design lessons that represent both concepts using physical models or drawings.
- **What needs unpacking? What topics need emphasizing?** As noted, the most logical content sequencing approach for your team is to consider these expectations as applications of prior work with fractions and multiplication and division. However, measurement should not be considered a once-and-done unit for you and your colleagues. Problem-solving opportunities involving measurement should be an important content element that is integrated into your fourth-grade mathematics curriculum throughout the year.

Represent and interpret data is the second content standard cluster for the 4.MD domain. It involves measuring to the nearest half and one-fourth of a unit.

- **What's familiar?** Measuring to the nearest half and on-fourth of a unit should be familiar to many teachers at this grade level.
- **What's new? What's challenging?** For some teachers, the line plot will not be a well-recognized nor frequently used data-representation tool by the students. In addition, measuring in fractional units (particularly one-eighth or smaller units) will not be a familiar student learning expectation and may require you and your team to design new lessons for these expectations.
- **What needs unpacking? What topics need emphasizing?** The important content link with this standard is your student work with fractions—measuring and using the line plot as a way to compare measurements. This application of the fraction expectations at this grade level should bring lifelike application to student demonstrations for analyzing and comparing fraction data.

Geometric measurement: Understand concepts of angle, and measure angles is the third and final content standard cluster for the 4.MD domain. It consists of three learning standards and will be interesting to students and teachers.

- **What's familiar?** Working with angles and measuring angles should be familiar topics for students at this grade level, particularly identifying angles.
- **What's new? What's challenging?** The depth of your student development with angles will be new for most of your fourth-grade teaching colleagues. Lesson designs and plans built on concepts around angle measurement and the actual student measurement of angles will be a new learning outcome for many teachers of this grade level.

- **What needs unpacking? What topics need emphasizing?** The major challenge with this content standard cluster will be determining which concepts and skills to emphasize. The necessary time you will need for the expanded work with angles needs to be ensured as part of the fourth-grade curriculum. The expectations within the CCSS is much more than the typical vocabulary approach of merely naming angles (for example, right, acute, obtuse) that may have been the approach for previous state and local school district standards. Fourth-grade students are now expected to be able to demonstrate the ability to measure angles as well as the ability to solve mathematical problems involving unknown angles.

Geometry (4.G)

At the fourth-grade level, the Geometry domain (see appendix C, page 174) consists of one content standard cluster built on three standards. The domain focuses on drawing and identifying lines and angles, classifying two-dimensional figures, and recognizing and drawing lines of symmetry.

The 4.G Content Standard Cluster

The Geometry (4.G) domain has one content standard cluster, which contains three standards (see appendix C, page 174).

1. Draw and identify lines and angles, and classify shapes by properties of their lines and angles.

The Understanding Questions for the 4.G Content Standard Cluster

The three questions in table 3.2 (page 79) provide a framework for you and your team to use to develop a greater understanding of the intent of each content standard cluster for the Geometry domain.

Draw and identify lines and angles, and classify shapes by properties of their lines and angles, the single content standard cluster in the 4.G domain, is typical of the geometric student learning standards and expectations at this grade level.

- **What's familiar?** As your students respond to lessons in which they identify and classify shapes by their properties, their learning experiences extend from as far back as the early primary and even preschool levels. Thus, this element of the content standard cluster should be very much a review. Such identification is a typical expectation in most current or former state mathematics standards.
- **What's new? What's challenging?** The expectation that you will teach the classification of two-dimensional figures based on parallel or perpendicular lines or the presence or absence of particular angles will be new fourth-grade content and challenging for many students. This standard implies that student classification may be based on whether or not, for example, acute

angles occur in the shape. For students to classify this way implies prerequisite understandings related to the classification elements—parallel or perpendicular lines and types of angles. The lessons designed for this content standard cluster will need to ensure students are engaged in Mathematical Practice 6—Attend to precision (see appendix A, page 161).

- **What needs unpacking? What topics need emphasizing?** This standard's expectations could be addressed during a relatively brief three-day to one-week geometry unit. The important prerequisite work with angles, which could also be part of the unit, should be emphasized as part of the lesson development and design, and, as indicated, engage the Mathematical Practice 6—Attend to precision.

Grade 4 Analysis: Concluding Comment

As you reflect on the challenges of teaching and learning for fourth-grade mathematics, this grade may be considered an *extension grade.* What does that mean? Work with multiplication and division of whole numbers is *extended* to larger numbers. Work with fractions, established in grade 3, *extends* to include addition and subtraction of fractions and early work with multiplication of fractions. Importantly, as with grade 3, the focus for fourth grade is not only on number but also on geometry and early work with algebra concepts in the Operations and Algebraic Thinking domain. At this grade level, there is an emphasis on the appropriate use of varied conceptual representations and an *extended* focus on student understanding of the mathematics to be learned.

Grade 5: What's the Mathematics?

In a word, fifth grade is huge. There's a lot of mathematics to be taught and learned with student understanding extended at this grade level. You need to know and love mathematics to teach fifth grade—that's for sure. What's so important? In grade 5, you move into several standards that are clearly *algebra readiness* in focus. You also move students to fluency with whole-number operations, including division with a two-digit divisor and operations involving decimals. Fractions are extended to include addition and subtraction with unlike denominators and an important emphasis on multiplication and division of fractions.

Depending on how you judge the mathematics content (the domain and content standard cluster) impact and the need for instructional time emphasis, it's conservative to say that approximately 50 percent or more of the fifth-grade year will be spent on developing fluency and conceptual understanding related to work with whole numbers, fractions, and decimals. Importantly, the Mathematical Practices (see appendix A, page 159) must continue to play a key role in providing opportunities for you to authentically engage students in the mathematics developed and learned at this grade level. The learning-target expectations that are new for this grade level include applications involving measurement and data, including work with volume and line plots, as well as a geometry content standard cluster that includes the coordinate plane. Fifth grade provides closure for the whole-number operations standards but, more importantly, requires you to establish the critical and foundational work with fractions necessary for students to extend their learning of standards involving ratio, rate, and proportion and of the number system in grades 6 through 8.

The CCSS for mathematics specify that instructional time at this grade level should focus on three critical areas:

> (1) developing fluency with addition and subtraction of fractions, and developing understanding of the multiplication of fractions and of division of fractions in limited cases (unit fractions divided by whole numbers and whole numbers divided by unit fractions); (2) extending division to 2-digit divisors, integrating decimal fractions into the place value system and developing understanding of operations with decimals to hundredths, and developing fluency with whole number and decimal operations; and (3) developing understanding of volume. (NGA & CCSSO, 2010, p. 33)

The content standard clusters for this domain are listed in appendix D (page 175).

As noted previously on page 66, use table 3.3 as an analysis tool to consider what's familiar, what's new or challenging, and what needs unpacking or emphasizing in each content standard cluster. The understanding questions are designed to help you analyze the CCSS for mathematics in relation to your experience in working with other standards. We've provided answers to these questions for the standards in each domain.

Table 3.3: Grade-by-Grade Analysis Tool—Grade 5

Content Standard Cluster	Which Standards in the Cluster Are Familiar?	What's New or Challenging in These Standards?	Which Standards in the Cluster Need Unpacking or Emphasizing?
Operations and Algebraic Thinking (5.OA)			
Write and interpret numerical expressions.			
Analyze patterns and relationships.			
Number and Operations in Base Ten (5.NBT)			
Understand the place-value system.			
Perform operations with multidigit whole numbers and with decimals to hundredths.			

continued →

Content Standard Cluster	Which Standards in the Cluster Are Familiar?	What's New or Challenging in These Standards?	Which Standards in the Cluster Need Unpacking or Emphasizing?
Number and Operations—Fractions (5.NF)			
Use equivalent fractions as a strategy to add and subtract fractions.			
Apply and extend previous understandings of multiplication and division to multiply and divide fractions.			
Measurement and Data (5.MD)			
Convert like measurement units within a given measurement system.			
Represent and interpret data.			
Geometric measurement: Understand concepts of volume and relate volume to multiplication and addition.			
Geometry (5.G)			
Graph points on the coordinate plane to solve real-world and mathematical problems.			
Classify two-dimensional figures into categories based on their properties.			
General Comments			

Visit **go.solution-tree.com/commoncore** for a reproducible version of this table.

Operations and Algebraic Thinking (5.OA)

The Operations and Algebraic Thinking domain (see appendix D, pages 176–177) emphasizes the conceptual understanding of operations, including the importance of properties (such as the distributive property) in understanding operations and problem solving involving the operations and the foundations of algebra (for example, patterns, expressions, and equations).

The 5.OA Content Standard Clusters

The Operations and Algebraic Thinking (5.OA) domain has two content standard clusters, which contain three standards (see appendix D, pages 176–177).

1. Write and interpret numerical expressions.
2. Analyze patterns and relationships.

The Understanding Questions for the 5.OA Content Cluster Standards

The three questions in table 3.3 (page 93) provide a framework for you and your team to use to develop a greater understanding of the intent of each content standard cluster for the Operations and Algebraic Thinking domain.

Write and interpret numerical expressions is the first content standard cluster for the 5.OA domain. The two standards focus on the use of parentheses, brackets, or braces in expressing numerical statements.

- **What's familiar?** For some teachers, the use of parentheses, brackets, and braces to express mathematical relationships and order operations will be a familiar way for students to model with mathematics as part of your lesson design (see Mathematical Practice 4, appendix A, page 160).
- **What's new? What's challenging?** These standards are clearly *prealgebra-ish.* The order of operations and the use of parentheses and, particularly, connecting this work to expressions may not be familiar to your students. Your teaching for this content standard cluster is essentially an extension of student work with whole numbers and provides an initial step toward generalizing the language of number and particularly arithmetic.
- **What needs unpacking? What topics need emphasizing?** Lessons for this cluster are not as much content related as they are Mathematical Practice related. This standard cluster emphasizes a way for students to model with mathematics and calls attention to representations of the mathematics (see Mathematical Practice 4, appendix A, page 160). The learning target is essentially designed to help students transition to algebraic thinking. To further the team's discussion about this topic, you should review the activities recommended in chapter 2 for Mathematical Practice 4 (see chapter 2, pages 42–43).

Analyze patterns and relationships is the second content standard cluster for the 5.OA domain. It should be a familiar topic for all of your fifth graders.

- **What's familiar?** Your students have had experience with patterns—numeric and geometric—since their early years of schooling and as recently as grade 4 within the CCSS. So, the extension in this content standard cluster builds to creating expressions based on patterns and being able to both identify and generalize from patterns provided or created. For example, consider the *add 3 and add 6 pattern* suggested in the actual standard (see 5.OA.3, appendix D, page 177).
- **What's new? What's challenging?** This cluster represents prealgebra standards that require you to engage students in generating patterns and using a coordinate plane to graph ordered pairs from patterns. Your students may be unfamiliar with writing and understanding ordered pairs and with graphing them on a coordinate plane.
- **What needs unpacking? What topics need emphasizing?** A one- to two-day lesson involving patterns organized as ordered pairs and then graphed on the coordinate plane will establish beginning work on these algebra-related topics. Your students should be given opportunities to graph ordered pairs on a coordinate plane and interpret data presented on a coordinate plane throughout the year. Such work will also provide engagement opportunities for students to both model with mathematics and use appropriate tools (see Mathematical Practice 4, Mathematical Practice 5, and others in appendix A, page 159). Figure 3.2 provides a sample input-and-output table and graph.

Score on Mrs. Burker's Game

Round	Score
1	4
2	5
3	6
4	7
5	8
6	?
?	?

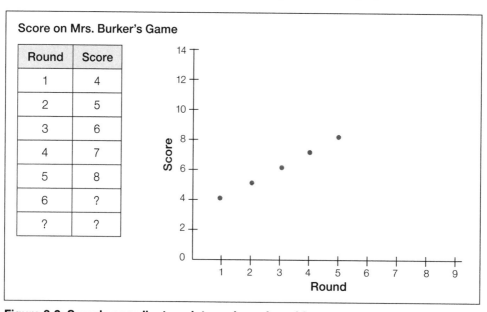

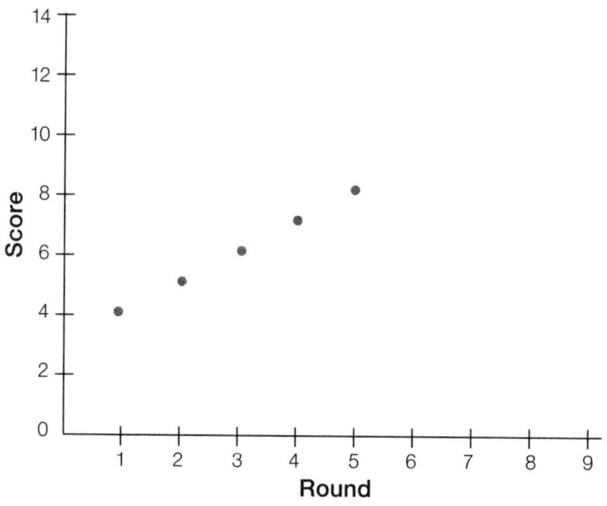

Figure 3.2: Sample coordinate points and graph problem.

The three-part analysis of each content standard cluster will enable your team to build understanding and extend insights into how to most effectively teach the CCSS for mathematics. The following Collaborative Team Task is a model that you can use to plan implementation of the selected domain standards. The template for the model is shown for the 5.OA domain. This template is available as a reproducible for each of the five content domains in fifth grade. You can use these guides to support your team's discussion and planning for the CCSS standards implementation at your school.

Collaborative Team Task:
Planning Implementation of Domain 5.OA

Based on your analysis of the standards for Operations and Algebraic Thinking, select a content standard cluster that you know is new and challenging for your students (and possibly for you, too). Use the questions in the table to guide development of your unit design plans. Ask one of your team members to be video recorded while teaching the lesson you design. You could also share a digital version of your notes in an interactive document, such as a pencast (see page 111), of the mathematics within the lesson that is developed in this activity. Use your video or pencast for discussion in a subsequent meeting as you provide formative feedback to your team about student progress toward mastery of the chosen content standard cluster and the 5.OA standards in that cluster.

Content standard cluster (see appendix D, pages 176–177): ______

Reason for selecting the content standard cluster: ______

What Content Needs to Be Unpacked for Lesson Design Around This Cluster?	Which Topics Needs to Be Emphasized?	How Will Students Be Engaged in the Mathematical Practices as They Learn This Content?	What Resources Will Be Needed?	How Will Students Demonstrate Learning of This Content Standard Cluster?

Visit **go.solution-tree.com/commoncore** for a reproducible version of this feature box.

Number and Operations in Base Ten (5.NBT)

The Number and Operations in Base Ten domain at this level (see appendix D, pages 177–178) focuses on place value, including decimal place value. Operations (addition, subtraction, multiplication, and division) with whole numbers and decimals are also an integral aspect of the content standard clusters in this domain.

The 5.NBT Content Standards Clusters

The Number and Operations in Base Ten (5.NBT) domain has two content standard clusters, which contain seven standards (see appendix D, pages 177–178).

1. Understand the place-value system.
2. Perform operations with multidigit whole numbers and with decimals to hundredths.

The Understanding Questions for the 5.NBT Content Standard Clusters

The three questions in table 3.3 (page 93) provide a framework for you and your team to use to develop a greater understanding of the intent of each content standard cluster for the Number and Operations in Base Ten (5.NBT) domain.

Understand the place-value system is the first content standard cluster in the 5.NBT domain. The four standards should be reasonably familiar teaching content for fifth-grade teachers.

- **What's familiar?** Work with place value should be a familiar topic. Place value at this level is extended to powers of ten, exponents, and decimals.
- **What's new? What's challenging?** What may be new and challenging for you will be the expectation that students work with the exponential value of numbers and reading, writing, and comparing decimals to thousandths, along with a strong connection to prior work with fractions. For many students at this grade level, work with decimals may have extended only through hundredths in the past.
- **What needs unpacking? What topics need emphasizing?** Your planning for this particular collection of standards will be continuous throughout the instructional year. While the focus on the work with powers of ten will connect directly to place-value lessons and related activities, which would typically occur early in the year, the extended work with decimals—comparing, using expanded form, and rounding—will be more focused within several lessons related to decimals. As your students complete activities involving computation with decimals, they will need to continuously apply place-value understandings in these standards. These standards are critical to your students' development and understanding of a sense of number particularly focused on decimals.

Perform operations with multidigit whole numbers and with decimals to hundredths is the second content standard cluster in the 5.NBT domain. It represents an important set of familiar learning targets for fifth-grade students.

- **What's familiar?** Multiplication and division of whole numbers have always been topics of important focus at the fifth-grade level. Similarly, related student work with operations involving decimals is also typical at this level, with addition and subtraction involving decimals often called for in earlier grade levels in prior state curriculum guidelines. It should be noted that this is the sole standard that places an emphasis on all four operations involving decimals.

- **What's new? What's challenging?** There are a number of considerations for you regarding these standards. First, emphasizing fluency with multiplication using the standard algorithm is no surprise, as for many students this will be a grade 4 outcome. The teaching challenge for you in this cluster may be the actual student use of the standard algorithm for multiplication. Specifically, if students have not had such experiences prior to this capstone year for multiplication, you may need to design support lessons for these underlying skills. However, as long as the learning trajectory related to the multiplication standards in the CCSS is followed, prior work at the fourth-grade level with the standard algorithm can merely be extended to this grade level. Your success with this standard cluster will depend to some extent on prior student experiences with multiplication, linking all the way back to the second-grade level. This points to the importance of your participation in occasional vertical-grade collaborative teamwork, as discussed in chapter 1.

  Division with a two-digit divisor has been a fifth-grade expectation for decades. The teaching challenge for your lesson designs will be to develop this important operation with *understanding*. Similarly, the expectations involving decimals will involve significant instructional planning time for you and your team, and your planning and instruction should connect back to prior and current work with fractions.

- **What needs unpacking? What topic needs emphasizing?** Your assessment of student mastery and subsequent closure related to the content standards for multiplication of whole numbers will be an early-in-the-year review and extension. Division with two-digit divisors is a multiweek topic for your fifth-grade students; while not a surprise, the work related to multiplication and division comes during the year with the heaviest instructional load related to fractions.

  Finally, you may consider the standard related to operations with decimals as an extension to maintenance activities involving student work with whole-number operations. Your preference should be to consider decimal operations as lesson components or lessons that parallel your student lessons for fraction operations, emphasizing the level of student understanding suggested by using representations and by connecting this work to the Mathematical Practices (see appendix A, page 159). Far too often, students fail to see the connections between decimal operations and fractions; this is the opportunity for you to build such understanding as part of your lesson and unit design for this cluster.

Number and Operations—Fractions (5.NF)

The Number and Operations—Fractions domain (see appendix D, pages 178–179) is a solely grade 3–5 content domain that emphasizes foundational work with fractions. At this level, the focus is on using equivalent fractions as strategy for the addition and subtraction of fractions and extending multiplication and division of whole numbers to work with multiplication and division of fractions.

The 5.NF Content Standards Clusters

The Numbers and Operations—Fractions (5.NF) domain has two content standard clusters, which contain seven standards (see appendix D, page 178–179).

1. Use equivalent fractions as a strategy to add and subtract fractions.
2. Apply and extend previous understandings of multiplication and division to multiply and divide fractions.

The Understanding Questions for the 5.NF Content Standard Clusters

The three questions in table 3.3 (page 93) provide a framework for you and your team to use to develop a greater understanding of the intent of the two content standard clusters and seven standards for the Number and Operations—Fractions domain.

Use equivalent fractions as a strategy to add and subtract fractions is the first content standard cluster in the 5.NF domain. It is fairly typical of student content expectations at this grade level.

- **What's familiar?** Addition and subtraction of fractions involving unlike denominators has been a typical fifth-grade content expectation.
- **What's new? What's challenging?** While not new, the challenge for your team is to teach and support the level of student proficiency and preparation (from prior grades) with a level of understanding related to equivalent fractions and their connection to addition and subtraction of fractions with unlike denominators, which is very important. Note that the typical use of factors and multiples leading to common multiples and common factors and then the least common multiple and greatest common factor are *not* the primary emphasis points for the expected student learning targets with addition and subtraction. This will be a change for many of your fifth-grade colleagues.
- **What needs unpacking? What topic needs emphasizing?** Although you will need to give these standards their own particular focus, you should spread out applications of these standards during the entire school year as part of your overall lesson and unit design. You will need to provide a series of lessons, perhaps one to two weeks' worth, involving addition and subtraction of fractions with particular emphasis on extending student work with equivalent fractions to now include adding and subtracting fractions with unlike

denominators. Providing students related experiences with mixed numbers and ensuring time for the use of visual models and benchmark fractions will be very important too. Opportunities for problem solving should be an emphasis during your instructional focus on the topic, but your team should also provide problem-solving opportunities involving addition and subtraction of fractions into lessons throughout the instructional year.

Apply and extend previous understandings of multiplication and division to multiply and divide fractions is the second content standard cluster in the 5.NF domain. It consists of five standards within the cluster and multiple parts to each standard. This cluster is very comprehensive and may have some aspects that are familiar.

- **What's familiar?** Student work with multiplication and division of whole numbers springboards the proposed work in this cluster. However, multiplication and division involving fractions may only be a familiar topic for some students.
- **What's new? What's challenging?** For you and your fifth-grade colleagues, work with multiplication and division of fractions will be new—*very new.* Here's the challenge: student work with number—wholes, fractions, and decimals—will occupy a significant portion of your instructional year at the fifth-grade level. See table 3.4 (page 105) for one view; approximately half the year will be spent on these content standard cluster topics. Finding time to do so *and* deeply developing the fraction aspects of number with understanding are both challenging and critically important as students leave grade 5 and move on to grade 6 expectations for mathematics, often in a middle school setting.
- **What needs unpacking? What topic needs emphasizing?** The emphasis at this grade level will be in developing student understanding of multiplication and division of fractions, which for many teachers was previously a sixth-grade expectation. This student work should occur in the second half of the instructional year and, as noted in the standards, should build from prior work with the operations of multiplication and division involving whole numbers. As with addition and subtraction involving fractions, providing problem-solving opportunities and engaging students in the other Mathematical Practices (see appendix A, page 159) should be integral components of your work with these standards.

Measurement and Data (5.MD)

The Measurement and Data domain for grade 5 (see appendix D, pages 179–180) consists of five standards within three content standard clusters and provides the opportunity for your students to represent and interpret data, convert measurement units with a given measurement system, and continue work in geometric measurement, with particular emphasis related to volume.

The 5.MD Content Standards Clusters

The Measurement and Data (5.MD) domain has three content standard clusters, which contain five standards (see appendix D, pages 179–180).

1. Convert like measurement units within a given measurement system.
2. Represent and interpret data.
3. Geometric measurement: Understand concepts of volume and relate volume to multiplication and to addition.

The Understanding Questions for 5.MD Content Standard Clusters

The three questions in table 3.3 (page 93) provide a framework for you and your team to use to develop a greater understanding of the intent of the three content standard clusters and five standards for the Measurement and Data domain.

Convert like measurement units within a given measurement system is the first content standard cluster in the 5.MD domain. It provides an opportunity for you to create lessons that provide a student measurement connection to prior work with fractions—represented as decimals.

- **What's familiar?** This standard provides a familiar and typically assessed measurement application of prior student work with fractions represented as decimals (the metric system).
- **What's new? What's challenging?** There is nothing particularly new with this standard cluster, but connections for converting centimeters to meters, as an example, will require a student understanding of decimal place value and equivalence.
- **What needs unpacking? What topics need emphasizing?** Student work with this standard should occur within a relatively brief measurement unit or chapter, or could be taught as an application within a one- to two-day lesson involving conversions within the metric system of measurement.

Represent and interpret data is the second content standard cluster in the 5.MD domain. It will be familiar content as part of your fifth-grade curriculum.

- **What's familiar?** Displaying data sets is a typical learning target activity for fifth grade. Similarly, interpreting and analyzing data using particular types of graphs—bar and line—will be familiar learning standards as part of your lesson or unit design.
- **What's new? What's challenging?** For some of your colleagues, a line plot will not be a familiar display tool. It should be noted that this standard extends work with line plots from grade 4 and involves operations with fractions. Given the expectations of this content standard cluster, the teaching challenge will include developing student confidence in representing and interpreting a line plot when using data from operations with fractions as the analysis source.

The suggested application of this standard presents an informal method for determining average or mean with your students.

- **What needs unpacking? What topics need emphasizing?** This standard cluster provides an opportunity within a variety of contexts for you to apply student work with fractions. This could occur during that slice of instructional emphasis—or elsewhere—based on your sequencing choices. As indicated, there are multiple learning targets you must address in your unit and lesson development—using a line plot, interpreting fractional data on a line plot, and informally applying average or mean. After your initial instruction on this cluster, applications involving the line plot must occur throughout the school year.

Geometric measurement: Understand concepts of volume, and relate volume to multiplication and to addition is the third and final content standard cluster in the 5.MD domain. It will be important at this grade level and includes three extensive learning standards.

- **What's familiar?** Some student work with volume should be familiar to you as a fifth-grade teacher.
- **What's new? What's challenging?** A challenge for this cluster is the level of student *understanding* sought in the content standard cluster related to volume. The standard begins by developing volume conceptually and then moves to applications of volume by counting unit cubes in both customary and metric measurements. Volume is then related to multiplication and division, as your students are expected to determine the volume of varied solid figures.
- **What needs unpacking? What topics need emphasizing?** This standard will take some time for you to teach and for students to learn. What is intended by these standards is much more than a one- or two-day lesson related to volume. The topic connects directly to student work with solids or three-dimensional figures and extends to the *area* of two-dimensional figures as well (see 3.MD standards, appendix B, pages 167–168).

Geometry (5.G)

At fifth grade, the Geometry domain consists of two content standard clusters built on four standards (see appendix D, pages 180–181). The focus is on graphs in the coordinate plane and the attributes of two-dimensional figures based on their properties.

The 5.G Content Standard Clusters

The Geometry (5.G) domain has two content standard clusters, which contain four standards (see appendix D, pages 180–181).

1. Graph points on the coordinate plane to solve real-world and mathematical problems.
2. Classify two-dimensional figures into categories based on their properties.

The Understanding Questions for the 5.G Standards

The three questions in table 3.3 (page 93) provide a framework for you and your team to use to develop a greater understanding of the intent of the two content standard clusters and four standards in the 5.G domain.

Graph points on the coordinate plane to solve real-world and mathematical problems is the first content cluster standard in the 5.G domain. It is the initial CCSS standard involving coordinates.

- **What's familiar?** Students may have had some prior experience with coordinates, such as playing coordinate-like games.
- **What's new? What's challenging?** Your teaching challenge will be related to the depth of students' prior work with coordinates and graphing points on the first quadrant of the coordinate plane. This will be a new topic for many fifth-grade teachers and students. What will be especially new for most is the prealgebra focus of these standards.
- **What needs unpacking? What topics need emphasizing?** Student work for this cluster could be achieved within a geometry unit or could connect back to or extend lessons involving patterns and relationships within the Operations and Algebraic Thinking domain (see appendix D, pages 176–177). Your team will need to decide where in the fifth-grade curriculum this standard cluster will be first introduced to students.

Classify two-dimensional figures into categories based on their properties is the second content standard cluster in the 5.G domain. It should be a very familiar topic for your team at this grade level.

- **What's familiar?** Students at this level have seemingly been classifying shapes since their preschool days. Prior CCSS expectations related to describing and classifying shapes occur within the geometry domain standards for third and fourth grades (see appendix B, page 168, and appendix C, page 174). These expectations for describing and classifying shapes are also addressed in the CCSS for kindergarten and grades 1 and 2 (NGA & CCSSO, 2010).
- **What's new? What's challenging?** The major teaching challenge with these related classification standards will be student background and demonstration of understanding of the elements of the classification—sides and angles.
- **What needs unpacking? What topics need emphasizing?** The standards in this cluster are an extension and review of prior student work and should be a component of a geometry unit or chapter, which would include geometric measurement. You would most likely teach these standards during the second half of the school year.

Grade 5 Analysis: Concluding Comment

Fifth-grade mathematics provides the capstone student curriculum experiences for the five elementary-level content domains of the CCSS—Operations and Algebraic

Thinking, Number and Operations in Base Ten, Number and Operations—Fractions, Measurement and Data, and Geometry. The sixth- to eighth-grade CCSS domains are related, to an extent, but different than these departing expectations and domains. What this means for the fifth-grade teacher—you—is a different sort of capstone. Note the following:

- Fluency with all whole-number operations—done!
- Completion of work involving fraction foundations and addition, subtraction, and multiplication of fractions—done!
- Work with foundational understandings and operations involving decimals—done!

As indicated at the beginning of this grade level's discussion, fifth grade is a huge year of mathematical proficiency for your students. A full sense of number and fluency with number is an aspiration for teachers and students at this grade level. Additionally, algebraic seeds related to expressions and coordinates are firmly planted in fifth grade. Your student learning experiences with measurement and data should be sure to connect to the fluency expectations for number with problem-based experiences that fully engage the Mathematical Practices (see appendix A, page 159).

Mathematics Content: A Different Look at Emphasis

Table 3.4 emphasizes the number of K–5 standards within a domain and the number of standards per grade level. As you review the table, one of your conclusions may be *less is more,* in that there are fewer standards per grade level as compared with existing state, provincial, or school district standards. Such a distinction implies that more time can now be provided to *drill down* and truly engage students in activities designed to develop understanding and mathematical proficiency. Use the data in table 3.4 and the reflection questions in figure 3.3 (page 106) to guide your collaborative team discussions for content focus and emphasis throughout the year.

Table 3.4: CCSS—Content Analysis, Grades K–5

Domains	K	1	2	3	4	5	Totals
Counting and Cardinality	9						5%
Operations and Algebraic Thinking	5	8	4	9	5	3	20%
Number and Operations in Base Ten	1	8	10	3	6	8	21% (K–5); 17% (3–5)
Number and Operations—Fractions				7	12	11	31% (3–5)

continued →

Domains	K	1	2	3	4	5	Totals
Measurement and Data	3	4	10	12	8	8	26%
Geometry	6	3	3	2	3	4	12%
Totals	24	23	27	33	34	34	

Note: Please consider this table for discussion only as to the impact of the CCSS. The totals are only a count of the standards (including substandards: a, b, c, and so on) within a content standard cluster. This is not an attempt to consider weight, emphasis, or time needed for particular standards, which is another factor for your consideration. Standards *is defined here as the full content standard cluster of expectations under a particular domain (such as Geometry).*

Visit **go.solution-tree.com/commoncore** for a reproducible version of this table.

1. Number and Operations in Base Ten and Fractions—48 percent of grades 3–5.

   How do you feel about the implication that close to half of your instructional year will be focused on number? Is the data set accurate? Should the emphasis be here? Should it be elsewhere? What do you wonder or worry about here?

2. Number-related domain emphasis (Operations and Algebraic Thinking, Number and Operations in Base Ten, and Number and Operations—Fractions):

   - 52 percent in grade 3
   - 68 percent in grade 4
   - 65 percent in grade 5

Does the number emphasis at these grades make sense to you? What do you wonder or worry about here?

Figure 3.3: Content analysis reflection considerations and questions.

Content Analysis by Domain

As your collaborative team becomes more comfortable with considering the mathematical prerequisites leading into particular grade levels, a logical next step will be for you to examine the hierarchical nature of the mathematics across the grades. Clements and Sarama (2009) and others have written about the importance of learning trajectories as students encounter mathematics concepts and develop understandings. Table 3.5 provides a domain-by-domain analysis of the mathematics within the CCSS for grades 2 through 5. As professional development opportunities are expanded to consider growth across the domains in the CCSS, your collaborative team should be able to track, for instance, the importance of place-value understanding as it is developed and extended across grades 3 to 5. Using table 3.5 will also allow your collaborative team to review specific standards—beyond the general standard statements provided in table 3.5—to consider growth and gaps from grade to grade. This across-domain analysis will also help you to again recognize the concentration and focus on particular topics at these grade levels.

Table 3.5: Domain-by-Domain Cross-Grade Analysis

Grade 2	Grade 3	Grade 4	Grade 5
Operations and Algebraic Thinking			
Represent and solve problems involving addition and subtraction.	Represent and solve problems involving multiplication and division.		
Add and subtract within 20.	Multiply and divide within 100.		
Work with equal groups of objects to gain foundations for multiplication.	Understand properties of multiplication and the relationship between multiplication and division.		
	Solve problems involving the four operations, and identify and explain patterns in arithmetic.	Use the four operations with whole numbers to solve problems.	
		Gain familiarity with factors and multiples.	
		Generate and analyze patterns.	Analyze patterns and relationships.
			Write and interpret numerical expressions.
Number and Operations in Base Ten			
Understand place value.		Generalize place-value understanding for multidigit whole numbers.	Understand the place-value system.
Use place-value understanding and properties of operations to add and subtract.	Use place-value understanding and properties of operations to perform multidigit arithmetic.	Use place-value understanding and properties of operations to perform multidigit arithmetic.	Perform operations with multidigit whole numbers and with decimals to hundredths.
Number and Operations—Fractions			
	Develop understanding of fractions as numbers.	Extend understanding of fraction equivalence and ordering.	Use equivalent fractions as a strategy to add and subtract fractions.

continued →

Grade 2	Grade 3	Grade 4	Grade 5
		Build fractions from unit fractions by applying and extending previous understandings of operations on whole numbers.	Apply and extend previous understandings of multiplication and division to multiply and divide fractions.
		Understand decimal notation for fractions, and compare decimal fractions.	
Measurement and Data			
Measure and estimate lengths in standard units.			
Relate addition and subtraction to length.			
Work with time and money.			
Represent and interpret data.	Represent and interpret data.	Represent and interpret data.	Represent and interpret data.
	Solve problems involving measurement and estimation of intervals of time, liquid volumes, and masses of objects.	Solve problems involving measurement and conversion of measurements from a larger unit to a smaller unit.	Convert like measurement units within a given measurement system.
	Geometric measurement: Understand concepts of area and relate area to multiplication and to addition.		Geometric measurement: Understand concepts of volume and relate volume to multiplication and to addition.
	Geometric measurement: Recognize perimeter as an attribute of plane figures and distinguish between linear and area measures.		

Grade 2	Grade 3	Grade 4	Grade 5
		Geometric measurement: Understand concepts of angle and measure angles.	
Geometry			
Reason with shapes and their attributes.	Reason with shapes and their attributes.		
		Draw and identify lines and angles, and classify shapes by properties of their lines and angles.	Classify two-dimensional figures into categories based on their properties.
			Graph points on the coordinate plane to solve real-world and mathematical problems.
General Comments			

Source: Adapted from NGA & CCSSO, 2010.

Visit **go.solution-tree.com/commoncore** for a reproducible version of this table.

Content Considerations

This chapter has provided a number of tools to support you as you work in your collaborative team to determine and analyze the CCSS mathematics content. The chapter's tables support the discussion of the mathematics content you must now teach in grades 3, 4, and 5. You can then determine the depth desired for your analysis of the content and when and how your collaborative team will engage in the analysis suggested. The ultimate goal will be for each member of your collaborative team to have a clear understanding of the important mathematics that impact his or her grade—to realize that what's provided within the CCSS is not all that different in terms of content from what you have experienced and to truly recognize the differences and understand that the CCSS do provide opportunities to dig deep and to really make less (fewer expectations) become more (provide a depth of understanding).

Finally, the questions you will need to ask within your collaborative team and then address as part of your CCSS content professional development efforts will help you determine next steps to take in the coming months and next school year. These questions are shown in figure 3.4 (page 110).

- Which grade levels will implement the CCSS next year?
- How many of the CCSS standards will you address at your grade level?
- What is your plan for the amount of instructional time spent on each standard?
- Do you have the instructional tools (Mathematical Practice 5) to accomplish your proposed plan? If not, what materials are needed?
- How will your students be engaged in the CCSS Mathematical Practices through their experiences in Operations and Algebraic Thinking, Number and Operations in Base Ten, Number and Operations—Fractions, Measurement and Data, and Geometry?

Figure 3.4: Anticipation questions for future planning.

Visit **go.solution-tree.com/commoncore** for a reproducible version of this figure.

This chapter should guide your school's professional development efforts in thinking about, analyzing, and unpacking the content domains and standards of the CCSS as your collaborative team takes responsibility for implementing and assessing the expectations of the Common Core State Standards.

Chapter 3 Extending My Understanding

1. Examine the CCSS domains, clusters, and standards at a particular grade level (or grade band).
    - Which are considered critical areas for instructional emphasis at each grade level 3–5?
    - Conduct a side-by-side comparison with your current mathematics curriculum standards, spending time unpacking and looking for comparative emphasis.
    - As a collaborative team, identify the familiar, new, or challenging content. How might this impact your implementation plan?
2. Examine a specific CCSS content standard. Discuss the meaning of the standard, analyze and interpret new or unfamiliar language, and describe student understandings and proficiency expected.
3. Examine the instructional materials currently used to support your mathematics curriculum. Determine the extent to which these materials are aligned with the CCSS by using the Mathematics Curriculum Materials Analysis Project tools discussed in the online resources (page 111). How will you use this information to guide planning, delivery of instruction, and effective assessment?
4. Examine a CCSS content standard that is new and challenging for a selected group of your students. Determine how the Mathematical Practices you use will help students achieve this standard.

Online Resources

Visit **go.solution-tree.com/commoncore** for links to these resources.

- **CCSS Mathematics Curriculum Materials Analysis Project (Bush et al., 2011; www.mathedleadership.org/docs/ccss/CCSSO%20Mathematics%20Curriculum%20Analysis%20Project.Whole%20Document.6.1.11.Final.docx):** The CCSS Mathematics Curriculum Analysis Project provides a set of tools to assist K–12 textbook selection committees, school administrators, and teachers in the analysis and selection of curriculum materials that support implementation of the CCSS for mathematics.
- **Illustrative Math Project (http://illustrativemathematics.org):** The main goal for this project is to provide guidance to states, assessment consortia, testing companies, and curriculum developers by illustrating the range and types of mathematical work that students will experience in implementing the Common Core State Standards for mathematics.
- **Progressions Documents for the Common Core Math Standards (Institute for Mathematics and Education, 2007; http://math.arizona.edu/~ime/progressions):** The CCSS for mathematics were built on progressions—narrative documents describing the progression of a topic across a number of grade levels informed by research on children's cognitive development and by the logical structure of mathematics. The progressions detail why standards are sequenced the way they are, point out cognitive difficulties and provide pedagogical solutions, and provide more detail on particularly difficult areas of mathematics. The progressions documents on this site are useful in teacher preparation, professional development, and curriculum organization, and they provide a link between mathematics education research and the standards.
- **Recommendations for CCSS Professional Development (the Institute for Mathematics & Education, the Center for Science, Mathematics & Computer Education, & the Institute for Research on Mathematics and Science Education, 2011; http://commoncoretools.files.wordpress.com/2011/05/2011_04_27_gearing_up.pdf):** These initial recommendations are from the Gearing Up for the Common Core State Standards in Mathematics conference. They can serve as guidelines for K–8 mathematics professional development for states transitioning to the CCSS.
- **Livescribe Pencasts (www.livescribe.com/en-us/pencasts):** Consider using Livescribe Pencasts of student work to help drive collaborative discussions related to student understanding of important standards within each of the content domains for grades 3–5 as one way to engage your colleagues.

CHAPTER 4

Implementing the Teaching-Assessing-Learning Cycle

The vision of the Common Core State Standards for mathematics (NGA & CCSSO, 2010) is one that interprets the learning of important mathematics as consisting of both mathematics content and mathematical practices—a vision the National Council of Teachers of Mathematics (2010) shares in *Making It Happen*. Much of your implementation effort surrounding the Common Core will focus on making sure your instruction is aligned with the more coherent and focused Common Core content standards and that the Mathematical Practices are interpreted as both essential mathematics to be learned and as ways in which your students should engage in learning the mathematics content. These are crucial steps in implementing the CCSS. However, ensuring these interpretations are implemented in your classroom is just the beginning work necessary for student attainment of the CCSS.

A Major Shift in the Function of Grades 3–5 Mathematics Assessment

This chapter examines the paradigm shift from the traditional use of summative assessment instruments to grade and evaluate student performance to the use of collaboratively developed formative assessment processes to guide your instruction. When implemented effectively, assessment practices are a critical instructional tool to improve teaching and student learning. Since the enactment of the No Child Left Behind Act of 2001 (NCLB, 2002), most of the assessment focus has been directed at preparing all students to perform well on state accountability tests. In many states, this led to tests and instruction that essentially narrowed the curriculum to focus on lower-level procedural skills—skills that make up but one component of the more balanced vision of the CCSS, which states that "mathematical understanding and procedural skill are equally important" (NGA & CCSSO, 2010, p. 4). Consequently, past improvements on state accountability tests may not reflect actual improved student learning in the broader set of skills and concepts called for in the CCSS. Think about the process of assessment teachers in your school typically use at your grade level. What is it like? More than likely, it has been an isolated activity that served the primary summative purpose of grading. For student mathematics learning to improve according to the CCSS, you will need to shift your assessment work from (1) preparing for external summative assessments used for accountability and (2) creating summative assessment instruments strictly to assign grades to using *formative assessment* processes that continuously improve your instruction and student learning.

Popham (2008) points out that it is important to be clear on the definition of formative assessment: "Formative assessment is a planned process in which assessment-elicited evidence of students' status is used by teachers to adjust their ongoing instructional procedures or by students to adjust their current learning tactics" (p. 6). Wiliam (2011) offers a similar definition:

> An assessment functions formatively to the extent that evidence about student achievement is elicited, interpreted, and used by teachers, learners, or their peers to make decisions about the next steps in instruction that are likely to be better, or better founded, than the decisions they would have made in the absence of that evidence. (p. 43)

According to both Popham (2008) and Wiliam (2011), formative assessment isn't just an assessment instrument but rather a planned process whose defining characteristic is its use to improve student learning. Formative assessment only takes place when you use the results of assessments to advance student learning. As Wiliam (2007a) concludes:

> So the big idea of formative assessment is that evidence about student learning is used to adjust instruction to better meet student needs; in other words, teaching is adaptive to the student learning needs and assessment is done in real time. (p. 191)

According to Popham (2008), at the highest levels of implementation, formative assessment "consists of schoolwide adoption . . . chiefly through the use of professional development and teacher learning communities" (p. ix). Therefore, collaborative teams are the primary mechanism to shift your schoolwide culture toward an emphasis on using formative assessment as the process to improve mathematics instruction and student learning. This is often referred to as assessment *for* student learning. When this is accomplished, assessment becomes the critical *feedback bridge* between improved instruction and student learning (Wiliam, 2011). According to Wiliam (2011):

> When formative assessment practices are integrated into the minute-to-minute and day-by-day classroom activities of teachers, substantial increases in student achievement—of the order of a 70 to 80% increase in the speed of learning are possible. . . . Moreover, these changes are not expensive to produce. . . . There is nothing else remotely affordable that is likely to have such a large effect. (p. 161)

The National Mathematics Advisory Panel (2008), in its final report, *Foundations for Success,* under its strict standard for scientific research, made this definitive recommendation to improve mathematics achievement at the K–8 level: "Teachers' regular use of formative assessment improves their students' learning. . . . The results are sufficiently promising that the Panel recommends regular use of formative assessment for students in the elementary grades" (p. xxiii).

Because formative assessment can be such a powerful instructional tool, highly effective assessment practices in grades 3–5 in mathematics integrate formative assessment *for* learning with summative assessment *of* learning. Formative assessment *for* learning is used to adapt, modify, and direct instruction. Summative assessment *of* learning is used to evaluate students' achievement, assign grades, and evaluate the overall effectiveness of the mathematics program based on school, district, state, province, or consortia assessments. In other words, *every* assessment instrument, whether or not it is used for grading or evaluation purposes, can and should serve a formative function and become an essential aspect of your work in collaborative teams.

The PLC Teaching-Assessing-Learning Cycle

Assessment can no longer solely serve a summative function—that of assigning grades and providing accountability—if the goal is to improve student learning and successfully implement the CCSS. For mathematics teaching and learning to improve, the formative assessment process must become the assessment focus of collaborative teams.

Figure 4.1 lists the critical questions you need to ask in your collaborative team in order to begin the process of implementing formative assessment in a planned way. When you address these questions in your collaborative team, their use supports growth toward assessment practices that bridge the gap between teaching and learning in order to improve student learning.

1. In advance of teaching the lesson, chapter, and unit of study (all three levels of planning), how well does each member of your grade-level collaborative team understand the student learning targets (content standard, depth of knowledge, and Mathematical Practices) and the assessments aligned with those learning targets?
2. Has your team collaboratively developed and agreed on scoring rubrics and procedures for both formative and summative assessments that will accurately reflect student achievement of the learning targets?
3. To what degree do your collaborative team's assessments build student confidence and encourage students to take responsibility for what they know and still have to learn?
4. How well does your collaborative team provide timely formative (and summative) assessment feedback that is both frequent and descriptive (versus evaluative), providing students with specific information regarding their strengths as well as strategies to improve?
5. How well does each member of your collaborative team, and the team as a collective group, modify instruction or provide additional instructional supports for students as necessary, based on the results of both formative and summative classroom assessments to improve student learning and future instruction?

Source: Adapted from Kanold, Briars, & Fennell, 2012.

Figure 4.1: Key assessment questions for grade-level collaborative teams.

Visit **go.solution-tree.com/commoncore** for a reproducible version of this figure.

When collaborative teams address these key questions, they support you in shifting the assessment emphasis from one that views assessment as primarily something that occurs at the end of instruction to determine if learning has occurred to an ongoing process that is used to improve teaching and learning. Thompson and Wiliam (2007) argue that teacher learning teams can play a key role in supporting this shift to assessment *for* learning because their sustained nature allows "change to occur developmentally, which . . . increases the likelihood of the change 'sticking' at both the individual and school level" (p. 17).

The teaching-assessing-learning cycle described in figure 4.2 outlines a process that not only includes the planned development of formative assessment within collaborative teams but also provides a framework you can use to review your use of current summative assessment tools, such as unit tests or quizzes. The process turns these summative assessments, which teachers use in collaborative teams as assessments *of* student learning for grading purposes, into formative learning opportunities—"the formative use of summative tests" (Wiliam, 2011, p. 38). Every student assessment opportunity, whether it is used for grading purposes or not, serves a formative function in the cycle and provides an opportunity for your collaborative team to monitor, adapt, and guide instruction.

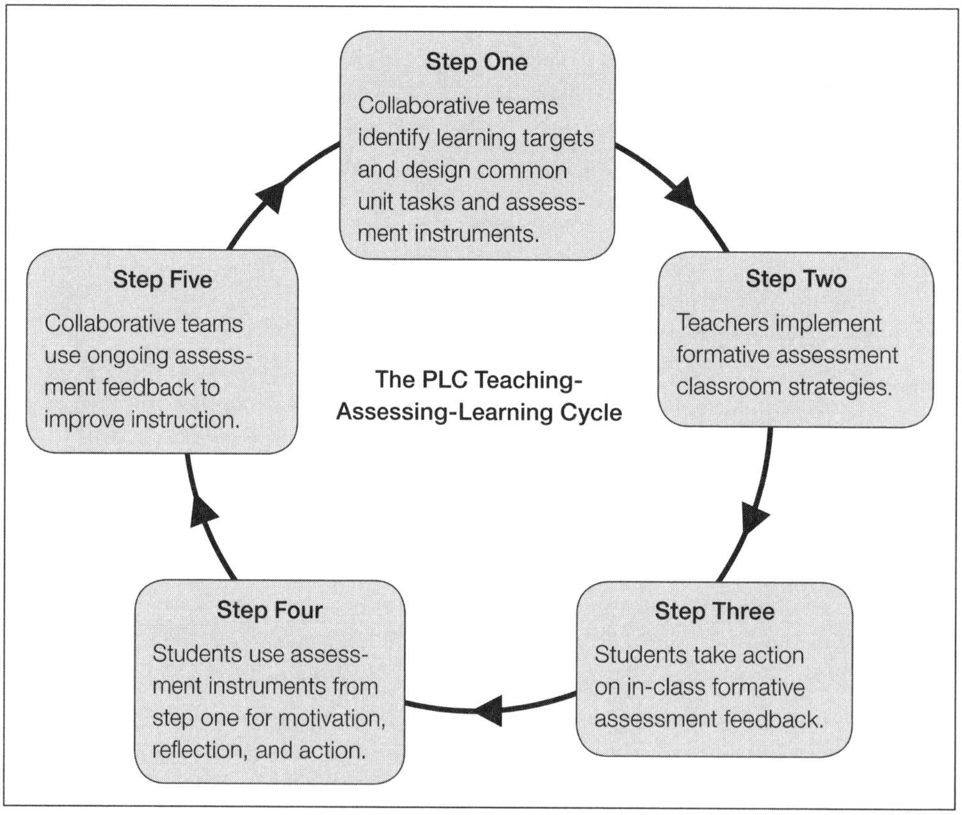

Figure 4.2: The PLC teaching-assessing-learning cycle.

Visit **go.solution-tree.com/commoncore** for a reproducible version of this figure.

This teaching-assessing-learning cycle—the PLC assessment cycle—requires you to work together within your grade-level collaborative team to design both common summative assessment instruments and formative assessment strategies in advance of beginning each one- to three-week period of mathematics instruction. The one- to three-week cycle is intentionally recommended because research suggests that formative assessment is only effective—resulting in improved student achievement—if done in short (within and between lessons) or medium cycles (one to four weeks; Wiliam & Thompson, 2007). During the process of creating a unit of summative and formative assessments, you and your other collaborative team members clearly define and develop a shared expectation for student performance. Your collaborative team must also determine how to communicate your learning expectations to students, which is done in part through the instructional tasks you select to use during the unit of instruction and the ongoing formative assessment tasks and strategies you design and implement (see step two in figure 4.2).

The assessment cycle begins with implementing a one- to three-week instructional unit of collaboratively developed lesson plans and the assessment tasks and tools designed to focus on the critical mathematics during that period of instruction. It is important to note that you do not have to move clockwise through the steps. That is, you can and should make adjustments, moving back and forth to different steps in the cycle as needed, based on results of formative assessment processes. This may mean your lesson plans and instructional time allocations have to be adjusted due to differences in student achievement within your class.

During instruction, you need to help students focus on performance and support them in making their own adjustments with respect to their learning strategies (see question three in figure 4.1, page 115; Popham, 2008). You need to remain reflective concerning the effectiveness of your lesson plans and keep notes throughout the unit of instruction so that your collaborative team can discuss successes and challenges and make appropriate adjustments for the following year. The cycle then repeats itself for the next one to three weeks of instruction.

It is important to note that effective formative assessment during a unit of instruction, which appears as a step in figure 4.2, is not an isolated event but rather an ongoing process embedded within instruction that is carried out continuously as lessons unfold (Wiliam, 2007a, 2011). This is possible to do because there are levels of *formality* with respect to formative assessment that are described more fully in step two (Ginsburg & Dolan, 2011; Marzano, 2007).

Step One: Collaborative Teams Identify Learning Targets and Design Common Unit Tasks and Assessment Instruments

In a professional learning community, before the first lesson of the next unit of mathematics instruction begins, your collaborative team reaches agreement on the design and proper use of high-quality, rigorous common assessment instruments for all students in your grade level. When grade-level collaborative teams create these common assessment instruments together, they enhance the coherence and fidelity to the student learning expectations. The wide variance in student task performance expectations (an inequity creator) from teacher to teacher is minimized when you work collaboratively with your colleagues to design assessments and tasks appropriate to the identified learning targets for the unit.

You can use figure 4.3 as a resource to guide your collaborative team discussions and evaluate your collaborative team readiness to teach, assess, and learn before the unit begins.

1. **Student opportunity to learn:** Do all teachers at your grade level have access to the same content? By the end of the unit will every teacher have covered the same content with the same rigor?
2. **Depth of knowledge:** Are cognitive requirements between the formative assessment tasks and the learning targets in the unit consistent for each teacher? Is the same complexity of knowledge (and skill) sought and required by all teachers for the mathematics unit?
3. **Range of knowledge:** Is the range of content covered under each of the content clusters for the unit of knowledge similar from teacher to teacher in the grade level? Do all teachers of the course include daily tasks that prepare students for procedural fluency as well as the conceptual understanding tasks that will be part of the common assessment instruments that all teachers use in the grade level?
4. **Balance of representation:** Are learning targets for a particular cluster of standards given the same emphasis on the common assessment instruments all teachers on the teacher team use?
5. **Source of challenge:** Does student assessment (test) performance actually depend on mastering the learning targets and not on irrelevant knowledge or skills?

Figure 4.3: Aligning learning targets with assessment instruments and tasks.

Visit **go.solution-tree.com/commoncore** for a reproducible version of this figure.

As each one- to three-week period of instruction approaches, your collaborative team meets to design lessons based on three essential assessment issues (Kanold et al., 2012; Stiggins, Arter, Chappuis, & Chappuis, 2006): (1) What are the identified learning standards? (2) What are the identified common summative assessments? (3) What are the identified daily formative mathematical tasks to be used?

What Are the Identified Learning Standards?

One of the advantages of the CCSS is the more clearly defined standards for each grade level. The number of standards per grade level is reduced in the CCSS compared with most traditional state standards to allow an instructional emphasis on developing student understanding, in part by engaging students in using the Mathematical Practices. This in turn creates an expectation that assessment of student learning will include assessing students' *understanding* of the conceptual knowledge necessary for developing procedural fluency through the Mathematical Practices. Consider the following questions to help identify learning standards.

- What are the mathematical skill- and concept-level CCSS learning standards for proficiency?
- What does proficiency look like?
- What are the mathematical understanding-level learning standards for proficiency?
- What does understanding look like for this unit of study?
- What are the Mathematical Practices that will be emphasized within this unit of instruction?

Figure 4.4 shows grade 5 standards from the CCSS for mathematics domain Number and Operations in Base Ten and the content standard cluster *Understand the place-value system* (see appendix D, page 177).

Understand the Place-Value System

1. Recognize that in a multidigit number, a digit in one place represents ten times as much as it represents in the place to its right, and one-tenth of what it represents in the place to its left.
2. Explain patterns in the number of zeros of the product when multiplying a number by powers of 10, and explain patterns in the placement of the decimal point when a decimal is multiplied or divided by a power of 10. Use whole-number exponents to denote powers of 10.
3. Read, write, and compare decimals to thousandths.
    a. Read and write decimals to thousandths using base-ten numerals, number names, and expanded form; for example, 347.392 = (3 × 100) + (4 × 10) + (7 × 1) + (3 × 1/10) + (9 × 1/100) + (2 × 1/1000).
    b. Compare two decimals to thousandths based on meanings of the digits in each place, using >, =, and < symbols to record the results of comparisons.
4. Use place-value understanding to round decimals to any place.

Source: Adapted from NGA & CCSSO, 2010, p. 35.

Figure 4.4: CCSS grade 5 Number and Operations in Base Ten (5.NBT).

As these fifth-grade standards from the CCSS illustrate, there is an emphasis on both skills and understanding as students are expected to *represent, explain, compare,* and *use understanding.* Expecting a student to understand implies that you will assess whether a student has understood. According to the CCSS (NGA & CCSSO, 2010):

> Asking a student to understand something means asking a teacher to assess whether the student has understood it. But what does mathematical understanding look like? One hallmark of mathematical understanding is the ability to justify, in a way appropriate to the student's mathematical maturity, why a particular mathematical statement is true or where a mathematical rule comes from. Mathematical understanding and procedural skill are equally important, and both are assessable using mathematical tasks of sufficient richness. (p. 4)

Determining whether or not a student is developing conceptual understanding requires continuous formative assessment during a lesson (informal) and across the span of a one- to three-week unit of instruction. The fifth-grade standards in figure 4.4 illustrate the connection between the CCSS content standards and the Mathematical Practices. The emphasis on explaining patterns in place value provides an opportunity to instructionally emphasize and also assess—Mathematical Practice 3—Construct viable arguments and critique the reasoning of others, and Mathematical Practice 7—Look for and make use of structure (see chapter 2 for descriptions of these Mathematical Practices). The formative assessment component during a unit of instruction provides your collaborative team the opportunity to discuss the Common Core vision of mathematics instruction and learning, emphasizing both content and student processes for learning the content.

What Are the Identified Common Assessment Instruments?

Based on the standards for the one- to three-week unit of instruction, collaborative teams have to develop the *common* assessment instruments that each collaborative team member will use during the unit of instruction. What are the quizzes, tests, or performance assessment instruments that will be used for the purpose of determining a student's grade or mastery level? In addition, the collaborative team must agree on the common *scoring rubrics* used for grading student work on the established performance targets. How will these rubrics, which define student performance expectation levels, be shared with your students during instruction to communicate the expectation level? How will students be provided descriptive feedback on their progress so they can make appropriate adjustments to their own learning strategies to advance their mastery on the summative assessment instruments?

Figure 4.5 highlights an adapted five-stage summative assessment instrument development process (Kanold et al., 2012) you can use to develop more effective summative assessment tools.

What Are the Identified Daily Formative Mathematical Tasks?

Working backward from the collaboratively designed summative assessment instruments that will be used for the one- to three-week unit of instruction, what are the common mathematical tasks that need to be part of each grade-level teacher's daily lessons in order to ensure students are prepared for the rigor and expectations of the assessment instrument tasks? Collaboratively designing lessons as a grade-level team allows you and your collaborative team to discuss and share effective instructional approaches. More importantly, it provides you the support you need to ensure that your lesson designs address both skills and conceptual understanding, as well as problem-solving tasks and an emphasis on the Mathematical Practices appropriate to the mathematics content standards.

1. **Plan:** Assess what and how. How important is this topic? Is this one of the CCSS grade-level areas for critical focus? What is the breadth and depth of the learning targets for the topic? Are the learning targets—skill level and understanding level—clear to everyone on the collaborative team? How will they be made clear to the students? What role will the CCSS Mathematical Practices have in the assessment?
2. **Develop:** Determine the sample questions and tasks for the assessment. Select, create, or modify assessment items or tasks and scoring rubrics as needed to meet student needs. What will be the format and methods used for student demonstrations of proficiency? Are there tasks that assess both the CCSS content standards and Mathematical Practices?
3. **Critique:** Evaluate the assessment for quality. How does the collaborative team know it has written a high-quality assessment? Does the school have well-defined and understood criteria for high-quality assessment development?
4. **Administer and score:** A unit assessment is given to the students and immediately scored using the collaboratively developed scoring rubric, and students receive timely descriptive feedback concerning their performance. Ideally, grade-level collaborative teams grade unit assessments together to improve the accuracy of feedback students receive. Students receive results immediately—ideally, the next day, but at most within two class days (Reeves, 2011).
5. **Revise:** Evaluate assessment quality based on results, and revise as needed for the following year. The results should also be used to identify learning targets and assessment questions that may need to be repeated as part of the next unit of study to build student retention—for example, areas identified in the CCSS frameworks for a more critical focus and emphasis.

Source: Adapted from Stiggins et al., 2006, pp. 106–117.

Figure 4.5: Common assessment planning process.

Visit **go.solution-tree.com/commoncore** for a reproducible version of this figure.

Preparing to develop the conceptual understanding that underlies the CCSS content standards requires that students learn mathematics by engaging in the CCSS Mathematical Practices as described in chapter 2. You should spend significant time during your collaborative lesson-planning sessions determining how you will connect Mathematical Practices to the mathematics content. For example, if your collaborative team's lesson plan calls for a consistent depth of knowledge (see figure 4.3, page 118), you should include preplanned questions to engage students in explaining patterns in placing the decimal point when multiplying decimals and prompts to encourage student responses; then the lesson plan will embed instructional strategies to teach through Mathematical Practice 3. Implementing the CCSS Mathematical Practices during *planning* increases the opportunity for student learning to take place and increase student achievement.

Step one is the critical place that potentially manufactures inequities in student mathematics learning. If your collaborative team does not reach agreement on the mathematical tasks and the rigor of the tasks you plan to include in a unit's lessons and assessments, then the students' learning outcomes will vary. This point cannot be overstated. Differences in teacher effectiveness within schools are at least four times the size of differences between schools (Wiliam, 2011). Equity in mathematics education requires grade-level collaborative teams to ensure they use mathematical tasks of sufficient richness to engage students in observable mathematical discussions that can simultaneously serve as a form of ongoing formative assessment (Kanold et al., 2012).

Step Two: Teachers Implement Formative Assessment Classroom Strategies

In step two of the assessment cycle, grade-level collaborative teams select formative assessment strategies to determine if students are making progress developing skills and mathematical understandings. Formative assessments, particularly at the lesson level, do not have to be and should not always be formal pencil-and-paper tests or quizzes. Creating and implementing written or formal assessments during each lesson will both take time away from instruction and decrease the likelihood that team members will implement formative assessment strategies (Popham, 2008). Popham (2008) and others (Ginsburg & Dolan, 2011; Wiliam, 2011) have suggested several "informal" strategies of assessment *for* learning that can provide you valuable insight into the level of student understanding as a lesson unfolds. Some of these strategies are included in figure 4.6.

An additional advantage of these formative assessment strategies is that they increase the level of student engagement—a key characteristic of classroom environments that promote high student achievement (Wiliam, 2011). You should spend time in your collaborative team reflecting on the formative assessment strategies you use and their impact on student engagement, particularly with respect to the use of strategy one in figure 4.6. Effective questioning is a high-leverage strategy used not only to increase student engagement but also to maintain the cognitive demand of mathematics tasks as a lesson unfolds (Stein et al., 2007). Devoting collaborative team time to preplanning these formative assessment questions is critical (Boaler & Staples, 2008). During the middle of instruction, as a lesson unfolds, you simply don't have the time to generate on-the-spot questions that effectively assess emerging student understanding that you can use to guide your instruction (Popham, 2008; Smith & Stein, 2011). Formulating questions prior to a lesson that are *interpretable*—that is, that lead to incorrect answers that reveal student progress toward developing understanding, is a particularly valuable use of planning time (Wiliam, 2011). The use of effective questioning during instruction embeds formative assessment processes in instruction in nonintrusive ways. This strategy's potential to increase student learning, if you listen carefully to student responses for their level of understanding and respond accordingly, is significant (Wiliam, 2007b).

Strategy One: Key Questioning During Whole-Class Discussion

You use preplanned questions during critical points during the lesson to assess student understanding. "These pivotal adjustment-influencing questions must be carefully conceptualized before the class session in which the discussion will take place. . . . Teachers can't expect to come up with excellent adjustment-influencing questions on the spur of the moment" (Popham, 2008, p. 60). It is important to monitor who is called on to respond to questions to ensure that all members of the class have an essentially equal chance.

Strategy Two: Miniwhiteboard Responses

Every student is supplied with a miniwhiteboard. You ask a preplanned question or provide the students with a critical problem to solve. The students then hold up their responses on whiteboards, and you scan the responses to make a decision concerning the students' mastery levels and needed instructional modifications.

Strategy Three: Traffic Lights or Red and Green Disks

You supply students with colored plastic cups—green, yellow, and red—or a CD-sized disk that is red on one side and green on the other. At critical points during the lesson, ask students to display the cup or disk that corresponds to their level of understanding (green means that the student understands, while the red—or yellow—cup indicates the student does not understand and that instructional adjustments are necessary).

Strategy Four: All Student Response Systems

If you have access to SMART Boards and clicker systems in your classroom, you can design key multiple-choice questions that students can work on at critical points in the lesson and send their answers to you using the clickers. This displays a real-time chart indicating the class's response to the question and immediately lets you know the level of the class's understanding or common misconceptions (if the multiple-choice options are keyed to common misconceptions).

Strategy Five: Diagnostic Interview Questions

You ask individual students questions to reflect on, articulate, and uncover how students are thinking while they are working individually or in small groups. The key is for you to engage in evaluative listening—listening to assess the student's understanding in order to modify instruction.

Figure 4.6: Formative assessment strategies.

Visit **go.solution-tree.com/commoncore** for a reproducible version of this figure.

More formalized formative assessment strategies include sampling one or two homework items daily and giving quick quizzes with immediate feedback every two to three lessons. One of the differences between mathematics teachers in the United States and other higher-performing countries, such as China, is that U.S. teachers seldom collect and grade homework on a daily basis. Rather, they tend to check homework in class or give students completion grades to encourage students to do the work (Shuhua, 2004). If this is done, you are deprived of an important formative assessment opportunity to determine your students' levels of understanding and adjust your instruction based on your students' demonstrated understanding (Shuhua, 2004). Faced with teaching multiple subjects to thirty or more students, you likely do not have time to grade every practice problem on every assignment. However, it is important that you collect and use student homework results to modify and guide future instruction, but don't spend class time grading homework. Spot-checking three to five critical problems (item sampling) can provide you with valuable daily formative assessment evidence that can be used to modify and adjust your instruction to meet individual student needs.

Every two to three lessons, we recommend that your collaborative team administer a relatively short, quick screening assessment that you designed together to assess the content of the immediate two to three previous lessons. These quick assessments need not be lengthy. Ten or fewer items that take no more than ten to fifteen minutes to complete are sufficient to provide you with more formal evidence concerning the current level of students' understanding and can be used to trigger instructional adjustments as necessary during the unit. It is recommended that these more formal formative uses of assessment instruments are administered every two to three lessons because research indicates that more frequent assessment, assuming the results are used to target and tailor the next stages of instruction, is related to greater student learning gains (Marzano, 2007).

Part of the process of developing formative assessments, whether informal or formal, includes determining in advance the level of student performance that will signal your need to make instructional adjustments (Popham, 2008). For example, what is the minimum class performance necessary on a quick screening assessment that will indicate that no instructional adjustment is necessary? For example, you may decide as a collaborative team that if the class average on a common assessment is 90 percent or better, no instructional adjustment is necessary. To be effective, your feedback on a student's response to a preplanned question during a lesson or a student's work on a homework assignment must be specific and descriptive. Providing students with descriptive feedback on formative assignments, including strengths, weaknesses, and next steps, with respect to how to make progress toward learning targets, is more effective than simply marking the work correct or incorrect, or even marking it correct or incorrect *with* comments (Davies, 2007; Marzano, 2006; Wiliam, 2011).

According to Wiliam (2007b), in order to "improve the quality of learning within the system, to be formative, feedback needs to contain an implicit or explicit recipe for future action" (p. 1062). Feedback that provides students with a *recipe* they can use to improve their level of understanding can motivate students to continue to persevere in making sense of problems—Mathematical Practice 1. For example, suppose you have been working with a student on multidigit multiplication. In order to develop student understanding, you use an area model to illustrate the partial products in the standard U.S. algorithm. However, the student is still struggling with connecting the partial products in the area model to ways to record the multiplication. So your recipe, or plan, for the student during Tier 1 intervention (see chapter 5) is for the student to record the partial products in a way that emphasizes the rule of place value within the standard U.S. algorithm. (See figure 4.7 for an example.)

```
   349
 ×   7
    63 (7 × 9)
   280 (7 × 4 tens)
+2100 (7 × 3 hundreds)
  2443
```

Figure 4.7: Sample multiplication problem emphasizing place value.

Step Three: Students Take Action on In-Class Formative Assessment Feedback

Effective formative assessment is not only about you using evidence to modify and adjust your instruction but also about students using the data to make their own adjustments in the processes they use to achieve the learning targets (Popham, 2008; Wiliam, 2011). Do your students learn to take more responsibility for their learning by using the feedback you provide them? This is the goal of step three in the assessment cycle. Steps two and three may occur simultaneously during mathematics lessons. When implemented, these steps support your work by informing students about their progress and designing activities that allow students to make their own learning adjustments in addition to your own instructional adjustments in support of student learning. You and your students share responsibility for the effective implementation of formative assessment steps in the assessment cycle.

In order for students to use formative assessment data to make adjustments to their own learning strategies, you should make curricular expectations clear to students. Figure 4.8 describes three curricular clarifications you need to make so students can effectively use formative assessment data to self-monitor and adjust their learning strategies (Popham, 2008).

Clarification One: Provide a Clear and Understandable Vision of the Standard

At the beginning of every lesson, subset of lessons, or unit, you need to provide students with the curricular aim in language they can understand. For example, the fourth-grade CCSS domain Number and Operations in Base Ten includes the standard "Use place value understanding and properties of operations to perform multi-digit arithmetic" in order to "Multiply a whole number of up to four digits by a one-digit whole number, and multiply two two-digit numbers, using strategies based on place value and the properties of operations. Illustrate and explain the calculation by using equations, rectangular arrays, and/or area models" (NGA & CCSSO, 2010, p. 29). Fourth-grade students need to understand that they are not only expected to multiply two two-digit whole numbers, but that they are also expected to use models to explain how they performed the calculation. For example, students might be required to draw an area model to illustrate the partial products in the product of two two-digit numbers in addition to simply completing an algorithm.

Figure 4.8: Necessary curricular clarifications. continued →

Clarification Two: Clarify Evaluative Criteria

It is important to clarify the criteria that will be used to determine the quality of students' work. If the scoring rubric for assessments will assess students' understanding, then the scoring criteria and rubrics that reflect this should be shared with students. This can be facilitated by sharing with students anonymous student examples and models of strong and weak work to help students better visualize the nature of the targeted level of understanding.

Clarification Three: Share the Building Blocks

You need to share with students the major building blocks (subskills) they must master in order to reach the standard. The content standard clusters in the CCSS often represent these building blocks. Unless students know what the building blocks are, it is difficult for them to assess their progress. A function of grade-level collaborative learning teams is to unpack the CCSS content standards and identify the necessary essential understandings, both for you and your students.

Source: Adapted from Popham, 2008, pp. 76–81.

Stiggins et al. (2006) suggest strategies you can use to support students in taking more responsibility for their own learning. Several of these strategies are adapted in figure 4.9. They provide insight into the nature of teacher-designed but *student-led* formative assessment *actions.*

As your team plans the mathematics lessons for a unit of study, discuss the various formative assessment strategies that you'll use to ensure students know about their progress and act accordingly. You and your team must require student-led action steps for responding to the formative feedback students are receiving from you as well as *other students.*

Step Four: Students Use Assessment Instruments From Step One for Motivation, Reflection, and Action

As you read this chapter, it is possible the first three steps in the assessment cycle are already part of your current assessment paradigm. You and your team do write common formative assessment tasks and instruments together, you do design effective formative assessment classroom strategies, and you do ensure that students take action on the feedback you provide. However, it is very rare to find collaborative teams that use common assessment instruments such as mid- or end-of-unit tests as part of a formative process of learning. It is in this step that the old paradigm of testing for grading purposes (an end goal) fades away and the new paradigm of assessment instruments and tools for formative assessment purposes (a means goal) emerges.

Strategy One: Provide a Clear and Understandable Vision of the Learning Target

Share with your students the CCSS cluster, learning targets, and prior-knowledge understanding expectations in advance of teaching the lesson or unit, giving the assignment, or doing the activity. Provide students with scoring guides written in plain language so they can understand them. More importantly, develop and design scoring criteria and rubrics with them.

Strategy Two: Use Examples and Models of Strong and Weak Work

Use models of strong and weak work, such as anonymous student work, work from life beyond school, and your own work. Begin with work that demonstrates strengths and weaknesses related to problems students will commonly experience, especially the problems or tasks that require student demonstrations of understanding. Ask students to discuss with peers the strengths and weaknesses of given solutions or strategies used to obtain a solution to problems posed in class or on a common assessment instrument.

Strategy Three: Offer Regular Descriptive Feedback

During and after the unit, offer descriptive feedback instead of grades on practice work. Descriptive feedback should reflect students' strengths and weaknesses with respect to the specific learning targets they are trying to achieve in a given assignment. Feedback is most effective when it is timely and identifies what students are doing right as well as what they need to work on next and then requires students to act on that feedback.

Strategy Four: Teach Students to Self-Assess and Set Goals

Self-assessment is a necessary part of learning, not an add-on that we do if we have the time or the "right" type of students. Self-assessment includes asking students to do the following:

- Identify their strengths and areas for improvement for specific learning targets throughout the unit
- Offer descriptive feedback to classmates
- Use your feedback, feedback from other students, or their own self-assessment to identify what they need to work on and set goals for future learning and then take action on those goals

Source: Adapted from Stiggins et al., 2006, pp. 42–46.

Figure 4.9: Formative assessment strategies for student action.

Visit **go.solution-tree.com/commoncore** for a reproducible version of this figure.

Wiliam (2007b) argues that summative assessment can take on three different purposes: (1) monitoring, (2) diagnosing, or (3) formatively assessing.

> [Summative] assessment *monitors* learning to the extent it provides information about whether the student, class, school, or system is learning or not; it is *diagnostic* to the extent it provides information about what is going wrong, and it is *formative* to the extent it provides information about what to do about it. (p. 1062)

For example, the third-grade CCSS domain Number and Operations—Fractions includes the standard that students will, "Recognize and generate simple equivalent fractions" (NGA & CCSSO, 2010, p. 24). Suppose a third-grade teacher team administers a summative assessment at the end of instruction addressing this standard. If results of the summative assessment indicate 80 percent of the third graders meet or exceed the team's expectations according to a four-point grading rubric (4—exceeds the standard, 3—meets the standard, 2—approaches the standard, 1—does not meet the standard), then this represents the *monitoring* function of the assessment. Analysis of specific student performance is *diagnostic.* Suppose an individual third-grade student receives a 1 on the team's grading rubric. This is diagnostically indicating that he is not demonstrating success on that standard.

A *diagnostic* assessment, while necessary, is insufficient. *Diagnostic* assessment does not tell the student what he or she needs to do differently in order to make progress meeting the standard. The frequent admonition to "Try harder" or the tendency to assign more practice problems, is not likely to support the student in making progress. All too often, the solution when a student has not demonstrated mastery is to assign more practice. However, the primary function of practice is to solidify a student's current level of understanding. If the student does not understand the concept and continues to practice what he does not understand, then additional practice only results in the student solidifying his lack of understanding and increases his frustration. When you take the step to provide the student with additional instruction, such as by using a series of area representations utilizing fraction bar models to demonstrate the meaning of equivalent fractions, then the summative assessment becomes *formative* for the student and has the potential to advance his learning. The important point is that any form of assessment becomes an opportunity to provide students with feedback, both with respect to their procedural fluency *and* conceptual understanding, to improve their learning.

It is the combination of formative assessment *with* feedback on the assessment instrument that has the largest impact on student achievement (Reeves, 2011). Reeves (2011) goes on to state that all forms of grading need to be viewed as formative feedback to students; and to be effective, feedback must have four characteristics.

1. **Accuracy:** Students and other teachers understand the evaluation criteria.
2. **Fairness:** Feedback is based solely on the student's work, not other student characteristics.
3. **Specificity:** Feedback occurs within agreed-on boundaries, and it is consistently applied to all students.
4. **Timeliness:** Students receive feedback in enough time to act on it and improve their performance.

As Wiliam (2011) describes it, effective feedback:

> should cause thinking. It should be focused; it should be related to the learning goals that have been shared with students; and it should be more work for the recipient than the donor. Indeed, the whole purpose of feedback should be to increase the extent to which students are owners of their own learning. (p. 132)

This will require that students are provided the time necessary to use the feedback they receive to improve their work (Wiliam, 2011).

When the collaborative team uses summative assessment instrument (test or quiz) results for a third-grade class to modify instruction for the next instructional topic, or modifies lessons within the assessed unit of instruction in advance of teaching the content the following year, then the summative assessment assumes a *formative* function for the collaborative team as well. Using assessment results to continuously improve instruction (lesson design) and student learning requires that each member of the collaborative team designs and uses common assessments.

Step Five: Collaborative Teams Use Ongoing Assessment Feedback to Improve Instruction

Step five is a critical component of the assessment cycle. It is during this step, at the end of a unit, that your collaborative team uses the results of assessment instruments and tools to analyze the effectiveness of the lessons you designed for the unit during step one. Assessment will continue to serve as an ends only and have limited impact unless you and your collaborative team make necessary adjustments before teaching the next unit. This investment in careful lesson planning and revision is strongly recommended as a lever to continually improve mathematics education and reduce inconsistencies in instructional quality (Morris & Hiebert, 2011; Morris et al., 2009).

A focus during collaborative lesson-planning sessions should be on the development of your pedagogical content knowledge—instructional strategies to help students learn specific mathematics content. Without strong pedagogical content-knowledge expertise, the ability of your collaborative team to affect increases in student achievement is lessened (Bausmith & Barry, 2011). Your collaborative team should use the critical lesson-planning and lesson-revision questions to support the inclusion of the high-leverage mathematics instructional practices (figure 1.2, page 15). Figure 4.10 highlights critical questions to guide your collaborative team during the lesson-planning and lesson-revision process.

1. How much of the lesson and material was approached through student investigation of cognitively demanding tasks or preplanned student questioning (instead of teacher-centered lecture and demonstration)?

   What evidence is there of a climate of mutual respect as students participate in mathematical discussions and provide meaningful feedback and critique the reasoning of other students?

   How will students make, test, and justify their mathematical conjectures and conclusions with the teacher and with one another?
2. What kinds of in-class formative assessments did the teacher use to reflect on the effectiveness of the lesson?

Figure 4.10: Critical lesson-planning questions.

continued →

What descriptive feedback did the teacher provide to students? How did students show they were engaged in the lesson? Did the lesson design develop student interest and motivation to learn the content? How?

Did the teacher seek evidence of student understanding?

Did students have an opportunity to reflect on their learning as it relates to the learning target?

3. What CCSS Mathematical Practices did the teacher and students use to learn the mathematics content standards?

   What evidence is there that students were part of a learning community?

   How did students communicate their ideas to one another and the teacher?

   How did the teacher's questions elicit student thinking and other students' respectful critiquing of that reasoning?

4. What kinds of student-generated questions and conjectures were proposed in the lesson, and what type of student-led tasks were used to assess student understanding and learning?

Source: Adapted from Kanold et al., 2012.

Visit **go.solution-tree.com/commoncore** for a reproducible version of this figure.

Quality lesson planning that builds formative assessment *for* student learning into mathematics lessons is the first tier of an RTI approach to instruction (see chapter 5). Baroody (2011) writes, "The major source of most mathematical learning difficulties is how children are taught (psychologically inappropriate instruction), not their mental equipment (organic or cognitive dysfunction)" (p. 30). Therefore, in mathematics instruction, highly effective Tier 1 instruction—instruction that emphasizes the high-leverage instructional practices (figure 1.2, page 15) with planned formative assessment—is the most important tier and the tier that should receive the majority of your collaborative team's planning work. Research concerning the three-tier RTI model suggests that with effective Tier 1 instruction, approximately 80 percent of elementary students' mathematics learning needs can be met so learning difficulties are prevented (Gersten et al., 2009; Wixson, 2011).

Standards-Based Report Cards

The CCSS provide an excellent opportunity for you to implement standards-based report cards in the elementary grades. At the fourth-grade level, for example, students could receive report card marks in each of the five mathematical content domains (NGA & CCSSO, 2010) and in Mathematical Practices during each marking period:

1. Operations and Algebraic Thinking
2. Number and Operations in Base Ten
3. Number and Operations—Fractions

4. Measurement and Data
5. Geometry

The marks students receive in each of these content domains (and Mathematical Practices) can be a direct result of their performance on summative assessments designed for each standard cluster under each domain. For example, under Operations and Algebraic Thinking in grade 4, there are three content standard clusters (NGA & CCSSO, 2010):

> 1. Use the four operations with whole numbers to solve problems.
> 2. Gain familiarity with factors and multiples.
> 3. Generate and analyze patterns. (p. 29)

A single assessment tool would be designed to assess student mastery of each of these clusters and the connected Mathematical Practices. For example, an assessment instrument would be designed to measure student proficiency of the first cluster. This assessment instrument would have a number of tasks designed to measure proficiency in each of the three standards—interpret a multiplication equation (4.OA.1), multiply or divide to solve word problems (4.OA.2), and solve multistep word problems (4.OA.3)—listed in this cluster.

In addition, tasks could be designed to also assess student proficiency and improved attainment of the Mathematical Practices addressed while teaching these content standards. For example, in Mathematical Practice 6, Attend to precision, as fourth graders develop their mathematical communication skills, they should try to use clear and precise language in their discussions with others and in their own reasoning. Specifically, are students precise when specifying units of measure and stating the meaning of the symbols they choose when setting up and solving the equation? Do they appropriately use the equal sign when setting up an equation and solving the problem?

Suppose you grade student assessments and make report-card marks based on a 1–4 scale rubric:

1 = Does not meet the standard

2 = Approaches the standard

3 = Meets the standard

4 = Exceeds the standard

The mode of the marks students receive on the assessment tasks for each cluster would determine the overall cluster mark. The mode of the marks students receive on the three summative cluster assessment instruments for the domain Operations and Algebraic Thinking would be the grade they receive on their report card for this domain. Many teachers use the mean when determining students' grades. However, the mean is almost always an inaccurate reflection of what a student knows (Reeves, 2011). This is because the mean does not reflect student performance at the end of a grading period, but rather the average performance over the length of the grading period, which may or may not reflect what the student knows at the end of instruction. The mode is also recommended over the mean because it functions better in a standards-based grading environment and avoids the creation of complicated rounding rules for determining grades.

Two formative assessment issues are important for you to keep in mind during summative assessment. First, within each lesson, ongoing formative assessments must be embedded within instruction (as described in step two of the assessment cycle) and used to continuously modify your instruction to prepare students for success on summative assessments. Second, the previously described summative assessment and grading process also serves a formative function. Results on summative assessments serve a formative function because the results are used to identify students who may need additional and targeted instruction to reach proficiency.

Because the assessment cycle emphasizes the continuous modification of instruction and targeted reteaching to meet individual student needs, it is important that students' grades also reflect this continued learning. For example, if a student's initial grade during a marking period for the domain Operations and Algebraic Thinking is a 2 (approaches the standard), but after six weeks of targeted additional instruction on the standard cluster within this domain, the student can then demonstrate proficiency, then the student's grade should be changed to reflect this new level of understanding and performance.

The CCSS Consortia Assessments

Preparing for and responding to large-scale mathematics assessments consume much of the focus and effort of grades 3–5 teachers, elementary school principals, and school district administrators. Implementing the CCSS is unlikely to alter the scrutiny and pressure you face from large-scale assessments.

In 2010, the U.S. Department of Education awarded $330 million in Race to the Top funds to two consortia, representing the majority of states, to develop assessments aligned with the CCSS. The SMARTER Balanced Assessment Consortium (SBAC), representing more than thirty states, received $160 million, and the Partnership for Assessment of Readiness for College and Careers (PARCC), representing more than twenty-five states, received $176 million. As of this publication, eleven states are members of both consortia (Porter et al., 2011). Both consortia intend to implement their new state-level common assessments for grades 3–8 and high school during the 2014–2015 school year.

Both assessment consortia aim to design *common* state assessments that are consistent with the vision of the CCSS to include items that assess higher-order thinking, reasoning and conceptual understanding, and problem-solving abilities. If the assessments take the form their designers intend, then these new common state assessments will go beyond assessment of low-level procedural skills that typify many current state-administered assessments. Because "students' opportunities to learn mathematics are influenced by the assessment policies of the local district . . . [and influenced by] . . . the nature of pedagogy in the classroom" (Tate & Rousseau, 2007, p. 1222), these new common assessments can serve as a lever to promote desired instructional changes in favor of an emphasis on deep understanding and reasoning.

Both PARCC and SBAC intend to provide adaptive online tests that will include a mix of constructed-response items, performance-based tasks, and computer-enhanced items that require the application of knowledge and skills. Both assessment consortia are intending to provide a variety of assessment options within the assessment system. You should check your state website for the latest information about the progress of the assessment consortia, or visit www.smarterbalanced.org for more information.

For the state assessments to function as a potential learning tool, you will need to ensure they are used for formative purposes—that they are used to provide you and your students with accurate, timely, fair, and specific feedback that can move learning forward. This will require that you are provided time within your collaborative team to plan instructional adjustments and that students are supported in relearning content not yet mastered.

However, overreliance on the PARCC and SBAC interim assessments to provide a school district's formative assessment system is not recommended since the effectiveness of this structure to improve student learning is questionable (Popham, 2008). What will make the most difference in terms of student learning is the short-cycle classroom-based formative assessment described in this chapter. As Wiliam (2007a) writes, "If students have left the classroom before teachers have made adjustments to their teaching on the basis of what they have learned about students' achievement, then they are already playing catch-up" (p. 191).

It will be important for you to become engaged in your state and school's transition to the SMARTER or PARCC assessment initiative as you approach full implementation of the Common Core. How and when will you use interim assessments? How will collaborative teams inform families and other members of the school community? How will collaborative teams prepare all children in each grade level or school? Such questions are appropriate as your district and school-level PLC teams begin to link state-supported CCSS-related assessments to your implementation of the Common Core for mathematics content and practices.

Assessment for Equity

When you work within your collaborative team to implement the assessment cycle, you and your team take significant steps toward reducing inequities in student learning generated when individual teachers make widely variable decisions. These decisions can be regarding instructional design issues, particularly the rigor of mathematical tasks and daily formative assessment and unit assessment task expectations (Kanold et al., 2012). Ensuring all your collaborative team members implement the assessment cycle is a key strategy to promote the goal of equitable mathematics learning.

As research indicates, for assessment to be formative and lead to improvements in student learning, there needs to be an "explicit recipe for future action" (Wiliam, 2007b, p. 1062). Chapter 5 looks at the recipe your collaborative team can follow when assessment results indicate students have not met the learning targets during step two or step four in the assessment cycle.

Chapter 4 Extending My Understanding

1. Generate a list of common forms of assessment (such as teacher observations, teacher-made quizzes and tests, unit assessments, textbook chapter tests, district assessments, state-mandated assessments, and so on) that exist in mathematics at a particular grade level. Then classify these assessments as either formative or summative.
2. Examine all of the assessments your grade-level colleagues use, and determine which ones teacher teams collaboratively developed.
    - Which assessments incorporate the use of collaboratively developed scoring rubrics?
    - To what extent do the assessment items or tasks require students to demonstrate a balance of conceptual understanding and procedural fluency?
    - How are the results of each used to inform and improve teaching and learning (formative)? Measure proficiency (summative)?
    - Discuss your findings. How might you use this information to collaboratively develop common assessments in your grade-level collaborative team?

Online Resources

Visit **go.solution-tree.com/commoncore** for links to these resources.

- **Mathematics Common Core Coalition (www.nctm.org/standards/mathcommoncore):** This site includes materials and links to information and resources that the organizations of the coalition provide to the public and the education community about the CCSS for mathematics.
- **NCTM's Assessment Resources (www.nctm.org/resources/content.aspx?id=12650):** This webpage provides resources such as a framework for evaluating large-scale assessments, NCTM's position statement on high-stakes assessment, and various other publications.
- **Partnership for Assessment of Readiness for College and Careers (www.parcconline.org):** PARCC provides Common Core content frameworks, sample instructional units, sample assessment tasks, professional development assessment modules, and more.
- **SMARTER Balanced Assessment Consortium (www.smarterbalanced.org):** This site provides grade-level content specifications for the summative assessment of the CCSS for mathematics, assessment development timelines

and overviews, curriculum priorities and considerations, various assessment-related resources, computer adaptive testing fact sheets, sample grade-level tasks, and additional resources.

CHAPTER 5

Implementing Required Response to Intervention

All students are entitled to quality instruction within an equitable learning environment designed to meet their specific learning needs. You have a professional obligation to create and maintain an equitable learning environment and provide high-quality instruction. This chapter focuses on the final paradigm shift required to ensure successful CCSS implementation—the need to create directive response to intervention programs to support all students in meeting the expectations of the CCSS. When such programs are in place, then intervention serves the goal of equity.

The National Council of Teachers of Mathematics (2008) notes:

> Excellence in mathematics education rests on equity—high expectations, respect, understanding, and strong support for all students. Policies, practices, attitudes, and beliefs related to mathematics teaching and learning must be assessed continually to ensure that all students have equal access to the resources with the greatest potential to promote learning. A culture of equity maximizes the learning potential of all students. (p. 1)

A culture of equity that maximizes the learning of all students shifts the instructional focus from teaching to student learning and implements a system in which student learning is continuously monitored and instructional adjustments and targeted supports are put in place based on student need. Effective collaborative teams emphasize and foster this cultural shift from teaching to student learning.

Promoting and supporting equitable practices for students is a complex process and is best supported when your collaborative team examines several factors. The National Council of Supervisors of Mathematics' (2008) position statement on equity recommends that mathematics educators:

- Respond to equity as a meaningful process to address social justice issues of race, language, gender, and class bias
- Embrace a mindset shift from a student deficit perspective of equity to a focus on creating opportunities for equal access to meaningful mathematics
- Recognize underachievement not as a result of group membership but more likely a symptom of varying beliefs, opportunities, and experiences to learn mathematics

Recognizing and responding to these important facets of equity will promote the rich conversations needed in your collaborative team to promote high-quality instruction and equitable classrooms. Use the following discussion questions in your collaborative team to facilitate the conversation.

1. Do all students have access to high-quality, rigorous instruction regardless of mathematics placement? What evidence does and does not support this?
2. Are mathematics lessons planned with student strengths in mind (as opposed to only deficits)? How is this demonstrated?
3. Are lower-achieving groups overrepresented by ethnicity, sex, or socioeconomic status in comparison to the student representation in other mathematics classes? If not, how might the collaborative team address this concern?

By examining the equitable practices in your school, in your grade-level collaborative team, and in your own classroom, you can have the deep and honest conversations necessary to promote a culture of equity.

Variation in student achievement among U.S. schools serving demographically similar students indicates that achievement gaps can be narrowed and that demographic factors are less likely to influence low achievement if students receive high-quality instruction and targeted instructional supports (McKinsey & Company, 2009; Reeves, 2003). Research indicates that all students can learn mathematics when they have access to high-quality mathematics instruction and sufficient time and support to learn the curriculum (Burris, Heubert, & Levin, 2006; Campbell, 1995; Education Trust, 2005; Griffin, Case, & Siegler, 1994; Knapp et al., 1995; Silver & Stein, 1996; Slavin & Lake, 2008; Usiskin, 2007).

Far too frequently in the United States, mathematics has been perceived as a subject only a select few could master or should study. However, high-quality mathematics education is no longer just for those who want to study mathematics or science in college—it is a requirement for most levels of postsecondary education and careers (Achieve, 2005; American College Testing Program, 2006). In addition, the Common Core State Standards expects all students to study and attain at minimum the same set of high-quality standards. For too long, too many students—especially students who are economically disadvantaged, English learners, or racial minorities or who have special needs—have been victims of low expectations in mathematics. For example, *tracking* has consistently deprived groups of students by relegating them to low-status mathematics classes in which they repeat basic skills year after year, fall further and further behind their peers, and do not experience significant mathematical substance (Boaler, Wiliam, & Brown, 2000; Stiff, Johnson, & Akos, 2011; Tate & Rousseau, 2002). To help close the achievement gap, students who have traditionally been identified as underperformers in mathematics must be exposed to more rigorous standards-based instruction and conceptually rich mathematical tasks. The CCSS require all students be held to and supported in meeting the same rigorous standards.

Equity does not mean that all students will receive identical instruction or the same amount and intensity of instruction. The National Council of Teachers of Mathematics (2000) propose, "Equity does not mean that every student should receive identical instruction; instead, it demands that reasonable and appropriate accommodations be made as needed to promote access and attainment for all students" (p. 12). These accommodations, or targeted supports, must be designed so that all students have the opportunity to experience success in the challenging grade-level mathematics content and practices outlined in the Common Core State Standards.

You can use the equity questions in figure 5.1 in your collaborative team to reflect on the degree to which all students are provided access to a rigorous mathematics curriculum based on grade-level CCSS. When using these questions, you should think about the evidence you use to support your responses. For example, if the least-experienced teachers on your team are teaching the most-challenged students, is it reasonable to argue that all students are receiving equitable instruction? Some of these team or school decisions are often made in an effort to reward teacher seniority, but may inadvertently be contributing to inequitable learning opportunities and outcomes (Lubienski, 2007).

1. Do all students receive the same high-quality common instructional tasks by each teacher on our team?
2. Do all students receive equally rigorous instruction, balancing conceptual and procedural development and mathematical processes?
3. Do all students receive the same amount of teaching and learning time for mathematics each day?
4. Who teaches the most struggling students—the most experienced or least experienced teachers?
5. Do all students receive rich, compelling lessons with a focus on student understanding and learning?
6. Do all students receive grade-level (or above) mathematics instruction on the CCSS?
7. Are there any students identified as low achieving, and what is the team's intentional response for intervention and support?

Figure 5.1: Equity reflection questions.

Holding High Expectations for All Students

A component of promoting equity is holding and maintaining high expectations for all students: do all teachers on your team really believe all students can learn? Inherent in teaching are the beliefs teachers hold about the children they teach. While no teacher ever wants to admit to having low expectations for any student, the reality is that many well-meaning, caring, and passionate teachers do in fact believe that some of their struggling students will not progress at the rate of other students and cannot meet grade-level standards. Do these low expectations derive from students' socioeconomic backgrounds, race, or ethnicity or the fact that students were placed in a low group? These are hard questions to ask but lie at the very heart of addressing equitable instruction.

Students inherently know the expectations their teachers hold for them, and research supports the powerful role self-efficacy plays in student achievement. As Bandura (1993) notes:

> People who have a low sense of self-efficacy in a given domain shy away from difficult tasks, which they perceive as personal threats. They have low aspirations and weak commitment to the goals they choose to purse. They maintain a self-diagnostic focus rather than concentrate on how to perform successfully. When faced with difficult tasks, they dwell on their personal deficiencies, on the obstacles they will encounter, and on all kinds of adverse outcomes. They slacken their efforts and give up quickly in the face of difficulties. (p. 144)

In the following collaborative team activities, you can explore the influence of teacher and student self-efficacy on student achievement. Use the activities early in the school year to identify your beliefs about your students, and then examine how those beliefs might influence your daily instructional decision making. You can use figure 5.2 to record the number of students who you believe will easily make one year's academic progress in the Common Core State Standards, will have to work hard to achieve one year's growth, and finally will not make one year's progress. In the final row, provide a rationale for your predictions. After everyone in your collaborative team completes the table in figure 5.2 for their students, discuss the reflection questions.

Number of Students Who Will Easily Make One Year's Mathematics Growth	
Number of Students Who Will Need to Work Hard and Receive Additional Support to Achieve One Year's Mathematics Growth	
Number of Students Who Will Not Make One Year's Progress, Despite All Additional Support and Intervention	
Rationale for Predictions	

1. Think privately about your placement of the students. Does the placement of the students have any influence on your expectation for how they will achieve?
2. Does student placement change the delivery or content of your instruction in any way?
3. How might the expectations of the Common Core State Standards, both the content and the Mathematical Practices, influence the instructional decisions you will make regarding the students?
4. What teacher moves might you be making that demonstrate your beliefs about the mathematics progress your students are making?

Figure 5.2: Teacher expectations activity and reflection questions.

Visit **go.solution-tree.com/commoncore** for a reproducible version of this figure.

In discussing the reflection questions in figure 5.2, the focus should primarily be on developing a safe environment for you and your peers to think and reflect on your underlying expectations. It is critical for peers to develop a nonjudgmental atmosphere as you work together to reflect on the many classroom aspects that influence your beliefs about the students you teach.

In a follow-up activity, you can audio or video record yourself or another team member in short five- to ten-minute clips during key instructional times. As a collaborative team, you can then watch or listen to these audio or video artifacts and write down statements made and the levels of questions posed to students that may reveal the teacher's and students' learning expectations within the particular lessons. You can bring these statements to your collaborative team for discussion and reflection. These sessions will undoubtedly be revealing. In your practice are you promoting student discourse, Mathematical Practices, and so on? Are the students engaged? These are just two examples of questions that may occur in such sessions. You may also opt to have another nonevaluative observer come in and record comments, statements, and questions. The purpose of this discussion is to create an awareness of teaching behaviors that signal to students the teacher's beliefs and expectations for them. Once again, a safe and encouraging environment is critical for this discussion to be productive.

The audio or videotaped vignettes will also provide indicators of teacher and student responses that can guide professional development relative to equity. For example, common statements teachers might make include, "You don't have to do that problem—it's pretty hard" or "You don't have to answer all the questions." Such comments may be intended to nurture students to successfully complete the problems or assignment—and *that* may be the message the student hears. In an effort to nurture and support struggling students, teachers sometimes inadvertently lower their expectations for some students. A teacher who poses mostly recall versus analysis (inference) and synthesis questions might be doing this subconsciously but nevertheless demonstrates a sense of lowered expectations for her students. Often these students are relieved and do not aspire beyond the lower expectation. Additionally, teachers sometimes limit important student interaction and discussion in order to maintain a well-managed classroom. Together, the teacher and student have agreed that the material is too challenging, easier problems or tasks are more appropriate, and student learning is reduced. What a shame!

Using Required RTI in Mathematics

Intervention for students in mathematics has far too frequently been approached through a deficit model in which misconceptions and student shortcomings are identified and then addressed through targeted intervention groups, often in pullout programs that remove students from classroom instruction. Unfortunately, the net result is that students fall further behind their grade-level peers. Students receive this specialized or targeted instruction only after they have failed. The goal of these traditional intervention groups has been to improve achievement, but often the focus of this intervention has been on a narrow set of skills that is inconsistent with the broader set of instructional goals called for in the Common Core State Standards. The effect of this approach to intervention has been a superficial quick fix and a "hope for the best" attitude that in the long run does not serve students well, especially in the new, more rigorous environment of the Common Core State Standards. Clearly, students who have never been identified to receive intervention before may need additional support (NCTM, 2008) in content areas such as number and operations, with the increased expectation of conceptual understanding. The reality is that any student may require intervention; students who excel in some topics may need intervention support in others (NCTM, 2011).

In 2004, the reauthorization of the Individuals With Disabilities Education Act revised the law to align with the requirements of the No Child Left Behind Act. This change encouraged school systems to provide targeted interventions for all students in a delivery model commonly known as response to intervention. RTI is a framework to meet the needs of all learners and increase student achievement. At the elementary level, the purpose of RTI is to use screening to identify at-risk students, provide early intervention to all students, prevent misidentification, provide a system of early identification, prevent the need for special education identification, and use student interventions as part of disability determination (Johnson, Smith, & Harris, 2009). NCTM's (2011) position statement on intervention notes that "the long term goal of intervention should be to help students gain independent strategies and take responsibility for their own learning" (p. 1).

RTI is typically organized in a tiered intervention system that increases in intensity and is targeted to students' diagnosed needs to provide the support they need before they fall behind (Fennell, 2011). There are many forms of RTI, and all should be flexible in terms of implementation (NCTM, 2011). For the purpose of this book, the RTI model is a three-tiered system that includes the integration of research-based instructional practices, progress monitoring, and required support in a systematic approach to improve teaching and learning (Fuchs, Fuchs, & Vaughn, 2008; Fisher, Rothenberg, & Frey, 2011). The three tiers are summarized in figure 5.3.

Monitoring Grades 3–5 Student Assessment Performance to Identify Student Needs

Most school districts first implement RTI programs in reading. A key component of reading RTI programs is universal screening for students at risk (Davis, Lindo, & Compton, 2007; Gersten et al., 2008; Jenkins, Hudson, & Johnson, 2007; Johnson, Mellard, Fuchs, & McKnight, 2006). As implementation of RTI programs was broadened beyond reading to mathematics, the universal screening component of reading programs was applied to mathematics. In some cases, this has resulted in school personnel utilizing mathematics assessments that are extraneous to the curriculum and used exclusively for the purpose of identifying students who require Tier 2 or 3 interventions. This creates yet another assessment system that consumes precious instructional time and that is not necessarily linked to the CCSS mathematics content standards. The collaborative team approach we advocate for here, specifically with respect to the development and use of common formative assessments outlined in chapter 4, supersedes the need for the creation and implementation of a separate RTI screening and monitoring assessment. All students receive universal mathematics screening through implementation of the assessment cycle.

Tier 1: Differentiated Instructional Response

Tier 1 comprises the instructional and curriculum program that all students receive. These classroom-based supports often include the following: high-quality, research-based instructional practices (figure 1.2, page 15); differentiated instruction; guided instruction with scaffolded support; additional time spent on developing concepts; use of specific or alternate models, materials, and tools; and more time to practice concepts. The mathematics instruction in Tier 1 is focused on differentiating grade-level instruction based on continuous formative assessment processes and supporting grade-level instruction. The classroom teacher typically provides Tier 1 support.

Tier 2: Targeted Response to Learning

Tier 2 encompasses targeted instructional time added to daily mathematics instruction for students whose needs are not met in Tier 1. This is typically not a pullout program. Instead, the classroom teacher or interventionist delivers it in small groups during additional mathematics instructional time. Tier 2 intervention still focuses on supporting grade-level instruction but with prioritized instructional focus on the grade-level CCSS critical areas for students whose Tier 1 differentiated instruction was insufficient. In addition, Tier 2 intervention typically provides instruction when a student is diagnosed with missing prerequisite grade-level skills and concepts.

Tier 3: Intensive Response to Learning

Tier 3 intervention is intensive instruction for students demonstrating greater need. This supplemental instruction is typically recommended for students with specific learning needs and might include small-group work or one-on-one tutoring with a supplemental program in addition to remaining in Tier 1 classroom instruction to rebuild fundamental and missing foundational prerequisite grade-level skills and concepts. The classroom teacher, special educators, mathematics specialists, interventionists, or a combination of professionals may provide the concentrated mathematical conceptual work that provides the foundation for the more complex mathematical topics being covered in daily grade-level instruction.

Figure 5.3: Tiers of mathematics intervention.

Figure 5.4 illustrates the increasing intensity of the tiers of intervention.

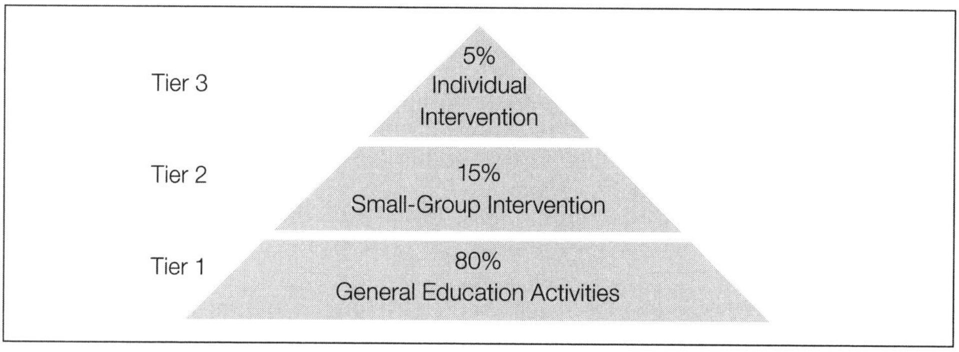

Source: Bender & Crane, 2011.

Figure 5.4: Pyramid of interventions.

The assessment cycle in chapter 4 (figure 4.2, page 116) outlines a process in which you work within your collaborative team to develop common assessments. These collaboratively developed assessments can and should also be seen and used as a universal system of screening and monitoring students for RTI services. This system of universal screening ensures all students an equal opportunity of having their learning needs identified. In addition, assessments you collaboratively developed are more likely to be aligned with the CCSS content standards and Mathematical Practices. It is critical that assessment results not be seen as a way to place students into a low or slower-paced group for mathematics instruction but rather be used to design instructional interventions and supports *in addition to* grade-level instruction to meet the needs of individual students.

Diagnosing Needs for Targeted Intervention in Tier 2 and Tier 3

Your collaborative team will need to decide whether individual student needs can be met within the daily mathematics lesson (Tier 1) or whether supplemental interventions (Tier 2 or Tier 3) are required. In order to effectively implement Tier 2 or Tier 3 interventions, you need to use student performance on formative and summative assessments to identify *and then diagnose* the specific needs of students. Traditionally, teachers have not received preservice training or professional development in the area of diagnosing students' conceptual or procedural mathematical misconceptions and gaps in prerequisite knowledge. A thorough diagnosis of student learning needs to not only consist of the identification of the misconceptions and instructional needs involving both skills and concepts but also include an analysis of the underlying or prerequisite knowledge that may be causing the student's current level of difficulty. This must all be carefully considered in order for Tier 2 or Tier 3 interventions to be strategically implemented. Moderate prerequisite conceptual and procedural difficulties may signal that the student needs Tier 2 support in addition to whole-class instruction. More severe fundamental conceptual and procedural knowledge gaps may signal that students need supplemental Tier 3 services in order to rebuild critical foundational skills and address conceptual knowledge gaps.

As you work in your collaborative team to examine student performance on formative and summative assessments, you can begin to develop your own diagnostic skills. As you examine student work to diagnose learning difficulties, you should consider the factors listed in figure 5.5.

In order to more accurately diagnose a student's conceptual difficulties with grades 3–5 mathematics, it may be necessary to conduct a *diagnostic interview*. A diagnostic interview consists of a series of prompts or questions that are asked to assess the considerations listed in figure 5.5. Table 5.1 provides an example of a fourth-grade diagnostic interview. The power of the diagnostic interview lies in how you use the results. Every mathematics teacher also needs to be a diagnostician. An everyday need exists to quickly determine the challenges, misconceptions, lack of prerequisites, and other issues that

1. **Student conceptual understanding:** Conceptual understanding is evidence of the student's knowledge of mathematical ideas and the ability to structure that knowledge in ways that facilitate making connections between ideas that are new to those that are known from prior experience.
2. **Student procedural fluency:** Procedural fluency refers to the development of procedures or algorithms for solving mathematical exercises. As an example, students learn to add by using terminology such as *carrying* and *borrowing* instead of using place-value manipulatives and vocabulary to develop rich understanding.
3. **Student disposition:** This includes students' attitudes or beliefs about learning mathematics, including positive or negative behaviors and self-efficacy. Student perseverance is a critical component of disposition.
4. **Teacher-introduced ineffective strategies:** These are the specific strategies or practices that teachers use to teach topics to students that may not advance student understanding. An example of this is the *Pac-Man* or *alligator* technique to teach the symbols used (<, >) when comparing and ordering quantities.
5. **Student prerequisite misconceptions:** This includes student misunderstandings about necessary underlying concepts in mathematics. This may include difficulties with language, symbols, concepts, or procedures. A true misconception is when the student consistently makes the same error or types of errors and demonstrates a lack of prerequisite knowledge.

Figure 5.5: Student work diagnoses and factors.

influence student achievement and, sooner than one might think, interest in mathematics (Fennell, 2011). The diagnostic interview has the potential to influence long-term and short-term planning and certain considerations for instructional strategies for students receiving Tier 2 or Tier 3 intervention time in order to address the identified student needs. A productive activity for you to engage in while working in your collaborative team is the creation of other diagnostic interview protocols, using table 5.1 as an example. The interview takes place when you ask a student to explain his or her thinking as you ask a question or provide a prompt. You are able to ask clarifying questions as the student solves the problem to determine the student's underlying conceptual understanding. When finished, you may want to make notes regarding the student's statements. Livescribe™ smartpens are a useful tool for conducting these interviews because they provide a real-time audio and visual record of the interview. These data can be collected and analyzed in collaborative teams to develop diagnostic skills and support intervention planning.

Table 5.1: Sample Fourth-Grade Diagnostic Interview

CCSS Domain and Standard (4.OA)	"**Use the four operations with whole numbers to solve problems.** Solve multistep word problems posed with whole numbers and having whole-number answers, using the four operations including problems in which remainders must be interpreted. Represent these problems using equations with a letter standing for the unknown quantity. Assess the reasonableness of answers using mental computation and estimation strategies including rounding" (p. 29).

continued →

Interview Prompt	Provide the student with the following problem. *The fourth-grade class went to Knoebels Amusement Resort, where 125 of them stood in line to ride the Radical Rollercoaster. At the last minute, 6 more students joined them in line. Each car could hold 4 students. How many cars would they need so all of them could have a ride?*
Conceptual Understanding	Have the student describe how he or she is solving the problem. Provide access to representational tools. Does the student use pictures, drawings, symbols, or manipulatives to represent the problem and its solution? Is the student able to interpret the language in the problem? Does the student connect the correct operations to the steps of the problem's solution? Does the student understand how to interpret the remainder in the problem's solution?
Procedural Fluency	Does the student use correct procedures to solve the problem? Does the student describe and identify the multistep nature of the problem?
Disposition	Does the student exhibit confidence and persist when solving the problem?
Ineffective Strategies	Does the student use tricks or specific nonthinking or nonproductive strategies to solve the problem?
Student Prerequisites and Misconceptions	Does the student demonstrate misunderstandings in solving the problem? For example, does he or she mistake the problem as a multiplication problem? Does the student lack prerequisite understandings and skills for solving the problem? For example, is he or she not fluent with division or working with remainders in division?

Visit **go.solution-tree.com/commoncore** for a reproducible version of this table.

Planning Your RTI System of Support

Planning is integral to the actions of your collaborative team. The efforts you have put forth in examining Mathematical Practices, defining which content standards need particular attention, and determining student learning needs through formative assessment culminate in the decisions you make for your RTI system of support.

Tier 1 Instructional Strategies

Baroody (2011) proposes, "The major source of most mathematical learning difficulties is how children are taught (psychologically inappropriate instruction), not their mental equipment (organic or cognitive dysfunction)" (p. 30). The goal of Tier 1 instruction in the three-tier RTI model is to provide effective classroom instruction—instruction that emphasizes the high-leverage instructional practices from chapter 1, figure 1.2 (page 15).

Collaborative teams embedding assessment processes—emphasizing steps two and four from the assessment cycle—to develop alternative pedagogical strategies to support student learning of grade-level CCSS in the classroom characterize highly effective Tier 1 instruction. In fact, approximately 80 percent of elementary students' mathematics learning needs can be met and learning difficulties prevented with highly effective Tier 1 instruction (Gersten et al., 2009; Wixson, 2011).

As noted earlier, core instruction and related assistance has too often not focused on developing key mathematical practices or processes, like making sense of problems and critiquing the reasoning of others, but more on rote or procedural thinking limited to computational proficiency. Students who struggle in mathematics, however, deserve and should receive instruction that emphasizes all aspects of mathematical proficiency and should have the opportunity to experience the same high-leverage instructional practices that other students experience (Baroody, 2011). Both the National Mathematics Advisory Panel (2008) and the National Research Council (2001) argue that all students need to experience a balanced and comprehensive curriculum. The National Mathematics Advisory Panel (2008) recommends:

> To prepare students for Algebra, the curriculum must simultaneously develop conceptual understanding, computational fluency, and problem solving skills. Debates regarding the relative importance of these aspects of mathematical knowledge are misguided. These capabilities are mutually supportive, each facilitating learning of the others. Teachers should emphasize these interrelations; taken together, conceptual understanding of mathematical operations, fluent execution of procedures, and fast access to number combinations jointly support effective and efficient problem solving. (p. xix)

Therefore, it is critical that instructional efforts not only focus on the CCSS content standards but also address Mathematical Practices at all levels.

Tier 2 and Tier 3 Intervention Strategies

Intervention instructional strategies in mathematics cannot simply be more of the same. Specifically, more instruction that repeats exactly what was done in the classroom, only at a slower pace and with more practice, is doomed to fail. Students who have not been successful in Tier 1 instruction need alternate approaches in Tier 2 or Tier 3. *Assisting Students Struggling With Mathematics* (Gersten et al., 2009) makes several instructional recommendations to support students who need intervention. Figure 5.6 (page 148) lists these recommendations. Discussing and developing a shared meaning of each of these strategies, and reflecting on their implementation and effectiveness during your collaborative meetings, are effective uses of your time.

1. Instruction during the intervention should be explicit and systematic. This includes providing models of proficient problem solving, verbalization of thought processes, guided practice, corrective feedback, and frequent cumulative review.
2. Interventions should include instruction on solving word problems that is based on common underlying structures.
3. Intervention materials should include opportunities for students to work with visual representations of mathematical ideas, and interventionists should be proficient in the use of visual representations of mathematical ideas.
4. Interventions at all grade levels should devote about ten minutes in each session to building fluent retrieval of basic arithmetic facts.
5. Tier 2 and Tier 3 interventions should include motivational strategies.

Source: Adapted from Gersten et al., 2009.

Figure 5.6: RTI instructional strategies.

Visit **go.solution-tree.com/commoncore** for a reproducible version of this figure.

Explicit Instruction

Research supports the use of explicit instruction for struggling or learning-impaired students (Clarke et al., 2011; Gersten et al., 2009; Gersten & Clarke, 2007; Jayanthi, Gersten, & Baker, 2008). Developing a shared understanding of explicit instruction is a particularly worthy topic of discussion in your collaborative team. Interpretations of *explicit instruction* can vary from teacher to teacher and often serve as a reason to begin *telling* students everything they need to know. These interpretations encourage rote memorization and student mimicking of teacher-demonstrated methods. Explicit teaching is more accurately viewed as an approach that directs student attention toward specific learning in a highly structured environment, but that does not take away from students' opportunity to think meaningfully about the mathematics they are learning, make connections, and develop deep understanding—and this distinction is critically important.

The effective use of explicit instruction supports students in developing conceptual understanding. Instruction is purposeful and meaningful, and students understand why they are learning a particular technique or strategy. A key component in delivering explicit instruction is using corrective feedback for students as they learn the material. One example of an explicit instructional strategy includes using bar models as a representational tool to assist in the teaching of whole-number addition, subtraction, multiplication, and division. (See figures 5.7 and 5.8.)

Figures 5.7 and 5.8 illustrate how students can be taught explicitly to recognize different types of problems and then use the bar diagrams to represent the problem's solution. Students are unlikely to generate this type of model or strategy on their own, so by explicitly modeling this technique with extensive guided practice and corrective feedback as students begin to use the representation, you empower students to recognize these problem structures and generalize solution strategies while building their understanding.

Jenna planted 43 flowers. Some of them started blooming. If 29 have blooms on them, how many do not?

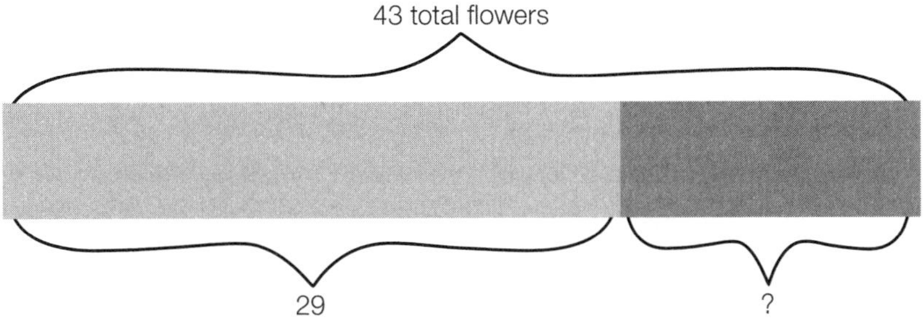

Figure 5.7: Bar model involving subtraction.

Robert has 7 baseball cards. He has 5 times as many football cards as baseball cards. How many more baseball cards than football cards does he have?

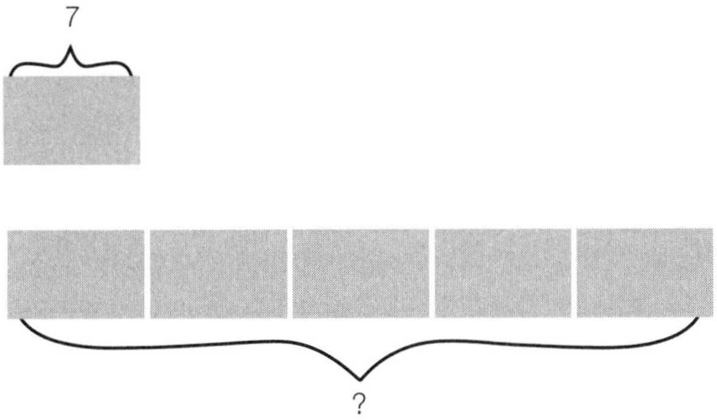

Figure 5.8: Bar model involving multiplication.

Word-Problem Structures

Word-problem structures are often confusing and difficult to interpret for students who need intervention. The language of word problems may appear to be misleading and confusing, especially if students have previously been taught keyword strategies (such as *how many in all, how many less*), which might actually inhibit understanding because students tend to focus on key words instead of the overall meaning of the problem. The Common Core State Standards (NGA & CCSSO, 2010) outline different types of word-problem situations students are likely to encounter. These common word-problem structures are found in table 5.2 (page 150) and table 5.3 (page 151). Explicit teaching of these word-problem structures during Tier 2 and Tier 3 intervention can enhance students' understanding and promote problem-solving success. These addition and subtraction word-problem structures provide contexts for all decompositions of number.

Table 5.2: Common Core Addition and Subtraction Problem Situations

	Result Unknown	Change Unknown	Start Unknown
Add to	Two bunnies sat on the grass. Three more bunnies hopped there. How many bunnies are on the grass now? 2 + 3 = ?	Two bunnies were sitting on the grass. Some more bunnies hopped there. Then there were five bunnies. How many bunnies hopped over to the first two? 2 + ? = 5	Some bunnies were sitting on the grass. Three more bunnies hopped there. Then there were five bunnies. How many bunnies were on the grass before? ? + 3 = 5
Take From	Five apples were on the table. I ate two apples. How many apples are on the table now? 5 – 2 = ?	Five apples were on the table. I ate some apples. Then there were three apples. How many apples did I eat? 5 – ? = 3	Some apples were on the table. I ate two apples. Then there were three apples. How many apples were on the table before? ? – 2 = 3
	Total Unknown	**Addend Unknown**	**Both Addends Unknown**
Put Together or Take Apart	Three red apples and two green apples are on the table. How many apples are on the table? 3 + 2 = ?	Five apples are on the table. Three are red and the rest are green. How many apples are green? 3 + ? = 5; 5 – 3 = ?	Grandma has five flowers. How many can she put in her red vase and how many in her blue vase? 5 = 0 + 5; 5 = 5 + 0 5 = 1 + 4; 5 = 4 + 1 5 = 2 + 3; 5 = 3 + 2
	Difference Unknown	**Bigger Unknown**	**Smaller Unknown**
Compare	***How many more?* version:** Lucy has two apples. Julie has five apples. How many more apples does Julie have than Lucy? **How many *fewer*? version:** Lucy has two apples. Julie has five apples. How many fewer apples does Lucy have than Julie? 2 + ? = 5; 5 – 2 = ?	**Version with *more*:** Julie has three more apples than Lucy. Lucy has two apples. How many apples does Julie have? **Version with *fewer*:** Lucy has three fewer apples than Julie. Lucy has two apples. How many apples does Julie have? 2 + 3 = ?; 3 + 2 = ?	**Version with *more*:** Julie has three more apples than Lucy. Julie has five apples. How many apples does Lucy have? **Version with *fewer*:** Lucy has three fewer apples than Julie. Julie has five apples. How many apples does Lucy have? 5 – 3 = ?; ? + 3 = 5

Source: Adapted from NGA & CCSSO, 2010, p. 88.

Table 5.3: Common Core Multiplication and Division Problem Situations

	Product Unknown	Group Size Unknown ("How Many in Each Group?" Division)	Number of Groups Unknown ("How Many Groups?" Division)
	3 × 6 = ?	3 × ? = 18 18 ÷ 3 = ?	? × 6 = 18 18 ÷ 6 = ?
Equal Groups	There are 3 bags with 6 plums in each bag. How many plums are there in all? **Measurement example**: You need 3 lengths of string, each 6 inches long. How much string will you need altogether?	If 18 plums are shared equally into 3 bags, then how many plums will be in each bag? **Measurement example:** You have 18 inches of string, which you will cut into 3 equal pieces. How long will each piece of string be?	If 18 plums are to be packed 6 to a bag, then how many bags are needed? **Measurement example:** You have 18 inches of string, which you will cut into pieces that are 6 inches long. How many pieces of string will you have?
Arrays, Area	There are 3 rows of apples with 6 apples in each row. How many apples are there? **Area example:** What is the area of a 3 cm by 6 cm rectangle?	If 18 apples are arranged into 3 equal rows, how many apples will be in each row? **Area example:** A rectangle has an area of 18 square centimeters. If one side is 3 cm long, how long is a side next to it?	If 18 apples are arranged into equal rows of 6 apples, how many rows will there be? **Area example:** A rectangle has an area of 18 square centimeters. If one side is 6 cm long, how long is a side next to it?
Compare	A blue hat costs $6. A red hat costs 3 times as much as the blue hat. How much does the red hat cost? **Measurement example:** A rubber band is 6 cm long. How long will the rubber band be when it is stretched to be 3 times as long?	A red hat costs $18, and that is 3 times as much as a blue hat costs. How much does a blue hat cost? **Measurement example:** A rubber band is stretched to be 18 cm long, and that is 3 times as long as it was at first. How long was the rubber band at first?	A red hat costs $18, and a blue hat costs $6. How many times as much does the red hat cost as the blue hat? **Measurement example:** A rubber band was 6 cm long at first. Now it is stretched to be 18 cm long. How many times as long is the rubber band now as it was at first?
General	$a \times b = ?$	$a \times ? = p$; $p \div a = ?$	$? \times b = p$; $p \div b = ?$

Source: Adapted from NGA & CCSSO, 2010, p. 89.

Fact Fluency

The Institute of Education Sciences (IES) Practice Guide, *Assisting Students Struggling With Mathematics: Response to Intervention (RtI) for Elementary and Middle Schools* (Gersten et al., 2009), recommends that students spend approximately ten minutes a day building fluency in basic arithmetic facts, defined here as the addition and related subtraction facts and the multiplication and related division facts. This recommendation is based on research indicating that students who lack foundational skills are at a disadvantage in subsequent mathematics learning (Gersten et al., 2005; Wallace & Gurganus, 2005). This recommendation might be interpreted as an opportunity to administer basic fact tests in an effort to reach fluency in students, but that is not the intent. For teachers to implement this recommendation requires them to build basic fact-strategy lessons for conceptual development, which will build fluency. Fact fluency must be based on an understanding of operations and thinking strategies (Fuson, 2003; NRC, 2001). Students must be able to connect facts to those they know, use mathematics properties to make associations, and construct visual representations to develop conceptual understanding. Discussing appropriate strategies to develop fact fluency with understanding is a productive use of your time when you meet in your collaborative team. Use the questions in figure 5.9 during collaborative team discussions to reflect on the effectiveness of instructional strategies to develop fact fluency and to ensure that such fluency instruction does not devolve to mere rote memorization.

1. How might you use ten minutes a day to develop fact fluency?
2. How might you use fact strategies to develop conceptual understanding of facts so students can become fluent?
3. What fact-fluency strategies might be best taught during this targeted instructional time?
4. What might be an effective method to screen for fact fluency?
5. How can fact fluency be monitored?
6. How might the use of the ten minutes be monitored?

Figure 5.9: Fact fluency discussion questions.

Visit **go.solution-tree.com/commoncore** to download a reproducible version of this table.

Monitoring Interventions

The questions and monitoring chart in figure 5.10 can support you as you work in your collaborative team to monitor student progress in intervention. Your team should revisit these questions and the monitoring chart following every formative and summative assessment to ensure that all students who need intervention to learn grade-level standards are receiving the support they need to be successful.

1. When will Tier 2 and Tier 3 intervention support be provided? (Tier 1 support will typically occur in the regular classroom.) This should include amount of time spent, number of intervention sessions, and who will provide interventions.
2. Who will provide Tier 1, 2, or 3 supports to identified students?
3. What are the expected outcomes for students in Tier 1, 2, or 3?
4. What will be the focus (specific standards or prerequisite standards) of the intervention?
5. How are the content standards and the Mathematical Practices being addressed during intervention?

Student	Responsible Teacher	Time	CCSS Content and Mathematical Practices	Tier 1	Tier 2	Tier 3	Specific Instructional Strategies
Jordyn	Mrs. K (Classroom teacher)	Twenty minutes—three times	Grade 3 **Domain:** Operations and Algebraic Standard three	✓			Use small-group targeted instruction, using word-problem structures and manipulatives.
Alicia	Mr. B	2:00–2:30	Grade 4 **Domain:** Operations and Algebraic Thinking Standard one			✓	Use one-on-one instruction focusing on explicit teaching of the bar-modeling strategy.

Figure 5.10: Intervention assignment questions and monitoring chart.

Visit **go.solution-tree.com/commoncore** for a reproducible version of this figure.

Prioritizing Intervention Efforts

As the academic year continues, many students will seemingly need intervention support on many content standards. Intervention time is not infinite and, at some point, it will become necessary to prioritize the content standards that will be the focus of intervention for some students. The standards and topics that fall under the Common Core State Standards' critical areas should be prioritized and emphasized during intervention. This will ensure a focus on the most important mathematics at each grade level. Grade-level collaborative teams develop timelines and long-range planning goals using the critical areas as a guide for optimizing the instructional time. (See appendices B, C, and D, pages 163, 169, and 175, for grades 3–5 critical areas.)

Developing Student Disposition and Motivation in Grades 3–5 RTI

Developing productive student dispositions is central to the success of any mathematics program. The National Research Council (2001) defines *productive disposition* as "habitual inclinations to see mathematics as sensible, useful, and worthwhile, coupled with a belief in diligence and one's own efficacy" (p. 5). These beliefs are often developed as a result of the student's classroom experiences and greatly influenced by his or her daily interactions with the teacher and fellow students. The National Mathematics Advisory Panel's (2008) recommendation regarding student self-efficacy is clear:

> Children's goals and beliefs about learning are related to their mathematics performance. Experimental studies have demonstrated that changing children's beliefs from a focus on ability to a focus on effort increases their engagement in mathematics learning, which in turn improves mathematics outcomes: When children believe that their efforts to learn make them "smarter," they show greater persistence in mathematics learning. (p. 20)

In a collaborative team activity focusing on student disposition, you may conduct interviews with students to assess student self-efficacy. For example, you could conduct three short interviews, using the sample interview questions in figure 5.11, with targeted students to determine their beliefs about their performance and progress. After interviewing the students, you could bring your notes from the interviews to a collaborative team meeting for discussion with your colleagues, using the reflection questions in figure 5.11.

Student Interview

1. When you get frustrated in mathematics class, what do you think you could do to overcome that frustration? (diligence)
2. Does hard work make a difference in learning mathematics? (diligence)
3. Are you a good mathematics student? Why or why not? (self-efficacy)
4. Is it important to know mathematics? Why or why not? (worthwhileness)
5. Is there anything that gets in your way of being successful in mathematics? (self-formative assessment) What would help you be a better mathematics student?
6. What are your strengths in learning mathematics? (using formative assessment data)
7. What strategies work well for you? (using formative assessment data)

Teacher Reflection

1. Were you surprised by the student answers or comments? Why or why not?
2. Do you think the students' beliefs are tied to their performance? Why or why not?
3. Are there any teacher moves or practices that might be reinforcing negative beliefs or dispositions? What might they be?
4. Are there any teacher moves or practices that might be reinforcing positive beliefs or dispositions for students? What might they be?

5. What moves could teachers make in the classroom to support more positive or constructive beliefs?
6. What specific actions might you take as a teacher now that you are more aware of specific student beliefs?

Figure 5.11: Student disposition interview and reflection questions.

Visit **go.solution-tree.com/commoncore** for a reproducible version of this figure.

The interview and reflection questions can be quite revealing because they allow you to compare your own perceptions with your students' beliefs. This reflection can provide a rich opportunity for you to make important changes in your classroom environment. Ensuring that students have positive dispositions toward mathematics and that you and your colleagues believe your students are capable of learning challenging grade-level mathematics are crucial steps to positioning successful intervention programs.

Serving All Students Well

For too long, mathematics education has not served all students equitably (NCTM, 2000). The expectations of the Common Core State Standards require that all students meet more rigorous grade-level standards in mathematics. Perhaps more importantly, equity concerns and economic demands make success in mathematics not only an immediate concern for all students but for society at large. The vast majority of students are capable of meeting these more rigorous expectations, but not necessarily within the same amount of instructional time or under the same instructional approach. An effective RTI program that systematically and continuously identifies student needs through a system of collaboratively developed assessments, and then provides students the appropriate targeted level of intervention support based on those assessment results, has the potential not only to ensure that all students have access to the conceptually rich mathematics outlined in the Common Core State Standards but also to close achievement gaps and promote equity in mathematics teaching and learning.

Chapter 5 Extending My Understanding

1. To what degree does your school provide RTI support as outlined in this chapter? Is there a systematic and timely structure that is a regular part of discussions in bimonthly grade-level or vertical collaborative team sessions?
2. Examine the descriptions of each tier of the RTI model (see pages 146–152). How might classroom teachers integrate this intervention model? How are students identified for targeted tier intervention? Do instructional approaches within the tiers supplement or replace whole-class instruction?
3. Considering your collaborative team's responses to questions one and two, how does the intervention reflect CCSS mathematics content and Mathematical Practices?

Online Resources

Visit **go.solution-tree.com/commoncore** for links to these resources.

- **Assisting Students Struggling With Mathematics: Response to Intervention (RtI) for Elementary and Middle Schools (Gerten et al., 2009; http://ies.ed.gov/ncee/wwc/pdf/practice_guides/rti_math_pg_042109.pdf):** Developed by a panel of RTI experts, the eight recommendations in this guide are designed to help teachers, principals, and administrators use RTI for the early detection, prevention, and support of students struggling with mathematics. View the multimedia companion website Response to Intervention in Elementary-Middle Math (Doing What Works website—http://dww.ed.gov) to download state and district tools and resource materials.
- **Classroom-Focused Improvement Process (School Improvement in Maryland, 2010; http://mdk12.org/process/cfip):** The Classroom-Focused Improvement Process (CFIP) is a six-step process for increasing student achievement that grade-level or cross-level teacher teams plan and carry out as a part of their regular lesson-planning cycle.
- **National Center on Response to Intervention (www.rti4success.org):** This site provides a wealth of resources to plan, implement, and screen RTI, including professional development modules that teacher learning teams can use to initiate or improve a RTI program in schools, districts, or states.
- **NCTM's Intervention Resources (www.nctm.org/resources/content.aspx?id=13198):** NCTM offers a collection of resources on intervention programs, intervention issues, intervention articles and research, Title I resources, and more.

EPILOGUE

Your Mathematics Professional Development Model

Implementing the Common Core State Standards for mathematics presents you with both new challenges and new opportunities. The unprecedented adoption of a common set of mathematics standards by nearly every state provides the opportunity for U.S. educators to press the reset button on mathematics education (Larson, 2011). Collectively, you and your colleagues have the opportunity to rededicate yourselves to ensuring that all students are provided with exemplary teaching and learning experiences, and you have access to the supports necessary to guarantee all students the opportunity to develop mathematical proficiency.

The CCSS college and career aspirations and vision for teaching, learning, and assessing students usher in an opportunity for unprecedented implementation of research-informed practices in your school or district's mathematics program. In order to meet the expectations of the five fundamental paradigm shifts described in this book, you will want to assess your current practice and reality as a school against the roadmap to implementation described in figure E.1 (page 158).

Figure E.1 describes the essential paradigm shifts in the four critical areas of curriculum, instruction, assessment, and intervention for your teams and in your mathematics program. As you professionally develop through your interaction and work as members of a collaborative team, your students will not only be better prepared for the CCSS assessment expectations but also for the college and career readiness that is an expectation for all students K–12—whether your state is part of the CCSS or not. Each sector in figure E.1 describes three vital collaborative team behaviors for that area of change. If you hope to break through any current areas of stagnation in your mathematics programs and achieve greater student success than ever before, then it is necessary to embrace these paradigms as part of a mindset for never-ending change, growth, and improvement within the reasoning and sense-making focus of the mathematics instruction your students receive in your school.

Working collaboratively in a grade-level team will make the Common Core obtainable not only for you but ultimately for your students. Working within a PLC culture is the best vehicle available to support you and your colleagues as you work together to interpret the Common Core State Standards, develop new pedagogical approaches through intensive collaborative planning, monitor student progress toward meeting the standards, and provide the targeted supports necessary to ensure that all students meet mathematical opportunities of the CCSS. But perhaps most significantly, collaborative

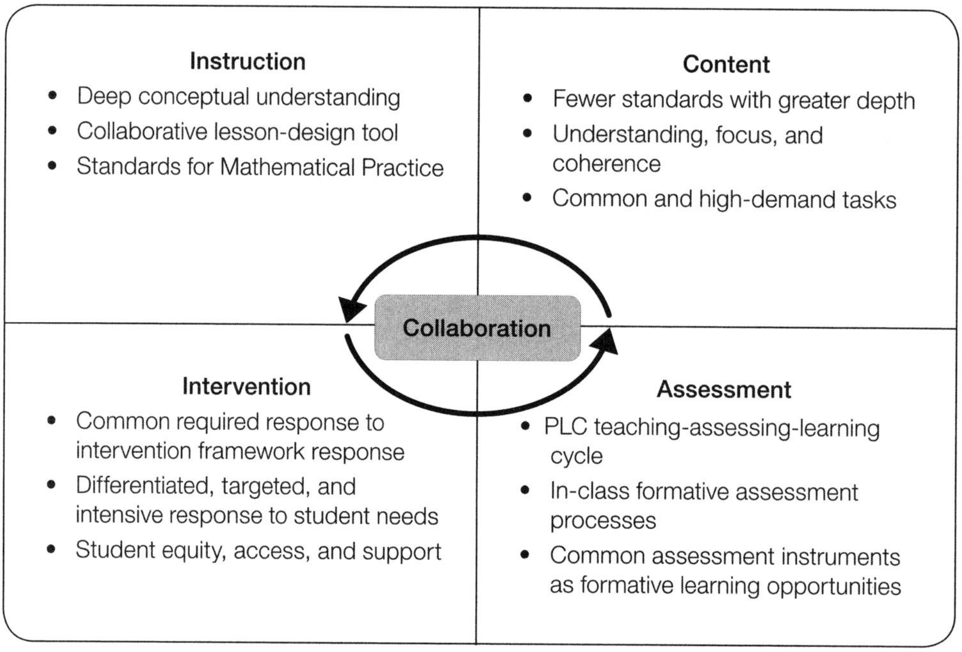

Figure E.1: PLCs at Work implementing Common Core mathematics.

learning teams in a PLC can foster an environment in which you work to support one another as you develop a fun culture focused on student learning and continuous instructional improvement.

APPENDIX A

Standards for Mathematical Practice

Source: NGA & CCSSO, 2010, pp. 6–8.

The Standards for Mathematical Practice describe varieties of expertise that mathematics educators at all levels should seek to develop in their students. These practices rest on important "processes and proficiencies" with longstanding importance in mathematics education. The first of these are the NCTM process standards of problem solving, reasoning and proof, communication, representation, and connections. The second are the strands of mathematical proficiency specified in the National Research Council's report *Adding It Up:* adaptive reasoning, strategic competence, conceptual understanding (comprehension of mathematical concepts, operations and relations), procedural fluency (skill in carrying out procedures flexibly, accurately, efficiently and appropriately), and productive disposition (habitual inclination to see mathematics as sensible, useful, and worthwhile, coupled with a belief in diligence and one's own efficacy).

1. Make sense of problems and persevere in solving them. Mathematically proficient students start by explaining to themselves the meaning of a problem and looking for entry points to its solution. They analyze givens, constraints, relationships, and goals. They make conjectures about the form and meaning of the solution and plan a solution pathway rather than simply jumping into a solution attempt. They consider analogous problems, and try special cases and simpler forms of the original problem in order to gain insight into its solution. They monitor and evaluate their progress and change course if necessary. Older students might, depending on the context of the problem, transform algebraic expressions or change the viewing window on their graphing calculator to get the information they need. Mathematically proficient students can explain correspondences between equations, verbal descriptions, tables, and graphs or draw diagrams of important features and relationships, graph data, and search for regularity or trends. Younger students might rely on using concrete objects or pictures to help conceptualize and solve a problem. Mathematically proficient students check their answers to problems using a different method, and they continually ask themselves, "Does this make sense?" They can understand the approaches of others to solving complex problems and identify correspondences between different approaches.

2. Reason abstractly and quantitatively. Mathematically proficient students make sense of quantities and their relationships in problem situations. They bring two complementary abilities to bear on problems involving quantitative relationships: the ability to decontextualize—to abstract a given situation and represent it symbolically and manipulate the representing symbols as if they have a life of their own, without necessarily attending to their referents—and the ability to contextualize, to pause as needed during the manipulation process in order to probe into the referents for the symbols involved. Quantitative reasoning entails habits of creating a coherent representation of the problem at hand; considering the units involved; attending to the meaning of quantities, not just how to compute them; and knowing and flexibly using different properties of operations and objects.

3. Construct viable arguments and critique the reasoning of others. Mathematically proficient students understand and use stated assumptions, definitions, and previously established results in constructing arguments. They make conjectures and build a logical progression of statements to explore the truth of their conjectures. They are able to analyze situations by breaking them into cases, and can recognize and use counterexamples. They justify their conclusions, communicate them to others, and respond to the arguments of others. They reason inductively about data, making plausible arguments that take into account the context from which the data arose. Mathematically proficient students are also able to compare the effectiveness of two plausible arguments, distinguish correct logic or reasoning from that which is flawed, and—if there is a flaw in an argument—explain what it is. Elementary students can construct arguments using concrete referents such as objects, drawings, diagrams, and actions. Such arguments can make sense and be correct, even though they are not generalized or made formal until later grades. Later, students learn to determine domains to which an argument applies. Students at all grades can listen or read the arguments of others, decide whether they make sense, and ask useful questions to clarify or improve the arguments.

4. Model with mathematics. Mathematically proficient students can apply the mathematics they know to solve problems arising in everyday life, society, and the workplace. In early grades, this might be as simple as writing an addition equation to describe a situation. In middle grades, a student might apply proportional reasoning to plan a school event or analyze a problem in the community. By high school, a student might use geometry to solve a design problem or use a function to describe how one quantity of interest depends on another. Mathematically proficient students who can apply what they know are comfortable making assumptions and approximations to simplify a complicated situation, realizing that these may need revision later. They are able to identify important quantities in a practical situation and map their relationships using such tools as diagrams, two-way tables, graphs, flowcharts and formulas. They can analyze those relationships mathematically to draw conclusions. They routinely interpret their mathematical results in the context of the situation and reflect on whether the results make sense, possibly improving the model if it has not served its purpose.

5. Use appropriate tools strategically. Mathematically proficient students consider the available tools when solving a mathematical problem. These tools might include pencil and paper, concrete models, a ruler, a protractor, a calculator, a spreadsheet, a computer algebra system, a statistical package, or dynamic geometry software. Proficient students are sufficiently familiar with tools appropriate for their grade or course to make sound decisions about when each of these tools might be helpful, recognizing both the insight to be gained and their limitations. For example, mathematically proficient high school students analyze graphs of functions and solutions generated using a graphing calculator. They detect possible errors by strategically using estimation and other mathematical knowledge. When making mathematical models, they know that technology can enable them to visualize the results of varying assumptions, explore consequences, and compare predictions with data. Mathematically proficient students at various grade levels are able to identify relevant external mathematical resources, such as digital content located on a website, and use them to pose or solve problems. They are able to use technological tools to explore and deepen their understanding of concepts.

6. Attend to precision. Mathematically proficient students try to communicate precisely to others. They try to use clear definitions in discussion with others and in their own reasoning. They state the meaning of the symbols they choose, including using the equal sign consistently and appropriately. They are careful about specifying units of measure, and labeling axes to clarify the correspondence with quantities in a problem. They calculate accurately and efficiently, express numerical answers with a degree of precision appropriate for the problem context. In the elementary grades, students give carefully formulated explanations to each other. By the time they reach high school they have learned to examine claims and make explicit use of definitions.

7. Look for and make use of structure. Mathematically proficient students look closely to discern a pattern or structure. Young students, for example, might notice that three and seven more is the same amount as seven and three more, or they may sort a collection of shapes according to how many sides the shapes have. Later, students will see 7×8 equals the well remembered $7 \times 5 + 7 \times 3$, in preparation for learning about the distributive property. In the expression $x^2 + 9x + 14$, older students can see the 14 as 2×7 and the 9 as $2 + 7$. They recognize the significance of an existing line in a geometric figure and can use the strategy of drawing an auxiliary line for solving problems. They also can step back for an overview and shift perspective. They can see complicated things, such as some algebraic expressions, as single objects or as being composed of several objects. For example, they can see $5 - 3(x - y)^2$ as 5 minus a positive number times a square and use that to realize that its value cannot be more than 5 for any real numbers x and y.

8. Look for and express regularity in repeated reasoning. Mathematically proficient students notice if calculations are repeated, and look both for general methods and for shortcuts. Upper elementary students might notice when dividing 25 by 11 that they are repeating the same calculations over and over again, and conclude they have a repeating decimal. By paying attention to the calculation of slope as they repeatedly check whether points are on the line through (1, 2) with slope 3, middle school students might abstract the equation $(y - 2)/(x - 1) = 3$. Noticing the regularity in the way terms cancel when expanding $(x - 1)(x + 1)$, $(x - 1)(x^2 + x + 1)$, and $(x - 1)(x^3 + x^2 + x + 1)$ might lead them to the general formula for the sum of a geometric series. As they work to solve a problem, mathematically proficient students maintain oversight of the process, while attending to the details. They continually evaluate the reasonableness of their intermediate results.

Connecting the Standards for Mathematical Practice to the Standards for Mathematical Content

The Standards for Mathematical Practice describe ways in which developing student practitioners of the discipline of mathematics increasingly ought to engage with the subject matter as they grow in mathematical maturity and expertise throughout the elementary, middle and high school years. Designers of curricula, assessments, and professional development should all attend to the need to connect the mathematical practices to mathematical content in mathematics instruction.

The Standards for Mathematical Content are a balanced combination of procedure and understanding. Expectations that begin with the word "understand" are often especially good opportunities to connect the practices to the content. Students who lack understanding of a topic may rely on procedures too heavily. Without a flexible base from which to work, they may be less likely to consider analogous problems, represent problems coherently, justify conclusions, apply the mathematics to practical situations, use technology mindfully to work with the mathematics, explain the mathematics accurately to other students, step back for an overview, or deviate from a known procedure to find a shortcut. In short, a lack of understanding effectively prevents a student from engaging in the mathematical practices.

In this respect, those content standards which set an expectation of understanding are potential "points of intersection" between the Standards for Mathematical Content and the Standards for Mathematical Practice. These points of intersection are intended to be weighted toward central and generative concepts in the school mathematics curriculum that most merit the time, resources, innovative energies, and focus necessary to qualitatively improve the curriculum, instruction, assessment, professional development, and student achievement in mathematics.

APPENDIX B

Standards for Mathematical Content, Grade 3

Source: NGA & CCSSO, 2010, pp. 21–26.

In Grade 3, instructional time should focus on four critical areas: (1) developing understanding of multiplication and division and strategies for multiplication and division within 100; (2) developing understanding of fractions, especially unit fractions (fractions with numerator 1); (3) developing understanding of the structure of rectangular arrays and of area; and (4) describing and analyzing two-dimensional shapes.

(1) Students develop an understanding of the meanings of multiplication and division of whole numbers through activities and problems involving equal-sized groups, arrays, and area models; multiplication is finding an unknown product, and division is finding an unknown factor in these situations. For equal-sized group situations, division can require finding the unknown number of groups or the unknown group size. Students use properties of operations to calculate products of whole numbers, using increasingly sophisticated strategies based on these properties to solve multiplication and division problems involving single-digit factors. By comparing a variety of solution strategies, students learn the relationship between multiplication and division.

(2) Students develop an understanding of fractions, beginning with unit fractions. Students view fractions in general as being built out of unit fractions, and they use fractions along with visual fraction models to represent parts of a whole. Students understand that the size of a fractional part is relative to the size of the whole. For example, $\frac{1}{2}$ of the paint in a small bucket could be less paint than $\frac{1}{3}$ of the paint in a larger bucket, but $\frac{1}{3}$ of a ribbon is longer than $\frac{1}{5}$ of the same ribbon because when the ribbon is divided into 3 equal parts, the parts are longer than when the ribbon is divided into 5 equal parts. Students are able to use fractions to represent numbers equal to, less than, and greater than one. They solve problems that involve comparing fractions by using visual fraction models and strategies based on noticing equal numerators or denominators.

(3) Students recognize area as an attribute of two-dimensional regions. They measure the area of a shape by finding the total number of same-size units of area required to cover the shape without gaps or overlaps, a square with sides of unit length being the standard unit for measuring area. Students understand

that rectangular arrays can be decomposed into identical rows or into identical columns. By decomposing rectangles into rectangular arrays of squares, students connect area to multiplication, and justify using multiplication to determine the area of a rectangle.

(4) Students describe, analyze, and compare properties of two-dimensional shapes. They compare and classify shapes by their sides and angles, and connect these with definitions of shapes. Students also relate their fraction work to geometry by expressing the area of part of a shape as a unit fraction of the whole.

Grade 3 Overview

Operations and Algebraic Thinking

- Represent and solve problems involving multiplication and division.
- Understand properties of multiplication and the relationship between multiplication and division.
- Multiply and divide within 100.
- Solve problems involving the four operations, and identify and explain patterns in arithmetic.

Number and Operations in Base Ten

- Use place value understanding and properties of operations to perform multi-digit arithmetic.

Number and Operations—Fractions

- Develop understanding of fractions as numbers.

Measurement and Data

- Solve problems involving measurement and estimation of intervals of time, liquid volumes, and masses of objects.
- Represent and interpret data.
- Geometric measurement: understand concepts of area and relate area to multiplication and to addition.
- Geometric measurement: recognize perimeter as an attribute of plane figures and distinguish between linear and area measures.

Geometry

- Reason with shapes and their attributes.

Operations and Algebraic Thinking 3.OA

Represent and solve problems involving multiplication and division.

1. Interpret products of whole numbers, e.g., interpret 5 × 7 as the total number of objects in 5 groups of 7 objects each. For example, describe a context in which a total number of objects can be expressed as 5 × 7.

2. Interpret whole-number quotients of whole numbers, e.g., interpret 56 ÷ 8 as the number of objects in each share when 56 objects are partitioned equally into 8 shares, or as a number of shares when 56 objects are partitioned into equal shares of 8 objects each. For example, describe a context in which a number of shares or a number of groups can be expressed as 56 ÷ 8.

3. Use multiplication and division within 100 to solve word problems in situations involving equal groups, arrays, and measurement quantities, e.g., by using drawings and equations with a symbol for the unknown number to represent the problem.

4. Determine the unknown whole number in a multiplication or division equation relating three whole numbers. For example, determine the unknown number that makes the equation true in each of the equations 8 × ? = 48, 5 = □ ÷ 3, 6 × 6 = ?.

Understand properties of multiplication and the relationship between multiplication and division.

5. Apply properties of operations as strategies to multiply and divide. Examples: If 6 × 4 = 24 is known, then 4 × 6 = 24 is also known. (Commutative property of multiplication.) 3 × 5 × 2 can be found by 3 × 5 = 15, then 15 × 2 = 30, or by 5 × 2 = 10, then 3 × 10 = 30. (Associative property of multiplication.) Knowing that 8 × 5 = 40 and 8 × 2 = 16, one can find 8 × 7 as 8 × (5 + 2) = (8 × 5) + (8 × 2) = 40 + 16 = 56. (Distributive property.)

6. Understand division as an unknown-factor problem. For example, find 32 ÷ 8 by finding the number that makes 32 when multiplied by 8.

Multiply and divide within 100.

7. Fluently multiply and divide within 100, using strategies such as the relationship between multiplication and division (e.g., knowing that 8 × 5 = 40, one knows 40 ÷ 5 = 8) or properties of operations. By the end of Grade 3, know from memory all products of two one-digit numbers.

Solve problems involving the four operations, and identify and explain patterns in arithmetic.

8. Solve two-step word problems using the four operations. Represent these problems using equations with a letter standing for the unknown quantity. Assess the reasonableness of answers using mental computation and estimation strategies including rounding.

9. Identify arithmetic patterns (including patterns in the addition table or multiplication table), and explain them using properties of operations. For example,

observe that 4 times a number is always even, and explain why 4 times a number can be decomposed into two equal addends.

Number and Operations in Base Ten 3.NBT

Use place value understanding and properties of operations to perform multi-digit arithmetic.

1. Use place value understanding to round whole numbers to the nearest 10 or 100.
2. Fluently add and subtract within 1000 using strategies and algorithms based on place value, properties of operations, and/or the relationship between addition and subtraction.
3. Multiply one-digit whole numbers by multiples of 10 in the range 10–90 (e.g., 9 × 80, 5 × 60) using strategies based on place value and properties of operations.

Number and Operations—Fractions 3.NF

Develop understanding of fractions as numbers.

1. Understand a fraction $1/b$ as the quantity formed by 1 part when a whole is partitioned into b equal parts; understand a fraction a/b as the quantity formed by a parts of size $1/b$.
2. Understand a fraction as a number on the number line; represent fractions on a number line diagram.
    a. Represent a fraction $1/b$ on a number line diagram by defining the interval from 0 to 1 as the whole and partitioning it into b equal parts. Recognize that each part has size $1/b$ and that the endpoint of the part based at 0 locates the number $1/b$ on the number line.
    b. Represent a fraction a/b on a number line diagram by marking off a lengths $1/b$ from 0. Recognize that the resulting interval has size a/b and that its endpoint locates the number a/b on the number line.
3. Explain equivalence of fractions in special cases, and compare fractions by reasoning about their size.
    a. Understand two fractions as equivalent (equal) if they are the same size, or the same point on a number line.
    b. Recognize and generate simple equivalent fractions, e.g., $1/2 = 2/4$, $4/6 = 2/3$). Explain why the fractions are equivalent, e.g., by using a visual fraction model.
    c. Express whole numbers as fractions, and recognize fractions that are equivalent to whole numbers. Examples: Express 3 in the form $3 = 3/1$; recognize that $6/1 = 6$; locate $4/4$ and 1 at the same point of a number line diagram.

d. Compare two fractions with the same numerator or the same denominator by reasoning about their size. Recognize that comparisons are valid only when the two fractions refer to the same whole. Record the results of comparisons with the symbols >, =, or <, and justify the conclusions, e.g., by using a visual fraction model.

Measurement and Data 3.MD

Solve problems involving measurement and estimation of intervals of time, liquid volumes, and masses of objects.

1. Tell and write time to the nearest minute and measure time intervals in minutes. Solve word problems involving addition and subtraction of time intervals in minutes, e.g., by representing the problem on a number line diagram.
2. Measure and estimate liquid volumes and masses of objects using standard units of grams (g), kilograms (kg), and liters (l). Add, subtract, multiply, or divide to solve one-step word problems involving masses or volumes that are given in the same units, e.g., by using drawings (such as a beaker with a measurement scale) to represent the problem.

Represent and interpret data.

3. Draw a scaled picture graph and a scaled bar graph to represent a data set with several categories. Solve one- and two-step "how many more" and "how many less" problems using information presented in scaled bar graphs. For example, draw a bar graph in which each square in the bar graph might represent 5 pets.
4. Generate measurement data by measuring lengths using rulers marked with halves and fourths of an inch. Show the data by making a line plot, where the horizontal scale is marked off in appropriate units—whole numbers, halves, or quarters.

Geometric measurement: understand concepts of area and relate area to multiplication and to addition.

5. Recognize area as an attribute of plane figures and understand concepts of area measurement.
    a. A square with side length 1 unit, called "a unit square," is said to have "one square unit" of area, and can be used to measure area.
    b. A plane figure which can be covered without gaps or overlaps by *n* unit squares is said to have an area of *n* square units.
6. Measure areas by counting unit squares (square cm, square m, square in, square ft, and improvised units).
7. Relate area to the operations of multiplication and addition.

a. Find the area of a rectangle with whole-number side lengths by tiling it, and show that the area is the same as would be found by multiplying the side lengths.

b. Multiply side lengths to find areas of rectangles with whole-number side lengths in the context of solving real world and mathematical problems, and represent whole-number products as rectangular areas in mathematical reasoning.

c. Use tiling to show in a concrete case that the area of a rectangle with whole-number side lengths *a* and *b* + *c* is the sum of *a* × *b* and *a* × *c*. Use area models to represent the distributive property in mathematical reasoning.

d. Recognize area as additive. Find areas of rectilinear figures by decomposing them into non-overlapping rectangles and adding the areas of the non-overlapping parts, applying this technique to solve real world problems.

Geometric measurement: recognize perimeter as an attribute of plane figures and distinguish between linear and area measures.

8. Solve real world and mathematical problems involving perimeters of polygons, including finding the perimeter given the side lengths, finding an unknown side length, and exhibiting rectangles with the same perimeter and different areas or with the same area and different perimeters.

Geometry 3.G

Reason with shapes and their attributes.

1. Understand that shapes in different categories (e.g., rhombuses, rectangles, and others) may share attributes (e.g., having four sides), and that the shared attributes can define a larger category (e.g., quadrilaterals). Recognize rhombuses, rectangles, and squares as examples of quadrilaterals, and draw examples of quadrilaterals that do not belong to any of these subcategories.

2. Partition shapes into parts with equal areas. Express the area of each part as a unit fraction of the whole. For example, partition a shape into 4 parts with equal area, and describe the area of each part as ¼ of the area of the shape.

APPENDIX C

Standards for Mathematical Content, Grade 4

Source: NGA & CCSSO, 2010, pp. 27–32.

In Grade 4, instructional time should focus on three critical areas: (1) developing understanding and fluency with multi-digit multiplication, and developing understanding of dividing to find quotients involving multi-digit dividends; (2) developing an understanding of fraction equivalence, addition and subtraction of fractions with like denominators, and multiplication of fractions by whole numbers; (3) understanding that geometric figures can be analyzed and classified based on their properties, such as having parallel sides, perpendicular sides, particular angle measures, and symmetry.

(1) Students generalize their understanding of place value to 1,000,000, understanding the relative sizes of numbers in each place. They apply their understanding of models for multiplication (equal-sized groups, arrays, area models), place value, and properties of operations, in particular the distributive property, as they develop, discuss, and use efficient, accurate, and generalizable methods to compute products of multi-digit whole numbers. Depending on the numbers and the context, they select and accurately apply appropriate methods to estimate or mentally calculate products. They develop fluency with efficient procedures for multiplying whole numbers; understand and explain why the procedures work based on place value and properties of operations; and use them to solve problems. Students apply their understanding of models for division, place value, properties of operations, and the relationship of division to multiplication as they develop, discuss, and use efficient, accurate, and generalizable procedures to find quotients involving multi-digit dividends. They select and accurately apply appropriate methods to estimate and mentally calculate quotients, and interpret remainders based upon the context.

(2) Students develop understanding of fraction equivalence and operations with fractions. They recognize that two different fractions can be equal (e.g., $15/9 = 5/3$), and they develop methods for generating and recognizing equivalent fractions. Students extend previous understandings about how fractions are built from unit fractions, composing fractions from unit fractions, decomposing fractions into unit fractions, and using the meaning of fractions and the meaning of multiplication to multiply a fraction by a whole number.

(3) Students describe, analyze, compare, and classify two-dimensional shapes. Through building, drawing, and analyzing two-dimensional shapes, students

deepen their understanding of properties of two-dimensional objects and the use of them to solve problems involving symmetry.

Grade 4 Overview

Operations and Algebraic Thinking

- Use the four operations with whole numbers to solve problems.
- Gain familiarity with factors and multiples.
- Generate and analyze patterns.

Number and Operations in Base Ten

- Generalize place value understanding for multi-digit whole numbers.
- Use place value understanding and properties of operations to perform multi-digit arithmetic.

Number and Operations—Fractions

- Extend understanding of fraction equivalence and ordering.
- Build fractions from unit fractions by applying and extending previous understandings of operations on whole numbers.
- Understand decimal notation for fractions, and compare decimal fractions.

Measurement and Data

- Solve problems involving measurement and conversion of measurements from a larger unit to a smaller unit.
- Represent and interpret data.
- Geometric measurement: understand concepts of angle and measure angles.

Geometry

- Draw and identify lines and angles, and classify shapes by properties of their lines and angles.

Operations and Algebraic Thinking 4.OA

Use the four operations with whole numbers to solve problems.

1. Interpret a multiplication equation as a comparison, e.g., interpret $35 = 5 \times 7$ as a statement that 35 is 5 times as many as 7 and 7 times as many as 5. Represent verbal statements of multiplicative comparisons as multiplication equations.
2. Multiply or divide to solve word problems involving multiplicative comparison, e.g., by using drawings and equations with a symbol for the unknown number to represent the problem, distinguishing multiplicative comparison from additive comparison.

3. Solve multistep word problems posed with whole numbers and having whole-number answers using the four operations, including problems in which remainders must be interpreted. Represent these problems using equations with a letter standing for the unknown quantity. Assess the reasonableness of answers using mental computation and estimation strategies including rounding.

Gain familiarity with factors and multiples.

4. Find all factor pairs for a whole number in the range 1–100. Recognize that a whole number is a multiple of each of its factors. Determine whether a given whole number in the range 1–100 is a multiple of a given one-digit number. Determine whether a given whole number in the range 1–100 is prime or composite.

Generate and analyze patterns.

5. Generate a number or shape pattern that follows a given rule. Identify apparent features of the pattern that were not explicit in the rule itself.

For example, given the rule "Add 3" and the starting number 1, generate terms in the resulting sequence and observe that the terms appear to alternate between odd and even numbers. Explain informally why the numbers will continue to alternate in this way.

Number and Operations in Base Ten 4.NBT

Generalize place value understanding for multi-digit whole numbers.

1. Recognize that in a multi-digit whole number, a digit in one place represents ten times what it represents in the place to its right. For example, recognize that $700 \div 70 = 10$ by applying concepts of place value and division.
2. Read and write multi-digit whole numbers using base-ten numerals, number names, and expanded form. Compare two multi-digit numbers based on meanings of the digits in each place, using >, =, and < symbols to record the results of comparisons.
3. Use place value understanding to round multi-digit whole numbers to any place.

Use place value understanding and properties of operations to perform multi-digit arithmetic.

4. Fluently add and subtract multi-digit whole numbers using the standard algorithm.
5. Multiply a whole number of up to four digits by a one-digit whole number, and multiply two two-digit numbers, using strategies based on place value and the properties of operations. Illustrate and explain the calculation by using equations, rectangular arrays, and/or area models.

6. Find whole-number quotients and remainders with up to four-digit dividends and one-digit divisors, using strategies based on place value, the properties of operations, and/or the relationship between multiplication and division. Illustrate and explain the calculation by using equations, rectangular arrays, and/or area models.

Number and Operations—Fractions 4.NF

Extend understanding of fraction equivalence and ordering.

1. Explain why a fraction a/b is equivalent to a fraction $(n \times a)/(n \times b)$ by using visual fraction models, with attention to how the number and size of the parts differ even though the two fractions themselves are the same size. Use this principle to recognize and generate equivalent fractions.
2. Compare two fractions with different numerators and different denominators, e.g., by creating common denominators or numerators, or by comparing to a benchmark fraction such as $1/2$. Recognize that comparisons are valid only when the two fractions refer to the same whole. Record the results of comparisons with symbols >, =, or <, and justify the conclusions, e.g., by using a visual fraction model.

Build fractions from unit fractions by applying and extending previous understandings of operations on whole numbers.

3. Understand a fraction a/b with $a > 1$ as a sum of fractions $1/b$.
    a. Understand addition and subtraction of fractions as joining and separating parts referring to the same whole.
    b. Decompose a fraction into a sum of fractions with the same denominator in more than one way, recording each decomposition by an equation. Justify decompositions, e.g., by using a visual fraction model. Examples: $3/8 = 1/8 + 1/8 + 1/8$; $3/8 = 1/8 + 2/8$; $2\ 1/8 = 1 + 1 + 1/8 = 8/8 + 8/8 + 1/8$.
    c. Add and subtract mixed numbers with like denominators, e.g., by replacing each mixed number with an equivalent fraction, and/or by using properties of operations and the relationship between addition and subtraction.
    d. Solve word problems involving addition and subtraction of fractions referring to the same whole and having like denominators, e.g., by using visual fraction models and equations to represent the problem.
4. Apply and extend previous understandings of multiplication to multiply a fraction by a whole number.
    a. Understand a fraction a/b as a multiple of $1/b$. For example, use a visual fraction model to represent $5/4$ as the product $5 \times (1/4)$, recording the conclusion by the equation $5/4 = 5 \times (1/4)$.

b. Understand a multiple of a/b as a multiple of $1/b$, and use this understanding to multiply a fraction by a whole number. For example, use a visual fraction model to express $3 \times (2/5)$ as $6 \times (1/5)$, recognizing this product as $6/5$. (In general, $n \times (a/b) = (n \times a)/b$.)

c. Solve word problems involving multiplication of a fraction by a whole number, e.g., by using visual fraction models and equations to represent the problem. For example, if each person at a party will eat $3/8$ of a pound of roast beef, and there will be 5 people at the party, how many pounds of roast beef will be needed? Between what two whole numbers does your answer lie?

Understand decimal notation for fractions, and compare decimal fractions.

5. Express a fraction with denominator 10 as an equivalent fraction with denominator 100, and use this technique to add two fractions with respective denominators 10 and 100.[4] For example, express $3/10$ as $30/100$, and add $3/10 + 4/100 = 34/100$.

6. Use decimal notation for fractions with denominators 10 or 100. For example, rewrite 0.62 as $62/100$; describe a length as 0.62 meters; locate 0.62 on a number line diagram.

7. Compare two decimals to hundredths by reasoning about their size. Recognize that comparisons are valid only when the two decimals refer to the same whole. Record the results of comparisons with the symbols >, =, or <, and justify the conclusions, e.g., by using a visual model.

Measurement and Data 4.MD

Solve problems involving measurement and conversion of measurements from a larger unit to a smaller unit.

1. Know relative sizes of measurement units within one system of units including km, m, cm; kg, g; lb, oz.; l, ml; hr, min, sec. Within a single system of measurement, express measurements in a larger unit in terms of a smaller unit. Record measurement equivalents in a two-column table. For example, know that 1 ft is 12 times as long as 1 in. Express the length of a 4 ft snake as 48 in. Generate a conversion table for feet and inches listing the number pairs (1, 12), (2, 24), (3, 36), . . .

2. Use the four operations to solve word problems involving distances, intervals of time, liquid volumes, masses of objects, and money, including problems involving simple fractions or decimals, and problems that require expressing measurements given in a larger unit in terms of a smaller unit. Represent measurement quantities using diagrams such as number line diagrams that feature a measurement scale.

3. Apply the area and perimeter formulas for rectangles in real world and mathematical problems. For example, find the width of a rectangular room given the area of the flooring and the length, by viewing the area formula as a multiplication equation with an unknown factor.

Represent and interpret data.

4. Make a line plot to display a data set of measurements in fractions of a unit ($\frac{1}{2}$, $\frac{1}{4}$, $\frac{1}{8}$). Solve problems involving addition and subtraction of fractions by using information presented in line plots. For example, from a line plot find and interpret the difference in length between the longest and shortest specimens in an insect collection.

Geometric measurement: understand concepts of angle and measure angles.

5. Recognize angles as geometric shapes that are formed wherever two rays share a common endpoint, and understand concepts of angle measurement:
    a. An angle is measured with reference to a circle with its center at the common endpoint of the rays, by considering the fraction of the circular arc between the points where the two rays intersect the circle. An angle that turns through $\frac{1}{360}$ of a circle is called a "one-degree angle," and can be used to measure angles.
    b. An angle that turns through *n* one-degree angles is said to have an angle measure of n degrees.
6. Measure angles in whole-number degrees using a protractor. Sketch angles of specified measure.
7. Recognize angle measure as additive. When an angle is decomposed into non-overlapping parts, the angle measure of the whole is the sum of the angle measures of the parts. Solve addition and subtraction problems to find unknown angles on a diagram in real world and mathematical problems, e.g., by using an equation with a symbol for the unknown angle measure.

Geometry 4.G

Draw and identify lines and angles, and classify shapes by properties of their lines and angles.

1. Draw points, lines, line segments, rays, angles (right, acute, obtuse), and perpendicular and parallel lines. Identify these in two-dimensional figures.
2. Classify two-dimensional figures based on the presence or absence of parallel or perpendicular lines, or the presence or absence of angles of a specified size. Recognize right triangles as a category, and identify right triangles.
3. Recognize a line of symmetry for a two-dimensional figure as a line across the figure such that the figure can be folded along the line into matching parts. Identify line-symmetric figures and draw lines of symmetry.

APPENDIX D

Standards for Mathematical Content, Grade 5

In Grade 5, instructional time should focus on three critical areas: (1) developing fluency with addition and subtraction of fractions, and developing understanding of the multiplication of fractions and of division of fractions in limited cases (unit fractions divided by whole numbers and whole numbers divided by unit fractions); (2) extending division to 2-digit divisors, integrating decimal fractions into the place value system and developing understanding of operations with decimals to hundredths, and developing fluency with whole number and decimal operations; and (3) developing understanding of volume.

(1) Students apply their understanding of fractions and fraction models to represent the addition and subtraction of fractions with unlike denominators as equivalent calculations with like denominators. They develop fluency in calculating sums and differences of fractions, and make reasonable estimates of them. Students also use the meaning of fractions, of multiplication and division, and the relationship between multiplication and division to understand and explain why the procedures for multiplying and dividing fractions make sense. (Note: this is limited to the case of dividing unit fractions by whole numbers and whole numbers by unit fractions.)

(2) Students develop understanding of why division procedures work based on the meaning of base-ten numerals and properties of operations. They finalize fluency with multi-digit addition, subtraction, multiplication, and division. They apply their understandings of models for decimals, decimal notation, and properties of operations to add and subtract decimals to hundredths. They develop fluency in these computations, and make reasonable estimates of their results. Students use the relationship between decimals and fractions, as well as the relationship between finite decimals and whole numbers (i.e., a finite decimal multiplied by an appropriate power of 10 is a whole number), to understand and explain why the procedures for multiplying and dividing finite decimals make sense. They compute products and quotients of decimals to hundredths efficiently and accurately.

(3) Students recognize volume as an attribute of three-dimensional space. They understand that volume can be measured by finding the total number of

same-size units of volume required to fill the space without gaps or overlaps. They understand that a 1-unit by 1-unit by 1-unit cube is the standard unit for measuring volume. They select appropriate units, strategies, and tools for solving problems that involve estimating and measuring volume. They decompose three-dimensional shapes and find volumes of right rectangular prisms by viewing them as decomposed into layers of arrays of cubes. They measure necessary attributes of shapes in order to determine volumes to solve real world and mathematical problems.

Grade 5 Overview

Operations and Algebraic Thinking

- Write and interpret numerical expressions.
- Analyze patterns and relationships.

Number and Operations in Base Ten

- Understand the place value system.
- Perform operations with multi-digit whole numbers and with decimals to hundredths.

Number and Operations—Fractions

- Use equivalent fractions as a strategy to add and subtract fractions.
- Apply and extend previous understandings of multiplication and division to multiply and divide fractions.

Measurement and Data

- Convert like measurement units within a given measurement system.
- Represent and interpret data.
- Geometric measurement: understand concepts of volume and relate volume to multiplication and to addition.

Geometry

- Graph points on the coordinate plane to solve real-world and mathematical problems.
- Classify two-dimensional figures into categories based on their properties.

Operations and Algebraic Thinking 5.OA

Write and interpret numerical expressions.

1. Use parentheses, brackets, or braces in numerical expressions, and evaluate expressions with these symbols.
2. Write simple expressions that record calculations with numbers, and interpret numerical expressions without evaluating them. For example, express the

calculation "add 8 and 7, then multiply by 2" as $2 \times (8 + 7)$. Recognize that $3 \times (18932 + 921)$ is three times as large as $18932 + 921$, without having to calculate the indicated sum or product.

Analyze patterns and relationships.

3. Generate two numerical patterns using two given rules. Identify apparent relationships between corresponding terms. Form ordered pairs consisting of corresponding terms from the two patterns, and graph the ordered pairs on a coordinate plane. For example, given the rule "Add 3" and the starting number 0, and given the rule "Add 6" and the starting number 0, generate terms in the resulting sequences, and observe that the terms in one sequence are twice the corresponding terms in the other sequence. Explain informally why this is so.

Number and Operations in Base Ten 5.NBT

Understand the place value system.

1. Recognize that in a multi-digit number, a digit in one place represents 10 times as much as it represents in the place to its right and $1/10$ of what it represents in the place to its left.
2. Explain patterns in the number of zeros of the product when multiplying a number by powers of 10, and explain patterns in the placement of the decimal point when a decimal is multiplied or divided by a power of 10. Use whole-number exponents to denote powers of 10.
3. Read, write, and compare decimals to thousandths.
    a. Read and write decimals to thousandths using base-ten numerals, number names, and expanded form, e.g., $347.392 = 3 \times 100 + 4 \times 10 + 7 \times 1 + 3 \times (1/10) + 9 \times (1/100) + 2 \times (1/1000)$.
    b. Compare two decimals to thousandths based on meanings of the digits in each place, using >, =, and < symbols to record the results of comparisons.
4. Use place value understanding to round decimals to any place.

Perform operations with multi-digit whole numbers and with decimals to hundredths.

5. Fluently multiply multi-digit whole numbers using the standard algorithm.
6. Find whole-number quotients of whole numbers with up to four-digit dividends and two-digit divisors, using strategies based on place value, the properties of operations, and/or the relationship between multiplication and division. Illustrate and explain the calculation by using equations, rectangular arrays, and/or area models.

7. Add, subtract, multiply, and divide decimals to hundredths, using concrete models or drawings and strategies based on place value, properties of operations, and/or the relationship between addition and subtraction; relate the strategy to a written method and explain the reasoning used.

Number and Operations—Fractions 5.NF

Use equivalent fractions as a strategy to add and subtract fractions.

1. Add and subtract fractions with unlike denominators (including mixed numbers) by replacing given fractions with equivalent fractions in such a way as to produce an equivalent sum or difference of fractions with like denominators. *For example,* $2/3 + 5/4 = 8/12 + 15/12 = 23/12$*. (In general,* $a/b + c/d = (ad + bc)/bd$.)
2. Solve word problems involving addition and subtraction of fractions referring to the same whole, including cases of unlike denominators, e.g., by using visual fraction models or equations to represent the problem. Use benchmark fractions and number sense of fractions to estimate mentally and assess the reasonableness of answers. *For example, recognize an incorrect result* $2/5 + 1/2 = 3/7$*, by observing that* $3/7 < 1/2$.

Apply and extend previous understandings of multiplication and division to multiply and divide fractions.

3. Interpret a fraction as division of the numerator by the denominator ($a/b = a \div b$). Solve word problems involving division of whole numbers leading to answers in the form of fractions or mixed numbers, e.g., by using visual fraction models or equations to represent the problem. *For example, interpret* $3/4$ *as the result of dividing 3 by 4, noting that* $3/4$ *multiplied by 4 equals 3, and that when 3 wholes are shared equally among 4 people each person has a share of size* $3/4$*. If 9 people want to share a 50-pound sack of rice equally by weight, how many pounds of rice should each person get? Between what two whole numbers does your answer lie?*
4. Apply and extend previous understandings of multiplication to multiply a fraction or whole number by a fraction.
   a. Interpret the product $(a/b) \times q$ as a parts of a partition of q into b equal parts; equivalently, as the result of a sequence of operations $a \times q \div b$. *For example, use a visual fraction model to show* $(2/3) \times 4 = 8/3$*, and create a story context for this equation. Do the same with* $(2/3) \times (4/5) = 8/15$*. (In general,* $(a/b) \times (c/d) = ac/bd$.)
   b. Find the area of a rectangle with fractional side lengths by tiling it with unit squares of the appropriate unit fraction side lengths, and show that the area is the same as would be found by multiplying the side lengths. Multiply fractional side lengths to find areas of rectangles, and represent fraction products as rectangular areas.

5. Interpret multiplication as scaling (resizing), by:
   a. Comparing the size of a product to the size of one factor on the basis of the size of the other factor, without performing the indicated multiplication.
   b. Explaining why multiplying a given number by a fraction greater than 1 results in a product greater than the given number (recognizing multiplication by whole numbers greater than 1 as a familiar case); explaining why multiplying a given number by a fraction less than 1 results in a product smaller than the given number; and relating the principle of fraction equivalence $a/b = (n \times a)/(n \times b)$ to the effect of multiplying a/b by 1.
6. Solve real world problems involving multiplication of fractions and mixed numbers, e.g., by using visual fraction models or equations to represent the problem.
7. Apply and extend previous understandings of division to divide unit fractions by whole numbers and whole numbers by unit fractions.
   a. Interpret division of a unit fraction by a non-zero whole number, and compute such quotients. *For example, create a story context for* $(1/3) \div 4$*, and use a visual fraction model to show the quotient. Use the relationship between multiplication and division to explain*
   b. Interpret division of a whole number by a unit fraction, and compute such quotients. *For example, create a story context for* $4 \div (1/5)$*, and use a visual fraction model to show the quotient. Use the relationship between multiplication and division to explain that* $4 \div (1/5) = 20$ *because* $20 \times (1/5) = 4$.
   c. Solve real world problems involving division of unit fractions by non-zero whole numbers and division of whole numbers by unit fractions, e.g., by using visual fraction models and equations to represent the problem. *For example, how much chocolate will each person get if 3 people share ½ lb of chocolate equally? How many ⅓-cup servings are in 2 cups of raisins?*

Measurement and Data 5.MD

Convert like measurement units within a given measurement system.

1. Convert among different-sized standard measurement units within a given measurement system (e.g., convert 5 cm to 0.05 m), and use these conversions in solving multi-step, real world problems.

Represent and interpret data.

2. Make a line plot to display a data set of measurements in fractions of a unit (½, ¼, ⅛). Use operations on fractions for this grade to solve problems involving information presented in line plots. *For example, given different measurements*

of liquid in identical beakers, find the amount of liquid each beaker would contain if the total amount in all the beakers were redistributed equally.

Geometric measurement: understand concepts of volume and relate volume to multiplication and to addition.

3. Recognize volume as an attribute of solid figures and understand concepts of volume measurement.
    a. A cube with side length 1 unit, called a "unit cube," is said to have "one cubic unit" of volume, and can be used to measure volume.
    b. A solid figure which can be packed without gaps or overlaps using n unit cubes is said to have a volume of n cubic units.
4. Measure volumes by counting unit cubes, using cubic cm, cubic in, cubic ft, and improvised units.
5. Relate volume to the operations of multiplication and addition and solve real world and mathematical problems involving volume.
    a. Find the volume of a right rectangular prism with whole-number side lengths by packing it with unit cubes, and show that the volume is the same as would be found by multiplying the edge lengths, equivalently by multiplying the height by the area of the base. Represent threefold whole-number products as volumes, e.g., to represent the associative property of multiplication.
    b. Apply the formulas $V = l \times w \times h$ and $V = b \times h$ for rectangular prisms to find volumes of right rectangular prisms with whole-number edge lengths in the context of solving real world and mathematical problems.
    c. Recognize volume as additive. Find volumes of solid figures composed of two non-overlapping right rectangular prisms by adding the volumes of the non-overlapping parts, applying this technique to solve real world problems.

Geometry 5.G

Graph points on the coordinate plane to solve real-world and mathematical problems.

1. Use a pair of perpendicular number lines, called axes, to define a coordinate system, with the intersection of the lines (the origin) arranged to coincide with the 0 on each line and a given point in the plane located by using an ordered pair of numbers, called its coordinates. Understand that the first number indicates how far to travel from the origin in the direction of one axis, and the second number indicates how far to travel in the direction of the second axis, with the convention that the names of the two axes and the coordinates correspond (e.g., x-axis and x-coordinate, y-axis and y-coordinate).

2. Represent real world and mathematical problems by graphing points in the first quadrant of the coordinate plane, and interpret coordinate values of points in the context of the situation.

Classify two-dimensional figures into categories based on their properties.

3. Understand that attributes belonging to a category of two-dimensional figures also belong to all subcategories of that category. For example, all rectangles have four right angles and squares are rectangles, so all squares have four right angles.
4. Classify two-dimensional figures in a hierarchy based on properties.

APPENDIX E

Changes in Mathematics Standards, 1989–2010

Helping students use their prior knowledge to enable them to recognize what is new and different in their learning is a key element of scaffolded instruction. Similarly, as you explore the CCSS for mathematics, it will be helpful to compare aspects of mathematics standards that have framed your previous instruction so that you can identify what is familiar, what is new and challenging, and what changes are required in the content delivered to your students. As you examine the CCSS mathematics standards for your grade level, you may find it helpful to refer to the standards that have formed the basis of your instruction. In all likelihood, these standards are based on the landmark documents that have influenced mathematics instruction since 1989, when the National Council of Teachers of Mathematics published *Curriculum and Evaluation Standards for School Mathematics* (NCTM, 1989). In 2000, NCTM updated these curriculum standards with the *Principles and Standards for School Mathematics* (PSSM), which has served as the blueprint for revised state standards throughout 2000–2010.

The placement of content standards and mathematical processes is an important consideration in any set of standards. The content and process standards within the *Principles and Standards for School Mathematics* are the same across all the grade-level bands (preK–2, 3–5, 6–8, and 9–12).

The Common Core State Standards (NGA & CCSSO, 2010) differ significantly from the *Principles and Standards for School Mathematics* (NCTM, 2000) in the descriptive language used to define the content standards. The CCSS reference content areas as *domains* rather than *content topics* or *strands*. Similarly, the content domains within the CCSS differ according to level rather than being the same from preK–12. These differences are illustrated in table E.1 (page 184), which shows content topics defined in the *Principles and Standards for School Mathematics* and the content domains defined in the Common Core State Standards. You can use this table with your collaborative learning team to focus discussion on these three questions:

1. How familiar are the terms describing content topics and content domains?
2. How does the sequence of content compare to the sequence you have followed in the past?
3. What are your teacher professional development needs as related to differences between the *Principles and Standards for School Mathematics* and the Common Core State Standards content?

Table E.1: Mathematics Content—*Principles and Standards for School Mathematics* and the Common Core State Standards

PSSM—Content Topics Grades PreK–12	CCSS—Content Domains Grades K–5	CCSS—Content Domains Grades 6–8
Number and Operations	Counting and Cardinality (K only)	Ratios and Proportional Relationships (grades 6–7 only)
Algebra	Operations and Algebraic Thinking	The Number System
Geometry	Number and Operations in Base Ten	Expressions and Equations
Measurement	Number and Operations—Fractions (grades 3–5 only)	Functions (grade 8 only)
Data Analysis and Probability	Measurement and Data	Geometry
	Geometry	Statistics and Probability

Visit **go.solution-tree.com/commoncore** for a reproducible version of this table.

In 2006, NCTM released the *Curriculum Focal Points.* The *Curriculum Focal Points* were intended to serve as a discussion document for states, school districts, and local schools as they began a conversation around the more important or *focus* topics at particular grades for levels K–8. Many states saw the Focal Points as an opportunity for their schools or school districts to identify areas of curricular focus within particular grades and also to provide the grade-by-grade essentials for all students. The Focal Points became one of the foundational guides to the Common Core State Standards. One aspect of the CCSS is the *critical areas* presented at the beginning of each grade level's discussion (see appendix B, page 163, for example). The critical areas are grade-level emphasis points and are, in essence, the *Curriculum Focal Points,* with some revision. The critical areas for grades 3–5 are shown in table E.2, which provides a second look at the important content across these grades. You can use this table to extend the discussion started with a review of table 3.1 (page 67) with your collaborative learning team. As your collaborative team begins work analyzing the content focus across the grades, you can draw on these questions to frame the discussion.

1. How much time do you think should be allotted for each critical area? How will these changes in time allocation be accommodated in building and classroom scheduling?
2. How are the critical areas similar to or different from topics you have emphasized in your teaching now or in the past?
3. What impact will work from the prior year have on the topics specified in the critical areas?

Table E.2: CCSS Critical Areas and NCTM Focal Points, Grades 3–5

Grade Level	CCSS Critical Areas	NCTM Focal Points
Grade 3	1. Develop an understanding of multiplication and division and strategies for multiplication and division within 100. 2. Develop an understanding of fractions, especially unit fractions (fractions with numerator 1). 3. Develop an understanding of the structure of rectangular arrays and of area. 4. Describe and analyze two-dimensional shapes.	1. Develop understandings of multiplication and division and strategies for basic multiplication facts and related division facts. 2. Develop an understanding of fractions and fraction equivalence. 3. Describe and analyze properties of two-dimensional shapes.
Grade 4	1. Develop understanding and fluency with multidigit multiplication, and develop understanding of dividing to find quotients involving multidigit dividends. 2. Develop an understanding of fraction equivalence, *addition and subtraction of fractions with like denominators,* and *multiplication of fractions by whole numbers.* 3. Understand that geometric figures can be analyzed and classified based on their properties, such as having parallel sides, perpendicular sides, particular angle measures, and symmetry.	1. Develop quick recall of multiplication facts and related division facts and fluency with whole-number multiplication. 2. Develop an understanding of decimals, including the connections between decimals and fractions. 3. Develop an understanding of area, and determine the areas of two-dimensional shapes. **Related Connections to the Focal Points*** **Measurement:** As part of understanding two-dimensional shapes, measure and classify angles. **Number and operations:** Develop strategies for multidigit division as the inverse of multiplication, as partitioning, or as successive subtraction.
Grade 5	1. Develop fluency with addition and subtraction of fractions, and develop understanding of the multiplication of fractions and of division of fractions in limited cases. 2. Extend division to two-digit divisors, integrating decimal fractions into the place-value system, and *develop understanding of operations with decimals to hundredths,* and develop fluency with whole-number and decimal operations. 3. Develop understanding of volume.	1. Develop an understanding of and fluency with division of whole numbers. 2. Develop an understanding of and fluency with addition and subtraction of fractions and decimals. 3. Describe three-dimensional shapes, and analyze their properties, including volume and surface area.

continued →

Note: *Italicized text indicates critical areas or elements of critical areas from the CCSS that were not in the considered* Curriculum Focal Points *(NCTM, 2006).*

**The* Curriculum Focal Points *(NCTM, 2006) presents the most important mathematical topics and connections to the other content areas for each grade level. The listing of related connections to the Focal Points at grade 4 indicates that a connection to measurement and number and operations was used to provide four critical areas for this grade.*

Visit **go.solution-tree.com/commoncore** for a reproducible version of this table.

The National Mathematics Advisory Panel (2008) identified the Critical Foundations of Algebra. These clusters of concepts and skills are essentials for all students prior to formal coursework in algebra and include the following major content topics, with suggested grade-level benchmarks for grades 3–5.

1. **Fluency with whole numbers:**
   a. By the end of grade 3, students should be proficient with the addition and subtraction of whole numbers.
   b. By the end of grade 5, students should be proficient with multiplication and division of whole numbers.
2. **Fluency with fractions:**
   a. By the end of grade 4, students should be able to identify and represent fractions and decimals and compare them on a number line or with other common representations of fractions and decimals.
   b. By the end of grade 5, students should be proficient with comparing fractions and decimals and common percentages and with addition and subtraction of fractions and decimals.
3. **Particular aspects of geometry and measurement:**
   a. By the end of grade 5, students should be able to solve problems involving perimeter and area of triangles and of all quadrilaterals having at least one pair of parallel sides (such as trapezoids).

Discussing the critical areas of the CCSS and the NCTM's Focal Points (see table E.2, page 185), as well as the NMAP's Critical Foundations, will build on your team's initial examination of the general mathematics content (see table E.1, page 184) of the CCSS. This subsequent discussion of their similarities and how they outline points and emphasize topics within the CCSS provides a second-level professional development opportunity for collaborative teams on the important mathematics for grades 3–5. This should prepare your collaborative teams to engage in meaningful discussions about what's mathematically important across these three grade levels. Additionally, these historical documents provide a precedent for curricular standards and eliminate major surprises regarding actual content topics when experienced teachers review the CCSS domains, standards, and clusters for grades 3–5.

References and Resources

Achieve. (2005). *Rising to the challenge: Are high school graduates prepared for college and work?* Washington, DC: Author.

American College Testing Program. (2006). *Ready for college and ready for work: Same or different?* Iowa City, IA: Author.

Baker, S., Gersten, R., & Lee, D. (2002). A synthesis of empirical research on teaching mathematics to low-achieving students. *The Elementary School Journal, 103*(1), 51–73.

Ball, D. L., & Bass, H. (2003). Making mathematics reasonable in school. In J. Kilpatrick, W. G. Martin, & D. Schifter (Eds.), *A research companion to principles and standards for school mathematics* (pp. 27–44). Reston, VA: National Council of Teachers of Mathematics.

Bandura, A. (1993). Perceived self-efficacy in cognitive development and functioning. *Educational Psychologist, 28*(2), 117–148.

Barber, M., & Mourshed, M. (2007). *How the world's best performing school systems come out on top.* Accessed at www.mckinseyonsociety.com/downloads/reports/Education/Worlds_School_Systems_Final.pdf on January 23, 2012.

Barnett-Clarke, C., Fisher, W., Marks, R., & Ross, S. (2010). *Developing essential understanding of rational numbers for teaching mathematics in grades 3–5.* Reston, VA: National Council of Teachers of Mathematics.

Baroody, A. J. (2011). Learning: A framework. In F. Fennell (Ed.), *Achieving fluency: Special education and mathematics* (pp. 15–53). Reston, VA: National Council of Teachers of Mathematics.

Bausmith, J. M., & Barry, C. (2011). Revisiting professional learning communities to increase college readiness: The importance of pedagogical content knowledge. *Educational Researcher, 40*(4), 175–178.

Bender, W. N., & Crane, D. (2011). *RTI in math: Practical guidelines for elementary teachers.* Bloomington, IN: Solution Tree Press.

Black, P., & Wiliam, D. (1998). Assessment and classroom learning. *Assessment in Education, 5,* 7–74.

Boaler, J., & Staples, M. (2008). Creating mathematical futures through an equitable teaching approach: The case of Railsdale School. *Teachers College Record, 110,* 608–645.

Boaler, J., Wiliam, D., & Brown, M. (2000). Students' experiences of ability grouping—disaffection, polarisation, and the construction of failure. *British Educational Research Journal, 26,* 631–648.

Buffum, A., Mattos, M., & Weber, C. (2009). *Pyramid response to intervention: RTI, professional learning communities, and how to respond when kids don't learn.* Bloomington, IN: Solution Tree Press.

Burris, C. C., Heubert, J. P., & Levin, H. M. (2006). Accelerating mathematics achievement using heterogeneous grouping. *American Educational Research Journal, 43*(1), 105–136.

Bush, W. S., Briars, D. J., Confrey, J., Cramer, K., Lee, C., Martin, W. G., et al. (2011). *Common core state standards (CCSS) mathematics curriculum materials analysis project.* Accessed at www.mathedleadership.org/docs/ccss/CCSSO%20Mathematics%20Curriculum%20Analysis%20Project.Whole%20Document.6.1.11.Final.docx on November 15, 2011.

Campbell, P. F. (1995). *Project IMPACT: Increasing mathematics power for all children and teachers. Phase 1, final report.* College Park: Center for Mathematics Education, University of Maryland.

Campbell, P. F. (2011). Elementary mathematics specialists: A merger of policy, practice, and research. In W. F. Tate, K. D. King, & C. R. Anderson (Eds.), *Disrupting tradition: Research and practice pathways in mathematics education* (pp. 93–103). Reston, VA: National Council of Teachers of Mathematics.

The Center for Comprehensive School Reform and Improvement. (2009). *Professional learning communities: Web sites.* Accessed at www.centerforcsri.org/plc/websites.html on November 15, 2011.

Clarke, B., Smolkowski, K., Baker, S. K., Fien, H., Doabler, C. T., & Chard, D. J. (2011). The impact of a comprehensive Tier 1 core kindergarten program on the achievement of students at risk in mathematics. *The Elementary School Journal, 111,* 561–584.

Clements, D. H., & Sarama, J. (2009). *Learning and teaching early math: The learning trajectories approach.* New York: Routledge.

Clements, T. B. (2011). *The role of cognitive and metacognitive reading comprehension strategies in the reading and interpretation of mathematical word problem texts: Reading clinicians' perceptions of domain relevance and elementary students' cognitive strategy use.* Unpublished doctoral dissertation, University of Central Florida.

Cobb, P. (2000). Conducting teaching experiments in collaboration with teachers. In A. E. Kelly & R. A. Lesh (Eds.), *Handbook of research design in mathematics and science education* (pp. 307–333). Mahwah, NJ: Erlbaum.

Cohen, D. K., & Ball, D. (2001). Making change: Instruction and its improvement. *Phi Delta Kappan, 83*(1), 73–77.

Common Core State Standards Initiative. (2011). *Mathematics: Introduction: Standards for mathematical practice.* Accessed at www.corestandards.org/the-standards/mathematics/introduction/standards-for-mathematical-practice on November 15, 2011.

Confrey, J., King, K. D., Strutchens, M. E., Sutton, J. T., Battista, M. T., Boerst, T. A., et al. (2008). Situating research on curricular change. *Journal for Research in Mathematics Education, 39*(2), 102–112.

Darling-Hammond, L. (2010). *The flat world and education: How America's commitment to equity will determine our future.* New York: Teachers College Press.

Darling-Hammond, L., Wei, R. C., Andree, A., Richardson, N., & Orphanos, S. (2009). *Professional learning in the learning profession: A status report on teacher development in the United States and abroad.* Dallas, TX: National Staff Development Council.

Davies, A. (2007). Involving students in the classroom assessment process. In D. Reeves (Ed.), *Ahead of the curve: The power of assessment to transform teaching and learning* (pp. 31–57). Bloomington, IN: Solution Tree Press.

Davis, G. N., Lindo, E. J., & Compton, D. L. (2007). Children at risk for reading failure: Constructing an early screening measure. *Teaching Exceptional Children, 39*(5), 32–37.

Dixon, J. K., Egendoerfer, L. A., & Clements, T. (2009). Do they really need to raise their hands? Challenging a traditional social norm in a second grade mathematics classroom. *Teaching and Teacher Education, 25,* 1067–1076.

DuFour, R., DuFour, R., & Eaker, R. (2008). *Revisiting professional learning communities at work: New insights for improving schools.* Bloomington, IN: Solution Tree Press.

DuFour, R., DuFour, R., Eaker, R., & Many, T. (2010). *Learning by doing: A handbook for professional learning communities at work* (2nd ed.). Bloomington, IN: Solution Tree Press.

Education Trust. (2005). *Gaining traction, gaining ground: How some high schools accelerate learning for struggling students.* Washington, DC: Author.

Erwin, J. C. (2004). *The classroom of choice: Giving students what they need and getting what you want.* Alexandria, VA: Association for Supervision & Curriculum Development.

Fennell, F. (Ed.). (2011). *Achieving fluency: Special education and mathematics.* Reston, VA: National Council of Teachers of Mathematics.

Fernandez, C., & Yoshida, M. (2004). *Lesson study: A Japanese approach to improving mathematics teaching and learning.* Mahwah, NJ: Erlbaum.

Ferrini-Mundy, J., Graham, K., Johnson, L., & Mills, G. (1998). *Making change in mathematics education: Learning from the field.* Reston, VA: National Council of Teachers of Mathematics.

Fisher, D., Frey, N., & Rothenberg, C. (2011). *Implementing RTI with English learners.* Bloomington, IN: Solution Tree Press.

Franke, M. L., Kazemi, E., & Battey, D. (2007). Mathematics teaching and classroom practice. In F. K. Lester (Ed.), *Second handbook of research on mathematics teaching and learning* (pp. 225–256). Charlotte, NC: Information Age.

Fuchs, D., Fuchs, L. S., & Vaughn, S. (2008). *Response to intervention: A framework for reading educators.* Newark, DE: International Reading Association.

Fuson, K. C. (2003). Toward computational fluency in multidigit multiplication and division. *Teaching Children Mathematics, 9,* 300–305.

Garet, M., Wayne, A., Stancavage, F., Taylor, J., Walters, K., Song, M., et al. (2010). *Middle school mathematics professional development impact study: Findings after the first year of implementation (NCEE 2010–4009).* Washington, DC: National Center for Education Evaluation and Regional Assistance.

Gersten, R., Beckmann, S., Clarke, B., Foegen, A., Marsh, L., Star, J. R., et al. (2009). *Assisting student struggling with mathematics: Response to intervention (RtI) for elementary and middle schools (NCEE 2009–4060).* Washington, DC: National Center for

Education Evaluation and Regional Assistance. Accessed at http://ies.ed.gov/ncee/wwc/pdf/practice_guide_rti_math_pg_042109.pdf on November 15, 2011.

Gersten, R., & Clarke, B. S. (2007). *Effective strategies for teaching students with difficulties in mathematics* (Research brief). Reston, VA: National Council of Teachers of Mathematics.

Gersten, R., Jordan, N. C., & Flojo, J. R. (2005). Early identification and intervention for students with mathematics difficulties. *Journal of Learning Disabilities, 38*(4), 293–304.

Ginsburg, H. P., & Dolan, A. O. (2011). Assessment. In F. Fennell (Ed.), *Achieving fluency: Special education and mathematics* (pp. 85–103). Reston, VA: National Council of Teachers of Mathematics.

Gresalfi, M. S., & Cobb, P. (2011). Negotiating identities for mathematics teaching in the context of professional development. *Journal for Research in Mathematics Education, 42*(3), 270–304.

Griffin, S. A., Case, R., & Siegler, R. S. (1994). Rightstart: Providing the central conceptual prerequisites for first formal learning of arithmetic to students at risk for school failure. In K. McGilly (Ed.), *Classroom lessons: Integrating cognitive theory and classroom practice* (pp. 25–49). Cambridge, MA: MIT Press.

Hanley, T. V. (2005). Commentary on early identification and intervention for students with math difficulties: Made sense—do the math. *Journal for Learning Disabilities, 38*(4), 346–349.

Hatfield, M. M., Edwards, N. T., Bitter, G. G., & Morrow, J. (2008). *Mathematics methods for elementary and middle school teachers.* Hoboken, NJ: Wiley.

Hiebert, J., & Grouws, D. A. (2007). The effects of classroom mathematics teaching on students' learning. In F. K. Lester (Ed.), *Second handbook of research on mathematics teaching and learning.* Charlotte, NC: Information Age.

Hiebert, J., & Stigler, J. W. (2004). A world of difference: Classrooms abroad provide lessons in teaching math and science. *Journal of the National Staff Development Council, 25*(4), 10–15.

Hill, J., Ball, D. L., & Schilling, S. (2008). Unpacking "pedagogical content knowledge": Conceptualizing and measuring teachers' topic-specific knowledge of students. *Journal for Research in Mathematics Education, 39*(4), 372–400.

Individuals With Disabilities Education Improvement Act of 2004, Pub. L. No. 108–446, 118 Stat. 2647 (2004).

Inside Mathematics. (2010a). *Common core standards for mathematical practice.* Accessed at http://insidemathematics.org/index.php/common-core-standards on November 15, 2011.

Inside Mathematics. (2010b). *Tools for coaches.* Accessed at www.insidemathematics.org/index.php/tools-for-teachers/tools-for-coaches on November 15, 2011.

Inside Mathematics. (2010c). *Tools for principals & administrators.* Accessed at www.insidemathematics.org/index.php/tools-for-teachers/tools-for-principals-and-administrators on November 15, 2011.

Institute for Mathematics and Education. (2007). *Progressions documents for the common core math standards.* Accessed at http://ime.math.arizona.edu/progressions on November 15, 2011.

Institute for Mathematics & Education, Center for Science, Mathematics & Computer Education, & Institute for Research on Mathematics and Science Education. (2011). *Gearing up for the common core state standards in mathematics: Five initial domains for professional development in grades K–8.* Accessed at http://commoncoretools.files.wordpress.com/2011/05/2011_04_27_gearing_up.pdf on November 15, 2011.

Jayanthi, M., Gersten, R., & Baker, S. (2008). *Mathematics instruction for students with learning disabilities or difficulty learning mathematics: A guide for teachers.* Portsmouth, NH: RMC Research Corporation.

Jenkins, J. R., Hudson, R. F., & Johnson, E. S. (2007). Screening for service delivery in an RTI framework: Candidate measures. *School Psychology Review, 36,* 560–582.

Jenkins, O. F. (2010). A professional collaboration model. *Mathematics Teaching in the Middle School, 16*(5), 288–294. Accessed at www.nctm.org/publications/article.aspx?id=27410 on November 15, 2011.

Johnson, E. S., Mellard, D. F., Fuchs, D., & McKnight, M. (2006). *Response to intervention: How to do it.* Lawrence, KS: National Research Center on Learning Disabilities.

Johnson, E., Smith, L., & Harris, M. (2009). *How RTI works in secondary schools.* Thousand Oaks, CA: Corwin Press.

Jordan, N., & Hanich, L. (2003). Characteristics of children with moderate mathematics deficiencies: A longitudinal perspective. *Learning Disabilities Research & Practice, 18,* 213–221.

Kanold, T. (2006). The flywheel effect. *Journal for Staff Development, 27*(2), 16–21.

Kanold, T., Briars, D., & Fennell, F. (2012). *What principals need to know about teaching and learning mathematics.* Bloomington, IN: Solution Tree Press.

Kantowski, M. G. (1980). Some thoughts on teaching for problem solving. In S. Krulik & R. Reys (Eds.), *Problem solving in school mathematics: 1980 yearbook* (pp. 195–203). Reston, VA: National Council of Teachers of Mathematics.

Kersaint, G. (2007). The learning environment: Its influence on what is learned. In W. G. Martin, M. E. Strutchens, & P. C. Elliott (Eds.), *The learning of mathematics: Sixty-ninth yearbook* (pp. 83–96). Reston, VA: National Council of Teachers of Mathematics.

Kinzer, C. J., Virag, L, & Morales, S. (2011). A reflective protocol for mathematics learning environments. *Teaching Children Mathematics, 17*(8), 480–484.

Knapp, M. S., Adelman, N. E., Marder, C., McCollum, H., Needels, M. C., Padilla, C., et al. (1995). *Teaching for meaning in high-poverty schools.* New York: Teachers College Press.

Larson, M. R. (2009). A curriculum decision-maker's perspective on conceptual and analytical frameworks for studying teachers' use of curriculum materials. In J. T. Remillard, B. A. Herbel-Eisenmann, & G. M. Lloyd (Eds.), *Mathematics teachers at work: Connecting curriculum materials and classroom instruction* (pp. 93–99). New York: Routledge.

Larson, M. R. (2011). *Administrator's guide: Interpreting the Common Core State Standards to improve mathematics education*. Reston, VA: National Council of Teachers of Mathematics.

Learning Forward. (2011). *Standards for professional learning*. Accessed at www.learningforward.org/standards/standards.cfm on November 15, 2011.

Leinwand, S. (2009). *Accessible mathematics: 10 instructional shifts that raise student achievement*. Portsmouth, NH: Heinemann.

Leithwood, K., & Seashore Louis, K. (Eds.). (1998). *Organizational learning in schools*. Lisse, The Netherlands: Swets & Zeitlinger.

Lezotte, L. W. (1991). *Correlates of effective schools: The first and second generation*. Okemos, MI: Effective Schools.

Little, J. W., & Horn, I. S. (2007). "Normalizing" problems of practice: Converting routine conversation into a resource for learning in professional communities. In L. Stroll & K. Seashore Louis (Eds.), *Professional learning communities: Divergence, depth, and dilemmas* (pp. 79–92). New York: McGraw-Hill.

Lubienski, S. T. (2007). What can we do about achievement disparities? *Educational Leadership, 65*(3), 54–59.

Marzano, R. J. (2006). *Classroom assessment and grading that work*. Alexandria, VA: Association for Supervision and Curriculum Development.

Marzano, R. J. (2007). Designing a comprehensive approach to classroom assessment. In D. Reeves (Ed.), *Ahead of the curve: The power of assessment to transform teaching and learning* (pp. 103–125). Bloomington, IN: Solution Tree Press.

McCall, M. S., Hauser, C., Cronin, J., Kingsbury, G. G., & Houser, R. (2006). *Achievement gaps: An examination of differences in student achievement and growth*. Lake Oswego, OR: Northwest Evaluation Association.

McKinsey & Company. (2009). *The economic impact of the achievement gap in America's schools*. Washington, DC: Author.

Morris, A. K., & Hiebert, J. (2011). Creating shared instructional products: An alternative approach to improving teaching. *Educational Researcher, 40*(1), 5–14.

Morris, A. K., Hiebert, J., & Spitzer, S. M. (2009). Mathematical knowledge for teaching in planning and evaluating instruction: What can preservice teachers learn? *Journal for Research in Mathematics Education, 40,* 491–529.

National Council of Supervisors of Mathematics. (2008). *Improving student achievement by leading the pursuit of a vision for equity*. Denver, CO: Author.

National Council of Supervisors of Mathematics. (2011). *Resources*. Accessed at www.mathedleadership.org/ccss/materials.html on November 15, 2011.

National Council of Teachers of Mathematics. (1980). *Agenda for action: Problem solving*. Accessed at www.nctm.org/standards/content.aspx?id=17279 on June 25, 2011.

National Council of Teachers of Mathematics. (1989). *Curriculum and evaluation standards for school mathematics*. Reston, VA: Author.

National Council of Teachers of Mathematics. (2000). *Principles and standards for school mathematics.* Reston, VA: Author.

National Council of Teachers of Mathematics. (2006). *Curriculum focal points for prekindergarten through grade 8 mathematics: A quest for coherence.* Reston, VA: Author.

National Council of Teachers of Mathematics. (2007). *Mathematics teaching today: Improving practice, improving student learning.* Reston, VA: Author.

National Council of Teachers of Mathematics. (2008). *Equity in mathematics education: Position statement.* Reston, VA: Author.

National Council of Teachers of Mathematics. (2008–2011). *Teaching with curriculum focal points* (Vols. 1–13). Reston, VA: Author.

National Council of Teachers of Mathematics. (2010). *Making it happen: A guide to interpreting and implementing common core state standards for mathematics.* Reston, VA: Author.

National Council of Teachers of Mathematics. (2010–2012). *Developing essential understanding* (Vols. 1–10). Reston, VA: Author.

National Council of Teachers of Mathematics. (2011). *Intervention: Position statement.* Reston, VA: Author.

National Governors Association Center for Best Practices & Council of Chief State School Officers. (2010). *Common core state standards for mathematics.* Washington, DC: Authors. Accessed at www.corestandards.org/assets/CCSSI_Math%20Standards.pdf on November 22, 2010.

National Governors Association Center for Best Practices & Council of Chief State School Officers. (2011). *Resources: Common Core implementation video series.* Accessed at www.ccsso.org/Resources/Digital_Resources/Common_Core_Implementation_Video_Series.html on November 15, 2011.

National Mathematics Advisory Panel. (2008). *Foundations for success: The final report of the National Mathematics Advisory Panel.* Washington, DC: U.S. Department of Education.

National Research Council. (2001). *Adding it up: Helping children learn mathematics.* Washington, DC: National Academies Press.

National Research Council. (2009). *Mathematics learning in early childhood: Paths toward excellence and equity.* Washington, DC: National Academies Press.

No Child Left Behind Act of 2001, Pub. L. No. 107–110, 115 Stat. 1425 (2002).

Noguera, P. (2004). Transforming high schools. *Educational Leadership, 68*(8), 26–31.

Olson, J. (2007). Developing students' mathematical reasoning through games. *Teaching Children Mathematics, 13*(9), 464–471.

Penuel, W. R., Fishman, B. J., Yamaguchi, R., & Gallagher, L. P. (2007). What makes professional development effective? Strategies that foster curriculum implementation. *American Educational Research Journal, 44*(4), 921–958.

Perry, B., & Dockett, S. (2002). Young children's access to powerful mathematical ideas. In L. D. English (Ed.), *Handbook of international research in mathematics education* (pp. 81–111). Mahwah, NJ: Erlbaum.

Perry, R., & Lewis, C. (2010). Building demand for research through lesson study. In C. E. Coburn & M. K. Stein (Eds.), *Research and practice in education: Building alliances, bridging the divide.* Lanham, MD: Rowman and Littlefield.

Pölya, G. (1957). *How to solve it* (2nd ed.). Princeton, NJ: Princeton University Press.

Popham, W. J. (2008). *Transformative assessment.* Alexandria, VA: Association for Supervision and Curriculum Development.

Porter, A., McMaken, J., Hwang, J., & Yang, R. (2011). Common core standards: The new U.S. intended curriculum. *Educational Researcher, 40*(3), 103–116.

Rasmussen, C., Yackel, E., & King, K. (2003). Social and sociomathematical norms in mathematics classrooms. In H. L. Schoen & R. I. Charles (Eds.), *Teaching mathematics through problem solving: Grades 6–12* (pp. 143–154). Reston, VA: National Council of Teachers of Mathematics.

Rathouz, M. (2011). 3 ways that promote student reasoning. *Teaching Children Mathematics, 18*(3), 182–189.

Reeves, D. (2003). *High performance in high poverty schools: 90/90/90 and beyond.* Englewood, CO: Center for Performance Assessment.

Reeves, D. (2011). *Elements of grading: A guide to effective practices.* Bloomington, IN: Solution Tree Press.

Reys, B., & Fennell, F. (2003). Who should lead instruction at the elementary level. *Teaching Children Mathematics, 9,* 277–282.

Reys, R., Lindquist, M. M., Lambdin, D. V., & Smith, N. L. (2012). *Helping children learn mathematics* (10th ed.). Hoboken, NJ: Wiley.

Reys, R., & Reys, R. (2011). The high school mathematics curriculum—what can we learn from history? *Mathematics Teacher, 105*(1), 9–11.

Rivkin, S. G., Hanushek, E. A., & Kain, J. F. (2005). Teachers, schools, and academic achievement. *Econometrica, 73*(2), 417–458.

Saunders, W. M., Goldenberg, C. N., & Gallimore, R. (2009). Increasing achievement by focusing grade-level teams on improving classroom learning: A prospective, quasi-experimental study of Title I schools. *American Educational Research Journal, 46*(4), 1006–1033.

Schmidt, W. H., Cogan, L. S., Houang, R. T., & McKnight, C. C. (2011). Content coverage differences across districts/states: A persisting challenge for U.S. education policy. *American Journal of Education, 117*(3), 399–427.

Schmoker, M. (2006). *Results now: How we can achieve unprecedented improvement in teaching and learning.* Alexandria, VA: Association for Supervision and Curriculum Development.

Schmoker, M. (2011). *Focus: Elevating the essentials to radically improve student learning.* Alexandria, VA: Association for Supervision and Curriculum Development.

School Improvement in Maryland. (2010). *Introduction to the classroom-focused improvement process (CFIP).* Accessed at http://mdk12.org/process/cfip on November 15, 2011.

Seeley, C. L. (2009). *Faster isn't smarter: Messages about math, teaching, and learning in the 21st century.* Sausalito, CA: Math Solutions.

Shuhua, A. (2004). *The middle path in math instruction: Solutions for improving math education.* Lanham, MD: Scarecrow Education.

Siegler, R., Carpenter, T., Fennell, F., Geary, D., Lewis, J., Okamato, Y., et al. (2010). *Developing effective fractions instruction for kindergarten through 8th grade: A practice guide (NCEE 2010–4039).* Washington, DC: National Center for Education Evaluation and Regional Assistance.

Silver, E. (2010). Examining what teachers do when they display their best practice: Teaching mathematics for understanding. *Journal of Mathematics Education at Teachers College, 1*(1), 1–6.

Silver, E. A., & Stein, M. K. (1996). The QUASAR project: The "revolution of the possible" in mathematics instructional reform in urban middle schools. *Urban Education, 30,* 476–521.

Slavin, R. E., & Lake, C. (2008). Effective programs in elementary mathematics: A best-evidence synthesis. *Review of Educational Research, 78*(3), 427–515.

Smith, M. S., & Stein, M. K. (2011). *5 practices for orchestrating productive mathematics discussions.* Reston, VA: National Council of Teachers of Mathematics.

Stein, M. K., & Kaufman, J. H. (2010). Selecting and supporting the use of mathematics curricula at scale. *American Educational Research Journal, 47,* 663–693.

Stein, M. K., Remillard, J., & Smith, M. S. (2007). How curriculum influences student learning. In F. K. Lester (Ed.), *Second handbook of research on mathematics teaching and learning* (pp. 319–370). Charlotte, NC: Information Age.

Stein, M. K., Russell, J., & Smith, M. S. (2011). The role of tools in bridging research and practice in an instructional improvement effort. In W. F. Tate, K. D. King, & C. R. Anderson (Eds.), *Disrupting tradition: Research and practice pathways in mathematics education* (pp. 33–44). Reston, VA: National Council of Teachers of Mathematics.

Stein, M. K., & Smith, M. S. (2010). The influence of curriculum on students' learning. In B. J. Reys, R. E. Reys, & R. Rubenstein (Eds.), *Mathematics curriculum: Issues, trends, and future directions, seventy-second yearbook* (pp. 351–362). Reston, VA: National Council of Teachers of Mathematics.

Stiff, L. V., Johnson, J. L., & Akos, P. (2011). Examining what we know for sure: Tracking in middle grades mathematics. In W. F. Tate, K. D. King, & C. R. Anderson (Eds.), *Disrupting tradition: Research and practice pathways in mathematics education* (pp. 63–75). Reston, VA: National Council of Teachers of Mathematics.

Stiggins, R. J., Arter, J. A., Chappuis, J., & Chappuis, S. (2006). *Classroom assessment for student learning: Doing it right—using it well.* Portland, OR: Educational Testing Service.

Stigler, J. W., Gonzales, P., Kawanaka, T., Knoll, S., & Serrano, A. (1999). *The TIMSS videotape classroom study: Methods and findings from an exploratory research project on eighth-grade mathematics instruction in Germany, Japan, and the United States.* Washington, DC: U.S. Department of Education, National Center for Education Statistics.

Stigler, J. W., & Hiebert, J. (1999). *The teaching gap: Best ideas from the world's teachers for improving education in the classroom.* New York: The Free Press.

Tate, W., & Rousseau, C. (2002). Access and opportunity: The political and social context of mathematics education. In L. D. English (Ed.), *Handbook of international research in mathematics education* (pp. 271–300). Mahwah, NJ: Erlbaum.

Tate, W. F., & Rousseau, C. (2007). Engineering change in mathematics education: Research, policy, and practice. In F. K. Lester (Ed.), *Second handbook of research on mathematics teaching and learning* (pp. 1209–1246). Charlotte, NC: Information Age.

Teacher Education Initiative Curriculum Group. (2008). *High-leverage teaching practices.* Unpublished manuscript, School of Education, University of Michigan, Ann Arbor.

Thompson, M., & Wiliam, D. (2007, April). *Tight but loose: A conceptual framework for scaling up school reforms.* Paper presented at the annual meeting of the American Educational Research Association, Chicago, IL.

Usiskin, Z. (2007). The case of the University of Chicago school mathematics project—Secondary component. In C. R. Hirsch (Ed.), *Perspectives on the design and development of school mathematics curricula* (pp. 173–182). Reston, VA: National Council of Teachers of Mathematics.

Walker, E. N. (2007). Why aren't more minorities taking advanced math? *Educational Leadership, 65*(3), 48–53.

Wallace, A. H., & Gurganus, S. P. (2005). Teaching for mastery of multiplication. *Teaching Children Mathematics, 12,* 26–33.

Waters, T., Marzano, R., & McNulty B. (2003). *Balanced leadership: What 30 years of research tells us about the effect of leadership on student achievement.* Denver, CO: McREL.

Wayne, A. J., Kwang, S. Y., Zhu, P., Cronen, S., & Garet, M. S. (2008). Experimenting with teacher professional development: Motives and methods. *Educational Researcher, 37*(8), 469–479.

Weiss, I. R., Heck, D. J., & Shimkus, E. S. (2004). Looking inside the classroom: Mathematics teaching in the United States. *NCSM Journal of Mathematics Education Leadership, 7*(1), 23–32.

Wiggins, G., & McTighe, J. (2000). *Understanding by design.* New York: Prentice Hall.

Wiliam, D. (2007a). Content then process: Teacher learning communities in the service of formative assessment. In D. Reeves (Ed.), *Ahead of the curve: The power of assessment to transform teaching and learning* (pp. 183–204). Bloomington, IN: Solution Tree Press.

Wiliam, D. (2007b). Keeping learning on track: Classroom assessment and the regulation of learning. In F. K. Lester (Ed.), *Second handbook of research on mathematics teaching and learning* (pp. 1053–1098). Charlotte, NC: Information Age.

Wiliam, D. (2011). *Embedded formative assessment.* Bloomington, IN: Solution Tree Press.

Wiliam, D., & Thompson, M. (2007). Integrating assessment with instruction: What will it take to make it work? In C. A. Dwyer (Ed.), *The future of assessment: Shaping teaching and learning* (pp. 53–82). Mahwah, NJ: Erlbaum.

Williams, B. (2003). Reframing the reform agenda. In B. Williams (Ed.), *Closing the achievement gap: A vision for changing beliefs and practices* (pp. 178–196). Alexandria, VA: Association for Supervision and Curriculum Development.

Wixson, K. (2011). A systemic view of RTI research. *The Elementary School Journal, 111*(4), 503–510.

Index

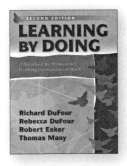

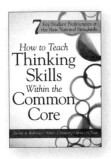

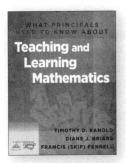

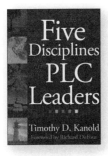